THE FILM SPECTATOR:
FROM SIGN TO MIND

FILM CULTURE IN TRANSITION

Thomas Elsaesser: General Editor

Double Trouble
Chiem van Houweninge on Writing and Filming
>*Thomas Elsaesser, Robert Kievit and Jan Simons (eds.)*
>(1994)

Between Stage and Screen
>*Egil Törnqvist*
>(spring 1995)

Fassbinder's Germany
>*Thomas Elsaesser*
>(summer 1995)

Film and the First World War
>*Karel Dibbets and Bert Hogenkamp (eds.)*
>(1994)

Writing for the Medium
>*Thomas Elsaesser, Jan Simons and Lucette Bronk (eds.)*
>(1994)

THE FILM SPECTATOR: FROM SIGN TO MIND

Edited by

WARREN BUCKLAND

AMSTERDAM UNIVERSITY PRESS

Cover photo: still from Fritz Lang's film *Dr. Mabuse, der Spieler*, (1921). By permission of the Stiftung Deutsche Kinemathek Berlin.

Cover design: Kok Korpershoek (KO), Amsterdam
Typesetting: A-zet, Leiden

ISBN 90 5356 170 6 (hardbound)
ISBN 90 5356 131 5 (paperback)

© Amsterdam University Press, Amsterdam, 1995

Dedicated to the Memory of Christian Metz

CONTENTS

Section 3: The Pragmatic Tendency in the New Film Semiology

FROM SIGN TO MIND:
A GENERAL INTRODUCTION

THOMAS ELSAESSER

Few can doubt that the encounter between linguistics and film which began in the early 1960s was a crucial moment in the life of film as a theoretical object.[1] Even today, when other practical concerns about the cinema's future within an ever more integrated audio-visual culture seem more pressing, or when other theoretical paradigms about a film's relation to subjectivity, identity-politics and gender seem to promise more relevance, a reminder of the first moves to introduce methods at once rigorous and systematic into film studies are of more than historical interest.

What initially brought our field – whose origins have never been properly examined[2] – into contact with linguistics was not the fact that the cinema (since its very beginnings) had combined images with language, whether spoken (during the film-performance) or written (in the form of intertitles). The appeal to language - as the essays that follow indicate - was prompted by a number of broadly theoretical and even philosophical issues around the question of signification. How can a photographic reproduction and representation of reality be a meaningful statement about this reality? As Christian Metz put it: we need 'to understand how films are understood'[3] or in Bill Nichols' phrase: we need 'to understand images *of* the world as speech *about* the world'.[4]

This collection sets out to document the recent and productive engagment with the Metzian heritage among European scholars, demonstrating that his thought was in some respects both richer and more open than its identification with Saussurean semiology would lead one to believe. But before handing over to the editor, I would like to mention briefly the other side of the Metzian oeuvre, associated with Metz's best-known book, *The Imaginary Signifier*, and to indicate how it connects the lingustic semiology of early Metz with the semio-pragmatics featured in this volume.[5] Known also as the 'second semiology' or 'psycho-semiology', the essays collected in *The Imaginary Signifier* have often been interpreted as a radical break, a kind of non-sequitur even, in relation to Metz's first semiological project, a half-admission of failure. And indeed, in the way they have sometimes been taken up, as a polemical tool and didactic shorthand, psycho-semiotics left behind crucial aspects of the linguistic agenda. Yet, as is only now becoming fully apparent, Metz's original formulations can also be seen as the first project's necessary 'verso', namely a bold attempt to theorize, from the position of a poetics or rhetoric, the linguistic place of the user. It was to bring him back, towards the end of his life, to the thought of his first masters, Jakobson, Benveniste and Barthes. The central essay of his last period, 'The Impersonal Enunciation or the Site of Film', reprinted and introduced below, is thus both a return to his own origins and the offer of a dialogue with his followers, whether sympathetic or critical.

On the question of the spectator or user, one can once more distinguish a 'European' approach (represented by part 2 of this collection) from an Anglo-American one. While the inclusion of the spectator as part of the structure and meaning of a film was the most important theoretical innovation for film studies in the mid-1970s, the 'pragmatics' embodied in psychoanalytical theories of spectatorship, and the more specifically linguistic pragmatics – still side by side in Metz – were in due course to develop in separate directions. What they nonetheless had in common was the fact that the spectator, understood as the instance that the text addresses, as well as the locus of the text's intelligibility, emerged as the producer of both meaning and subjectivity. It was Metz's reworking of Benveniste's theory of enunciation, together with his own version of Freudian psychoanalysis, redefined through structural linguistics and amplified by Jean-Louis Baudry's theory of the cinematic apparatus, which initially provided a two-pronged theoretical framework for the notion that any visual representation necessarily implies a subject. This subject, however, was not to be confused either with a physical spectator sitting in an auditorium, or with the individual who had to be imagined standing, as it were, 'behind' the camera. The subject of psycho-semiotics, in other words, was a textually constructed subject – a formulation which in itself begged many questions, not least whether it is appropriate to speak of a film as a text at all.

It also raised the question whether it was legitimate to conflate a 'linguistically' grounded theory of subjectivity, depending on such categories as personal pronouns, adverbs or the tense structure and modality of verbs, with a set of cinematic devices ranging from the point of view shot and the look of the characters, to framing, camera movement and off-screen space – devices which, as the 'negative linguistics' of Metz's first semiology had already made clear, do not have a unified level, such as syntax, to bind them together into a mutually interdependent system. Instead, they could at best be thought of as – more or less opportunistically – ganging up together, in order to constitute various cinematic and filmic codes, whose possibility and limits Metz had, in *Langage et cinéma*, painstakingly described.

The first semiology of the cinema arose out of a double movement: it wanted to distinguish itself both from the pseudo-objectivity of the cinema as the representation of the real (the post-war adulation of neo-realism), and from the pseudo-subjectivity of journalistic film-criticism and cinephile auteurism. As a consequence, the first semiology had given the spectator no definite role in the filmic process, concentrating instead on ascribing the meaning-generating power of moving images to 'codes' at work within the filmic text, the term 'code' (amenable, of course, also to a technical definition) situating itself at a level of hierarchy and interdependence somewhat less rigid than 'language-system' or 'syntax', while nonetheless connoting a logic more binding than that of 'convention' or 'shared belief'.

This is why Metz's work on the articulation of a film's temporality (his famous grande syntagmatique of the image track) remains so important, even though it seems to have preoccupied the film studies community only very briefly. Developed between 1965 and 1969, the grande syntagmatique was Metz's audacious attempt to analyze exhaustively one particular example of filmic speech. Once it became clear that the individual image and its sign status could not be the basis for film semiology, Metz tackled the level of image ordering, the relation between shots: combination rather than commutation would explain how film comes to be a species of discourse. Several times revised, the grande syntagmatique was Metz's initial response to his discovery that the cinema constituted a *langage* without a *langue*, but it also confirmed his belief that 'it is not because cinema is language that it can tell us such beautiful stories, it's because cinema has told us such beautiful stories that it has become a language'. More precisely, the grande syntagmatique set out to show how the spatio-temporal ordering of shots, which since Griffith articulated the narrative logic of a film, was not only responsible for conferring upon the pro-filmic event meanings not contained in the analogical relations between iconic signifiers and signifieds, but was governed by fairly strict rules. Furthermore, these combinations/articulations were not infinite – Metz identifies eight of them – and in the fiction film especially (but not only in the fiction film), they attained the status of a narrative syntax, even if their quasi-universality must not be confused with a filmic 'grammar'. Metz groups them in a hierarchy of complexity within an overall framework, that of the 'autonomous segment', where autonomy is generally defined by formal features (fade in/fade out) combining into a unit of sense, marked by a change of location, the termination of an event or action. Within the autonomous segment, Metz establishes eight types, ranging from the autonomous shot (characterised by spatio-temporal unity) to the sequence (differentiated according to a branching structure around single shot/multiple shots//a-chronological/chronological ///simultaneous/sequential). Metz also applied the grande syntagmatique to an individual film,

Adieu Philippine by Jacques Rozier,[6] and the combination of a theoretical exposition with a practical illustration made the grande syntagmatique the single most influential contribution to the semiology of the cinema.

Even if among the different syntagmatic types making up the grande syntagmatique some proved more convincing than others, it showed the possibility of isolating paradigmatic relations among filmic syntagms, after Metz had failed to find them on the level of the filmic image. This in turn led him to conclude that filmic syntax conforms to the rhetorical trope of *dispositio* (determined ordering of undetermined elements – in this case images) rather than to a grammar. Writers such as Bellour were to demonstrate to what extent parallelism, repetition, alternation and other rhetorical devices were to structure filmic discourse, and Metz himself has tried to define and delimit the pertinence to filmic articulation of the paradigm/syntagm/metaphor/metonymy relations.[7] Although it had laid the theoretical groundwork for the small-scale and large-scale formal analysis of so-called classical Hollywood narrative film (textual analysis), the grande syntagmatique was not without problems, recognized first of all by Metz himself: most significantly, the eight articulations identified were all modelled on narrative film, which meant that narrative appeared not as one form of image concatenation among others, but intrinsic to all filmic signification (thus raising the question of how it was possible to understand documentary, avantgarde or other non-narrative films).

Secondly, Metz still adhered to the photographic analogy, and the realist aesthetics it implied. Not only did the image remain meaningful in itself, which is especially clear in Metz's (inadequate, because too inclusive) definition of the autonomous shot, but equally problematic, the level of denotation (which in the grande syntagmatique organizes and hierarchizes the connotative levels) is supported by the presupposition of a time-space world existing independent from its filmic articulations. As becomes clear in Michel Colin's 'The Grande Syntagmatique Revisited' (reprinted in this volume), it is around the primacy of time-space relations and the concept of 'diegesis' that one part of cine-semiology redefined itself in the late 1980s.

The difficulties may have arisen from the fact that in the 'first semiology', the communication model of Jakobson, with its sender/addressee, transmitter/receiver, its notion of a message passed from one to the other proved a powerful if often under-examined basis. The spectator/receiver's job was merely to 'decode' the message 'correctly', which meant that 'subjectivity' was located in the 'phatic' dimension of the communication act, i.e. the materiality of the channel and the 'noise' it made when open and receiving. This was a line of inquiry which at the time was not the one pursued, but which this present collection reinvestigates in the context of Francesco Casetti's enunciative theory and Roger Odin's semio-pragmatics of the cinema.

Instead, what – under the influence of Stephen Heath – was taken to be the path which could transcend the impasses of the first semiology, was the notion that a film text has necessarily inscribed in it a spectator/addressee, whom it 'interpellated' as 'subject'. While Heath proposed this formulation as a reworking of Metz's early writings and as a reading of 'The Imaginary Signifier', Heath's theory owed much to the way a number of originally very distinct theoretical paradigms had become fused. We can distinguish a reading of Jacques Deslandes' history of the beginnings of cinema and of film technology in relation to post-Renaissance perspectival representation by Jean-Louis Comolli; this was further developed by Jean-Louis Baudry, who brought Comolli's ideas in contact with the psychoanalysis of Jacques Lacan, who had himself been read, in the light of Marxian theories of ideology, by Louis Althusser. This definition of psycho-semiotics in film theory thus names a very particular convergence of theoretical concerns, at a particular historical juncture.

It is therefore not altogether surprising that the psycho-semiotics which became successful in Anglo-American film studies in the late 1970s tried to analyse the film experience, intelligibility and the production of affect by concentrating on the conditions which made possible the illusion of an ideologically coherent (and in a subsequent move, gender-specific) subject. Less evident was the fact that this version of psycho-semiotics constantly skirted a danger some French proponents, notably Metz, had tried so studiously to avoid, namely to conflate the textually constructed subject with 'the spectator', and then possibly adding to the confusion by attributing to this 'spectator' a set of constraints and limiting conditions known as 'subject-positioning' which in turn were said to determine the way films were read by actual spectators.

It was, in trying to answer some of these problems that, in the wake of Metz's initial rejection of it, a return to the communication model seemed appropriate. Thus, the long shadow of Jakobson is visible in 'The Impersonal Enunciation' and in turn, surfaces more clearly in the unapologetic use of a communication framework present in the writings of Odin and Casetti. On the other hand, a certain polemical polarization seemed to open up between European and US scholarship, the latter rejecting both the notion of 'text' (in the sense used by Heath and others) and 'communication'. For instance, the case for 'narration' as the paradigm designed to compete with and replace Metz's account of textuality and filmic enunciation was put most forcefully by David Bordwell in his 1985 study *Narration and the Fiction Film*, and given an added sophistication by Edward Branigan's *Narrative Comprehension and Film* of 1992. Yet one could argue that 'narration' takes up the other side of Metz's interpretation of Benveniste, where *histoire* becomes merely a special case of *discours*, and where narration is simply a less inclusive term than enunciation. The main convergence is that, in either case, it is not the text as 'utterance' which carries with it situational markers or attributes of time or stance. Rather, when faced with certain features of a film which do not fit a given framework of expectations, it is the spectator who supplies the discursive coordinates, i.e. is forced to raise questions pertaining to the purportive motivation or intentionality of the text.

In France, psycho-semiotics of the cinema as theorized by Metz and Heath, and practiced in the form of textual analysis by Bellour and Thierry Kuntzel had a far less lasting effect than it did in Britain or the United States. Instead, the influence of literary narratology on French film theory has been and still is substantial. Its origins have been traced back to, for instance, Albert Laffay's *Logique du cinema*, published in 1964, but written as early as the late 1940s. This pioneer notwithstanding, narratology in France belongs more properly to the strand of structuralism identified with Claude Brémond, Gérard Genette and Tzvetan Todorov, where it arose from the debates over context-sensitive or context-free theories of the sign, which were then focused on the issue whether narratives preserved their meaning across the media and could be construed as independent from the recipients' situation, as had been claimed by Lévi-Strauss for myths, which – in the words of Jakobson – 'pass from hand to hand without being altered in the process'.

Against this notion of narrative as embodying a certain abstract logical structure (which A. J. Greimas had already tried to overcome with his notion of a contractual situation supplementing and regulating textual semantics), a number of theorists have in fact taken Metz's work on metaphor/metonymy not in the (Anglo-American) direction of psychoanalysis, but either back to transformational grammar – notably Michel Colin and his revision of Metz's grande syntagmatique – or to the work of Greimas and Genette, exploring what in film might correspond to literary perspectivism, to 'focalization' and the complex modalities of action and tense. In this sense, both French and American narratology has decisively moved away from the specular categories of identification, fetishism, voyeurism, and towards a semantics of temporality. Here, the work of François Jost and Dominique Chateau remains exemplary. An early example of 'applied' narratology was a study of French cinema in the 1930s, *Générique des années trentes: les Français en focalisation interne* by Marie-Claire Ropars, Michèle Lagny and Michel Marie (published in 1986). In a similar vein, André Gaudreault has studied the emergence of a particular logic of time and space in early cinema by means of categories derived from Greimas and Genette.[8]

One of the consequences of trying to understand narratives within a logical or grammatical model was to develop categories that could define what happens to the idea of a filmic deep structure. If, for example, one can agree that, as far as spectatorial competence is concerned, strictly linguistic terms such as grammatical/ungrammatical do not apply to film, alternative terms such as 'intelligibility' or 'acceptability' would still have to be understood to encompass and specify the set of rules or constraints that tell a viewer how to understand a shot or sequence. On the other hand, what one is looking for are the elements within film that point to the way an utterance is organised to allow the spectator to 'make sense' even when certain of these rules are flouted or transgressed, if surface features such as cohesion or progression are absent, or if certain norms are being violated. In this respect, a communication model – in line with recent thinking in pragmatics – would start from the assumption that the 'norm' or 'default value' is in fact failed or fallible communication, with sender and recipient always out of step with each other, unless their contact is regulated and constrained by a series of enunciative instances, framing and contextualizing the message.

On the other hand, one might say that as long as a film works in a consistent manner on the articulation of time and space, its particular narrative logic will be construed 'acceptable' by the viewer, since the ability to read spatio-temporal relations and cues seems to belong to a type of competence which film shares with language, as can be seen, for instance, by George Lakoff's studies of spatial and temporal metaphors organizing both abstract reasoning and subjectivity. Such a move, when applied to film, could not only refer itself usefully to Metz's work on metaphor/metonymy, determined as these figures of discourse are by their placing along the syntagmatic chain, but one might also look again at the abstract categories by which a spectator apprehends a film's diegesis through certain spatial features (left/right, next to/opposite to, characters entering the frame, movements of the camera) which function not simply as punctuation marks or syntactic features, but also semantically. This may help to understand how films establish (and spectators recognise, accept and maintain contact with) a 'total' story-world, on the basis of partial, incomplete or even conflicting information and data. Odile Bächler's work on John Ford's *Stage Coach* or Michel Colin's analysis of the television coverage of the Tour de France are examples that come to mind.[9]

Narratology, following Benveniste and Genette, made it its task to identify the linguistic marks of *discours* in narratives, developing in the process some very sophisticated models for narrators, narrative levels, and for how to read the modalities of verbs in respect of aspect, tense and mood when analyzing narrative texts. None of this applies in any strict sense to the cinema, where, as I have already suggested, and following among others, François Jost, the marks of enunciation are more like enunciative uses (or contexts) of which the viewer is either aware or not. A stylistic feature may 'draw attention to itself', but instead of functioning as a mark of enunciation, or designating an enunciator (as locus of 'intentionality'), its *enoncé* may connote a certain style, or point to the presence of something not shown. To use an example of Jost's: a hand-held camera shot might signify 'cheap production' or 'authenticity' or 'we are about to see someone running, and this is his point of view'. Similarly, the unclaimed point of view shots in many of Fassbinder's films may either be regarded as careless-ness, as self-conscious art-cinema narration or it may be the basis for constructing a wholly different system of cinematic space, one 'open' to a gaze not physically present in the shot, or present off-screen, but implied by the film's semantic deep-structure.

More generally, the question of point of view, extensively discussed by Edward Branigan in *Point of View in the Cinema* and by Elena Dagrada in Section 3, became the basis for renewed interest in narration and also of authorship (now consid-ered not as an individual, or as the enunciative instance whenever the text seems to speak about itself as text, but rather as a kind of default value invoked by imagining an origin or an intentionality when a given system breaks down) and spectatorial compe-tence (the author as an effect of narration, but narration as the product of the spec-tator).[10]

These remarks demonstrate the continuing importance of Metz's work in founding the agenda of Film Studies, and the diversity of responses it has provoked. Those who have followed Metz (Michel Colin, Roger Odin, Francesco Casetti among them), have inherited his rigor and analytical precision, while vigorously addressing themselves to shortcomings of previous attempts at systematic accounts of film as lan-guage, which asked the right questions, but restricted themselves to too narrow a view of language. To identify and reformulate the questions semiotics has left unresolved is one of the major challenges to film studies, and it is precisely one of the tasks under-taken by the 'new film semiologists', whose work is being featured in the present col-lection.

More specifically, the collection highlights that one of the major insights of film semiology has been the fact that the 'meaning' of a film cannot be adequately determined by its formal syntactic and semantic characteristics alone. The inter-pretation of a film is equally a function of its social context, defined as the set of rules and conventions that spectators in given circumstances bring to bear on the particular films they see. If the formal devices, as semiologists put it, 'inscribe' the spectator in the text, film semiotics has also identified – under such different labels as 'the filmic enun-ciation' (Casetti), 'the communicative contract' (Odin, Jost) – the way the spectator inscribes a text in his/her systems of knowledge, belief, symbolic action and social practice.

Publishing an anthology of what the editor calls the 'new film semiology' is not only a way of paying homage and commemorating one of the founders of our sub-ject: Christian Metz, who died in 1993. It is first and foremost a reminder of the fields of inquiry that film semiology has disclosed. As such, it should be understood as a contribution to a debate which allows scholars in Europe and the United States, to make decisive interventions, even as they seem to question and interrogate the only sophisticated methodology film studies has until now called its own.

Notes

[1]   For a fuller account, on which this Introduction is based, the reader is referred to Thomas Elsaesser and Emile Poppe, entry 'Film' in *The Encyclopedia of Language and Linguistics*, R.E. Asher, editor-in-chief, Oxford: Pergamon Press, 1994, vol 3, pp. 1225-1241.

[2]   But see Francesco Casetti, *Teorie del cinema, 1945-1990*, Milano: Bompiani, 1993.

[3]   Christian Metz, *Langage et Cinema*, Paris: Larousse, 1971, p. 56.

[4]   Bill Nichols, introduction to 'The Voice of Documentary', in Nichols (ed.), *Movies and Methods*, vol. 2, Berkeley: University of California Press, 1985, p. 259.

[5]   Metz, *Psychoanalysis and Cinema: The Imaginary Signifier*, trans. Ben Brewster, Celia Britton, Alfred Guzzetti, and Annwyl Williams, London: Macmillan, 1982.

[6]   Metz, *Film Language: A Semiotics of the Cinema*, trans. Michael Taylor, New York: Oxford University Press, 1974, pp. 149-182.

[7]   Metz, 'Metaphor/Metonymy, or the Imaginary Referent', *Psychoanalysis and Cinema*, pp. 149-314.

[8]   André Gaudreault, *Du litteraire au filmique: System du récit*, Paris: Meridiens Klincksieck, 1988.

[9]   See Odile Bächler, 'Où la lecture d'une image est aussi une image', *Recherches Sémiotiques/Semiotic Inquiry*, 13, 1/2, 1993, pp. 229-41; Michel Colin, 'Comprendre l'événement sportif à la télévision. L'exemple de la course cycliste', *Communications*, 51, 1990, pp. 79-110.

[10] Edward Branigan, *Point of View in the Cinema*, Berlin / New York: Mouton, 1984, pp. 12-13.

PREFACE

WARREN BUCKLAND

Christian Metz's name is synonymous with the study of cinema in an academic context. His film theoretical essays constitute the foundation of the semiological study of film. One aim of this anthology is to present the ways in which some of Metz's European colleagues have continued to refine, elaborate, reinterpret, and criticise this early theory without the need to dismiss it in favour of a significantly different (i.e. Marxist, feminist, psychoanalytic, cognitive) theoretical approach or non-theoretical (historical) approach to film.

Taken as a whole, Metz's work influenced the formation of what has come to be known as modern or 'contemporary' film theory. The many studies of contemporary film theory[1] generally recognise that it consists of two stages – a classic semiology (also known as the first or structural semiology) and a post-structural theory (sometimes known as the second or psycho-semiology). Classic semiology, covering the period from the mid-1960s to the early 1970s, was based primarily upon structural linguistics, whereas post-structural film theory, which reached its peak in the early 1980s, no longer drew upon autonomous linguistic theories, but based itself primarily upon the Marxism of Louis Althusser and the psychoanalysis of Jacques Lacan. Post-structuralism criticised the epistemological foundations of classic semiology, particularly the autonomy it conferred upon the text in articulating meaning. Instead, textual meaning was theorised as inherently incomplete and indeterminate, since it was perceived to be determined by external absent causes (which are ideological-psychical-patriarchal in nature). Rather than paying exclusive attention to the internal structure of the text, which implies that the structure is complete in itself and simply needs to be replicated in a theoretical analysis, the post-structuralists turned their critical attention to the way these external absent causes actually determine the structures and meanings of texts.

This shift from a classic semiology to a post-structural theory closely shadowed the shift from structural linguistics to a theory of enunciation, particularly Emile Benveniste's theory of deixis. Structural linguistics posited that meaning is generated from the syntagmatic and especially paradigmatic relations between linguistic signs. But such a theory of meaning excludes deictic words – grammatical categories such as personal pronouns (I, you), demonstrative pronouns (this, that), etc. which gain a specific meaning only from their use in concrete discursive situations. The function of deictic words is to grammaticalize the spatio-temporal reference points of context within the utterance itself. The theory of deixis influenced the post-structural film theorists' concept of subject positioning, which was defined in terms of those features of context (especially the spectator's look) 'grammaticalized' (i.e. formally represented) in the film itself. Rather than being theorised as a closed, autonomous entity, post-structural film theory began by theorising the filmic text as being organised around an external centre occupied by the spectator. This theory of meaning (which merely theorised the spectator as an absent point) was then enriched by Althusser's theory of interpellation (a discursive process that attempts to address each individual as a coherent and unified subject) and Lacan's sophisticated theory of subjectivity, which adroitly expanded the base of post-structural film theory because of Lacan's linguistic re-reading of Freudian metapsychology.

What is not generally recognised is that classic film semiology was challenged, not only by post-structuralism, but also by what I would call the 'new film semiology' – that is, a semiological approach to film influenced by Transformational Generative Grammar, a renewed interest in enunciation, and by pragmatics. For most Anglo-American film scholars, film semiology takes only one form – what I have identified here as classic film semiology, ranging from Metz's 1964 paper 'Le cinéma: langue ou langage?' leading to his remarkable paper on the grande syntagmatique of the image track, and finally to his monumental book *Langage et cinéma*, published in 1971.[2] But as Metz himself acknowledged in the opening chapter of this book: 'By its very nature, the semiological enterprise must expand or disappear'.[3] Although *Langage et cinéma* marks the logical conclusion to classic film semiology, it does not mark the end of film semiology *per se*. In his subsequent work (particularly his essay 'Le signifiant imaginaire'[4]), Metz adopted a psychoanalytical framework, which aided the formation of post-structural film theory. However, many of his students and colleagues continued to work within a semiological-based framework. Research in film semiology has continued unabated in the 1970s and 1980s, especially in France, Italy, and Holland. Far from disappearing, film semiology has expanded from a 'classic' framework to a 'new' framework, which encompasses transformational generative grammar, cognitive science, a renewed interest in enunciation theory (in both film and television), and pragmatics. Very little of this work has been translated into English or even acknowledged by Anglo-American film scholars. The function of this anthology is to collect together a representative set of papers in film semiology which go beyond – but which do not dismiss – its structural linguistic foundations.

The aim of this anthology is therefore to challenge the Anglo-American perception of film semiology as a brief period in academic film studies. Coupled with its intense popularity and scientific pretensions, film semiology's purported brief appearance retrospectively conferred upon it the impression of being an intellectually irresponsible fad. I wish to stress that there is a continuity between classic film semiology and the new film semiology (whereas there is a displacement between classic film semiology and post-structural film theory). I also wish to stress that there is a continuity between film semiology and the intellectual precedents of semiology – namely, what Karl Otto Apel calls the Language Analysis tradition.

Section 1 of this anthology, 'Film Semiology, Transformational Generative Grammar, and Cognitive Science', collects together a series of papers that attempt to expand Metz's structural linguistic-based film semiology by drawing on a number of concepts from Noam Chomsky's transformational generative grammar (TGG) and from cognitive science. Chomsky shifted the emphasis of linguistic analysis away from the actual, manifest level of language and towards the underlying rules and conventions that allow interlocutors to *produce* and *comprehend* this manifest level. This shift in emphasis raises the fundamental question of the psychological reality of these language rules. For Chomsky, the rules the TG grammarian constructs are mentalistic (i.e. psychologically real). In transposing the framework of TGG to film, the question immediately posed by this branch of the new film semiology is whether the resulting film theory is psychologically real or not. In other words, is the film theory describing the mental processes involved in the construction and comprehension of filmic sequences (i.e. does the theory correspond to mental processes performed by spectators) or is it merely a theoretical tool constructed by the film semiologist? The question is whether the new film semiology has changed its 'object' of study by focusing its attention away from filmic texts themselves and towards the cognitive rules underlying the production and comprehension of filmic texts. Positive answers to this question are to be found in the papers of section 1.

The papers in section 2, 'Film and Enunciation Revisited', represent new departures in the application of the linguistic theory of enunciation to filmic discourse. The issue of filmic enunciation is not unique to the new film semiology. Indeed, the conjunction of film and the linguistic theory of enunciation marked the transition from classic film semiology to post-structural film theory. But compared with the papers collected together in section 2 – by Francesco Casetti, Metz, François Jost, and Jan Simons – the post-structural theorisation of filmic enunciation appears *ad hoc* and superficial. There are two main reasons for this: (1) classic film semiology groped its way towards enunciation theory in order to resolve a number of fundamental contradictions arising from the theorisation of texts as autonomous entities. Enunciation theory therefore became a last ditch attempt to prop up an inconsistent framework. But for the new film semiologists represented in section 2, enunciation theory became the starting point of their work, which enabled them to theorise in a systematic and rigorous manner the conjunction between film and enunciation. This approach is particularly evident in Casetti's work in the 1980s (culminating in his book *Dentro lo sguardo* in 1986[5]), which draws exhaustively upon the theory of deixis to conceptualise the relation between film and spectator. In his paper 'The Impersonal Enunciation, or the Site of Film', Metz moves away from a deictic theory of enunciation and instead argues that filmic enunciation can be identified with reflexive (or metadiscursive) moments in a film – the moments when a film refers to itself as a discursive construct. (2) The second reason why the post-structural theory of enunciation appears *ad hoc* and superficial is that the new film semiologists, from their well-established theoretical base, are able to apply their work in a more coherent manner. This enabled them to expand the scope of application to non-filmic forms of discourse, especially television (there is a good demonstration of this at the end of Jost's paper 'The Authorized Narrative').

Section 3, 'The Pragmatic Tendency in the New Film Semiology', collects together a small but representative sample of the work of Roger Odin, together with Elena Dagrada's study of the point-of-view shot. Both authors are directly influenced by the discipline of pragmatics, which currently dominates the theorisation of meaning in linguistics. To put this work into context, and to explain its importance today, we simply need to note that the internal development of film theory's study of meaning closely follows the linguistic study of meaning. In other words, the classical film theory of André Bazin, etc. can be aligned to an extensional semantic theory of meaning, since it presupposes that meaning lies in the referent, not in the discourse that represents that referent. Classic film semiology developed an intensional semantic theory of filmic meaning, since it argued that meaning is generated from within the filmic text itself. Theories of enunciation are narrow theories of pragmatics, since they still focus on the formal configurations of language, but configurations that nonetheless gain a specific meaning only within a particular context. The post-structural film theorists' notion of subject positioning is therefore a narrow pragmatic theory of filmic meaning.

Roger Odin's work is largely influenced by a broad (or extrinsic) theory of pragmatics. Whereas the theory of enunciation is a narrow theory of pragmatics because it simply supplements a semantic theory of meaning (by accounting for those 'anomalous' grammatical forms that do not have an intensional meaning), a broad theory of pragmatics argues that the semantic form of all utterances is inherently incomplete and indeterminate. It is only enriched and completed by the interlocutor's inferential activities guided by contextual information. Much of the recent literature on pragmatics is concerned with discussing the nature of this knowledge and with outlining the principles that guide interlocutors in their generation of inferences (or, more specifically, non-demonstrative inferences). Roger Odin argues that the filmic text does not signify its own meaning. Instead, in 'For a Semio-Pragmatics of Film', he argues that reading a film consists of '"applying" to [the image] processes that are essentially external to it'. In 'A Semio-Pragmatic Approach to the Documentary Film' Odin states that spectators must take up the role of 'documentarizing' subjects in order to comprehend the film on screen as a documentary. Odin offers a useful definition of fiction to explain how, within a semio-pragmatic framework, a documentary film differs from a fiction film. Whereas the spectator of a fiction film posits the enunciator as absent, the documentary spectator must posit the enunciator as real (since the enunciator of a documentary must be able to guarantee the truth of what is articulated on screen). Finally, Elena Dagrada shows how a filmic text does not determine its own meaning by studying a number of point of view shots in *The Wrong Man* and *The Nutty Professor*. These studies demonstrate that the point of view shot is a unit of filmic language, not necessarily a representation of character subjectivity.

To end, I need to say something about the organisation of this anthology. The three sections capture the three fundamental directions film semiology has taken since its initial classic stage. Moreover, these three fundamental directions have in common a shift from 'sign to mind' – that is, a transformation of the research 'object', from formal structures in texts towards cognitive structures in film spectators' minds. The only main omission from this anthology, as far as I am aware, is the enormous amount of work carried out by European (especially French) film theorists on film narratology (although one of the most articulate French film narratologists – François Jost – is represented in this anthology). Doubtless, an additional section on film narratology could have been included, although its status would have been different to the other sections, since much of its insights overlap, to some extent, with work in film narratology carried out by American film theorists, whereas the three actual sections of this anthology represent work which is historically and conceptually distinct to European film studies. Nonetheless, the emphasis throughout this anthology is to articulate a possible reconciliation between European and American film studies.

More than any other text, an anthology is the product of many different voices. But as the editor, the point of passage of a bundle of determinations, I must function as the real enunciator who guarantees the truth of what is articulated here. But I can only stand as a confident guarantor of truth because of the help and advice of many others. Special thanks goes to Jan Simons, who took time off from his thesis to write one of the introductions, collaborate on another, and then write an inspiring essay especially for the anthology, one that encapsulates the anthology's spirit by opening up new areas of research in film theory. On top of all this, Jan also suggested to me the anthology's title. If I stand as the real enunciator, then Thomas Elsaesser stands as a figure analogous to the implied author, the agent who takes a general overview of the text, acting as the 'silent' guide for the other agents (especially myself). As with all implied authors, this text would not have been possible without Thomas's support, which required from him a great deal of tolerance, patience and persistence. I therefore wish to thank Thomas for his dedication to this anthology, and to his unyielding belief in the continuing importance and value of film theory as a branch of film studies. Other voices also helped to shape this text, not least all the authors and copyright holders who allowed their work to be freely reproduced here. I also wish to thank the British Academy, whose award of a postdoctoral fellowship has given me the time needed to complete this anthology, and the Supplementary Research Grant Committee in the School of English and American Studies, University of East Anglia, for its contribution towards translation costs. Finally, I would also like to thank Guy Austin, Andrew Higson, Frank Kessler, Emile Poppe, Claudine Tourniaire, and Michael Wedel.

Notes

[1]   For example, Richard Allen, *Representation, Experience, and Meaning in the Cinema: A Critical Study of Contemporary Film Theory*, unpublished Ph.D. thesis, University of California, Los Angeles, 1989; Dudley Andrew, *Concepts in Film Theory*, New York: Oxford University Press, 1984; Jacques Aumont, Alain Bergala, Michel Marie, Marc Vernet, *Aesthetics of Film*, trans. Richard Neupert, Austin: University of Texas Press, 1992; Warren Buckland, *Filmic Meaning: The Semantics-Pragmatics Interface*, unpublished Ph.D. thesis, University of East Anglia, 1992; Francesco Casetti, *Teorie del cinema, 1945-1990*, Milano: Bompiani, 1993; Robert Lapsley and Michael Westlake, *Film Theory: An Introduction*, Manchester: Manchester University Press, 1988; David Rodowick, *The Crisis of Political Modernism: Criticism and Ideology in Contemporary Film Theory*, Urbana and Chicago: University of Illinois Press, 1988; Philip Rosen, *The Concept of Ideology and Contemporary Film Theory: A Study of the Position of the Journal "Screen" in the Context of the Marxist Theoretical Tradition*, vols I and II, unpublished Ph.D. thesis, University of Iowa, 1978; Robert Stam, Robert Burgoyne, Sandy Flitterman-Lewis, *New Vocabularies in Film Semiotics: Structuralism, Post-Structuralism, and Beyond*, London: Routledge, 1992.

[2]   Christian Metz, 'Le cinéma: langue ou langage?', *Communications*, 4, 1964, pp. 52-90; translation to be found in *Film Language: A Semiotics of the Cinema*, trans.

Michael Taylor, New York: Oxford University Press, 1974, pp. 31-91; the definitive discussion of the grande syntagmatique, 'Problems of Denotation in the Fiction Film', is to be found in the same volume, pp. 108-146; *Langage et cinéma*, Paris: Larousse, 1971, translated as *Language and Cinema*, trans. Donna Jean Umiker-Sebeok, The Hague: Mouton, 1974.

3 Metz, *Language and Cinema*, p. 19; translation modified.

4 Metz, 'Le signifiant imaginaire', *Communications*, 23, 1975, pp. 3-55; translated in *Screen*, 16, 2, 1975, pp. 14-76 and in Christian Metz, *Psychoanalysis and Cinema: The Imaginary Signifier*, trans. Ben Brewster et. al., London: Macmillan, 1982, pp. 1-87.

5 An English translation of this book is forthcoming from Indiana University Press.

SECTION 1

FILM SEMIOLOGY, TRANSFORMATIONAL GENERATIVE GRAMMAR, AND COGNITIVE SCIENCE

INTRODUCTION

Warren Buckland

Film semiology is not some fad that grew out of the 1960s, for it has a more stable origin in the language analysis tradition and (implicitly) in Gaston Bachelard's philosophy of science.[1] The work carried out in the 1960s is only the starting point for film semiology. This section of the anthology represents one of the most important developments/transformations film semiology has undergone. More specifically, this section collects together a representative set of papers that highlight the limitations of a structural linguistic-based film semiology (or 'classic film semiology'). However, except for the final paper by Colin, these papers do not reject the linguistic approach to film, but attempt to expand it through the employment of more powerful linguistic theories – especially Transformational Generative Grammar (TGG). Generative grammar is a particularly complex discipline with its own complicated internal history of development. Some knowledge of generative grammar is required in order to comprehend the papers in this section. Here I shall attempt to offer a concise outline of the main concepts the new film semiologists draw from.

For Noam Chomsky, structural linguistics (more particularly, structural phonology) is merely a sophisticated form of textual description, for it analyses structural patterns at the expense of the systems of rules that constitute them:

> current work in phonology [i.e. generative phonology] is demonstrating that the real richness of phonological systems lies not in the structural patterns of phonemes but rather in the intricate systems of rules by which these patterns are formed, modified, and elaborated. The structural patterns that arise at various stages of derivation are a kind of epiphenomenon. The system of phonological rules makes use of the universal features in a fundamental way, but it is the properties of the systems of rules, it seems to me, that really shed light on the specific nature of the organization of language.[2]

Although structural linguistics did analyse rules of transformation, they were primitive and relatively unimportant compared to the resulting structural patterns. For this reason, Chomsky calls structural linguistics an observationally adequate theory of grammar – a theory whose scope is limited to the analysis of a corpus of language using taxonomic principles of segmentation and classification: 'structural linguistics ... assumes that the technique for discovering the correct hypothesis (grammar) must be based on procedures of successive segmentation and classification of the items in the corpus ...'.[3] From the late 1950s onwards, TGG moved away from this taxonomic procedure by attempting to develop a precise, algorithmic formulation of the rules that generate the grammatical sentences of a particular language. Furthermore, TGG claims that these rules constitute the knowledge of language the native speaker-hearer utilises to generate and comprehend sentences. For this reason, Chomsky calls TGG a descriptively adequate theory of grammar – a theory that 'assigns structural descriptions to sentences *in accordance with the linguistic competence of the native speaker*'.[4] Finally, Chomsky proposes an explanatory adequate theory of grammar, which must contain 'a way of evaluating alternative proposed grammars',[5] all of which are descriptively adequate. Part of this process involves ascertaining the similarities between these various grammars, which are then deemed to be revealing universal properties of language. In conclusion, we can say that TGG constructs a formal model that generates grammatical sentences, and also considers the psychological status of that model, whereas structural linguistics (and classic film semiology) merely segments and classifies the epiphenomenon – the output of a TGG.

For researchers in TGG, language structure consists not only of the structural elements of language but, more importantly, of the underlying system of rules that produce these structural elements. TGG's abstract and complex notion of structure includes a finite set of re-write rules that generate deep structure strings and a finite number of transformational rules that transform these deep structures into a potentially infinite number of surface structure sentences. This generation of an infinite number of surface structures from a finite number of rules characterises the economical and creative aspects of language, two important criteria for the authors represented in this section of the anthology.

Moreover, the grammatical rules of generation and transformation must be constrained so that they generate *all* and *only* the sentences that native speakers judge to be well-formed, or grammatical. Hence, for Chomsky, 'grammatical' is a technical, rather than an evaluative or prescriptive term. In this technical sense, a grammatical sentence is one that is generated according to the rules of a particular grammar (it is a sentence recognised by that grammar). Such a sentence can thereby be described as well-formed with reference to that grammar.

Chomsky summarizes this version of TGG (the Standard Theory) in the following way:

A grammar contains a syntactic component, a semantic component, and a phonological component. The latter two are purely interpretive; they play no part in the recursive generation of sentence structures. The syntactic component consists of a base and a transformational component. The base, in turn, consists of a categorical subcomponent and a lexicon. The base generates deep structures. A deep structure enters the semantic component and receives a semantic interpretation; it is mapped by the transformational rules into a surface structure, which is then given a phonetic interpretation by the rules of the phonological component. Thus the grammar assigns semantic interpretations to signals, this association being mediated by the recursive rules of the syntactic component.[6]

The categorical subcomponent (part of the base of the syntactic component) generates deep structures by means of a series of re-writing (or categorial) rules, which expand a single grammatical category into a string of other grammatical categories, such as S → NP + VP, which reads: re-write S(entence) as Noun Phrase + Verb Phrase. Re-writing rules also define the underlying grammatical relations of a sentence – or, more precisely, the deep structure of a surface structure sentence, which can be represented in the form of a tree-diagram (see the section of Colin's paper 'The Grande Syntagmatique Revisited' entitled 'Preliminary Remarks on the Table of the Grande Syntagmatique'). Tree-diagrams inter-relate three elements: a root node (the topmost node), preterminal nodes, which are dominated by the root node, and terminal nodes (the lexical entries). At the end of re-writing rules, the category symbols are replaced by lexical entries (for example, the category symbol N is re-written as a particular noun). Strings containing grammatical categories are called preterminal strings, whereas strings containing lexical entries are called terminal strings.

Category symbols such as N cannot simply be re-written in terms of any lexical entry belonging to the class of nouns. Each category symbol is analysable into a set of complex symbols, called *selectional features* (the inherent grammatical and semantic components of lexical items). Thus, a particular noun category symbol may be represented in terms of the following selectional features: [+N, +Common, +Count, +Animate, -Human]. Only a noun which posseses these particular features (such as 'dog', 'cat', etc.) can then be inserted into the preterminal string to form a terminal string. The selectional features therefore specify the conditions or constraints placed on the choice of lexical items which can be inserted into preterminal strings.

The two constant reference points for all the essays in this section are the formulation of the concept of filmic competence, which involves an assessment of the psychological reality of film semiology, and Metz's grande syntagmatique (or, more generally, the notion of filmic grammaticality). The grande syntagmatique is the founding moment of classic film semiology (because it identifies intensional filmic meanings – i.e. meanings specific to filmic discourse), while discussions of filmic competence constitute one of the most fundamental aspects of the new film semiologists' re-evaluation of classic film semiology.

The first paper in this section, by Dominique Chateau, highlights the limitations of classic film semiology and begin to discuss the necessity to move beyond it, primarily through the employment of TGG. It begins to explore what a TGG of film would look like, what its main 'objects' and tools of analysis would be, and what results it expects to achieve. The second paper, Michel Colin's detailed re-reading of Metz's grande syntagmatique in terms of TGG, is the most explicit indication of what a TGG of film looks like. The final paper illustrates Colin's attempt to continue this re-assessment of classic film semiology but with concepts drawn from non-linguistic areas of cognitive science.

The most characteristic aspect of the work of Chateau and Colin is that it is not, in relation to classic film semiology, merely a more complicated formal model of film (although it is that as well) because, more crucially, it attempts to make film semiology descriptively adequate by integrating into its framework cognitive theory. But here we must point out the differences between Chateau's and Colin's cognitive theories of film from that of the cognitive paradigm of film well known to Anglo-American film scholars (the work of 'the cognitivists', represented by David Bordwell, Edward Branigan, and Noël Carroll).[7] Whereas Chateau and Colin develop and transform classic film semiology using concepts drawn primarily from TGG and generative semantics, the cognitivists employ concepts drawn for the most part from non-linguistic areas of cognitive science. Furthermore, whereas the work of Chateau and Colin was formulated in relation to classic film semiology, the work of the cognitivists was formulated in relation to (more accurately, in opposition to) post-structural film theory. Both the cognitivists and post-structural film theorists study the film-spectator interface, but differ radically in the manner in which they theorise this interface. The cognitivists are primarily interested in how the spectator employs cognitive knowledge and processes to comprehend the basic level of the film's meaning (the cause-effect logic of its narrative, spatial and temporal relations, etc.). The post-structural film theorists were interested in the way film engaged with the spectator's unconscious psychic processes, such as fetishism, voyeurism, disavowal, the Oedipal narrative trajectory, etc., which were seen to function like other dominant discourses in strengthening each spectator's identity (which was implicitly posited as masculine, for the above psychic processes primarily act as defence mechanisms for masculine identity). Bordwell does not deny that both paradigms can be reconciled (because they operate on different but parallel levels),[8] although he offers no research that attempts such a reconciliation. However, in his disputation with me, Carroll is rather pessimistic about any reconciliation between the two paradigms.[9]

One of the most remarkable results of Colin's essay 'The Grande Syntagmatique Revisited' is that it explicitly transforms film semiology into a descriptively adequate discipline, not only by raising the issue of its psychological reality, but also by applying Chomsky's notion of creativity to film (the generation of infinite phenomena by finite rules). Colin achieves this by characterising the eight syntagmatic types of the grande syntagmatique in terms of selectional features. As I pointed out above, in TGG selectional features specify the inherent grammatical and semantic components of lexical items. In reformulating the grande syntagmatique in terms of selectional features, Colin makes explicit the inherent semantic features of the eight syntagmatic types. For example, Colin defines the descriptive syntagma in terms of the following selectional features:

<+diegetic, +specific, -narrative, +linear>

This reads: in the descriptive syntagma, the events depicted constitute part of the narrative world (in opposition to the generic events depicted in the parallel syntagma, for example); the events depicted exist in a specific space (in opposition to the catalogue of events depicted in the bracket syntagma and the generic events in the parallel syntagma); it is non-narrative (for there is no causality between the events depicted in each shot); and, a chronological relationship is signified between the events depicted in consecutive shots. (In the case of the descriptive syntagma, only spatial co-existence is signified.)

Due to this more explicit formulation of the syntagmatic types, Colin is able to iron out many of the asymmetries in the grande syntagmatique, particularly those not noticed before – including Metz's problematic definition of the distinction between the scene and sequence (which, for Colin, is based on the presence or absence of the feature <inclusive>), and the distinction between the parallel and bracket syntagmas (for Colin, based on the presence or absence of the feature <diegetic>).

But the most remarkable results of this re-reading of the grande syntagmatique is that Colin can brush aside the positivists' question of whether Metz's table is exhaustive. For, as with all generative models, the actual, manifest syntagmatic types merely constitute the end result (the epiphenomenon) of the generative process. Within the generative framework, we can identify and analyse, not only actual syntagmas, but also possible (i.e. potential) syntagmas and impossible syntagmas. Once all the finite selectional features have been identified, the potentially infinite number of syntagmatic types can be conceived and generated. Colin gives the example of a potential syntagma consisting of the following selectional features: <+diegetic, -specific, -linear>. This syntagma does not correspond to any of the eight identified by Metz, and may not have yet been manifest in a film (a phenomenon more common in verbal language, in which many of the sentences spoken and written everyday are manifest for the first time). But Colin also notes that some syntagmas can never be manifest in film, such as a non-linear sequence shot – due, of course, to the specific material traits/physical nature of film.

For Colin, then, the primary aim of the grande syntagmatique is not the identification of the actual syntagmatic types, but the identification of the more fundamental selectional features that combine to form these syntagmatic types. This generative conception of film is, for me, one of the most fruitful results of a generative grammar of film, for it enables the film semiologist to rethink the fundamental question of filmic 'grammar' or 'syntax' – or, to avoid the linguistic terminology, the question of the sequencing of shots. Ultimately, it enables the film semiologist to consider the possiblity of defining a non-prescriptive criterion of filmic grammaticality.

A second question posed by Colin's re-reading of Metz's grande syntagmatique is the psychological reality of film semiology, which is discussed briefly at the end of the 'The Grande Syntagmatique Revisited'. Within the context of TGG, film semiology is characterised as positing a relation of identity between its semiological descriptions and psychologically real structures – i.e. mental states and processing operations in the spectator's mind. But here we see Colin confusing the different types of theoretical adequacy of grammars. Metz proposes the grande syntagmatique as an observationally adequate model, since it is based upon the structural linguistic goal of segmenting and classifying the basic units of language. I regard Colin's re-reading of the grande syntagmatique as an attempt to raise it to the level of descriptive adequacy – as a model that attempts to represent each spectator's filmic competence (knowledge necessary for the comprehension of spatio-temporal relations in the image-track). However, in the conclusion to his paper, Colin characterises this shift as one from descriptive to explanatory adequacy. But this assumes that the grande syntagmatique already represents each spectator's competence, and that Colin's aim has been to compare the grande syntagmatique to other descriptively adequate models of film (which, clearly, is not the case).

Colin considers the psychological reality of the grande syntagmatique further in 'Film Semiology as a Cognitive Science'. But he also begins to employ concepts from non-linguistic areas of cognitive science to develop his own theory of the way spectators construct the spatial relations between shots. Colin analyses this with a scene from *The Barefoot Contessa*, and concludes that the (mental representation of) diegetic space is not fixed and solid, but fluid and open to revision. Furthermore, the spectator can 'correct' contradictions between different codes, as when screen direction is disrupted by the violation of the 180 degree rule.

To conclude we can note that, at first, classic film semiology asked whether film is a 'langue ou langage' and soon realised that it is a 'langage sans langue'. This directed classic film semiology away from attempts to discover in film a paradigmatic dimension (the basis of *la langue*) and towards the film's syntagmatic dimension. It is on this level that Metz in particular located (narrative) film's specific level of articulation, which he formalised in the eight syntagmatic categories of his grande syntagmatique. He identified these specific units of filmic meaning by employing the structural linguistic methodology of segmentation and classification. The driving force behind the grande syntagmatique is therefore the desire to define filmic specificity. A more comprehensive definition of filmic specificity was forthcoming in Metz's *Language and Cinema* where it is defined, not in terms of one code but a specific combination of codes. In the same book, Metz also defined classic film semiology's aim as the attempt to 'understand how film is understood'. This seemingly innocent phrase has been quoted time and again by the new film semiologists, and provides the link between classic film semiology and the new film semiology. Colin in particular confronts the consequences of this phrase in his paper 'Film Semiology as a Cognitive Science'. He equates the research areas of cognitive science and film semiology (vision, language, and problem solving), and makes it explicit that film semiology 'must describe the rules governing the links between visual representation of 3-D scenes and conceptual structures', which would then make it possible to show 'how the mental construction of diegetic space in film can be explained'.

These proclamations also prepare us for Roger Odin's work in section 3 of this anthology. Odin begins his paper 'For a Semio-Pragmatics of Film' by stating that the aim of film semiology is two-fold: to understand how film is understood, and to understand the mechanisms of the film-spectator relationship. It seems reasonable to claim that the aims of Colin and Odin are very close to those of the cognitivists (particularly Bordwell and Branigan).[10] The presentation of Colin's (and Odin's) work to an Anglo-American audience could then begin to reconcile the paradigms of European and American film theory.

Notes

1   For a discussion of the influence of the language analysis tradition and of Bachelard on film semiology, refer to my two papers: 'Filmic Meaning: The Semantics-Pragmatics Interface', *Kodikas/Code*, 14, 3/4, 1991, pp. 261-279; and 'The Structural Linguistic Foundation of Film Semiology', *Language and Communication*, 11, 3, 1991, pp. 197-216.

2   Noam Chomsky, *Language and Mind*, New York: Harcourt, Brace and World, Inc, 1968, pp. 65-66.

3   Noam Chomsky, *Aspects of the Theory of Syntax*, Cambridge, Mass.: MIT Press, 1965, p. 202.

4   Chomsky, ibid., p. 34; emphasis added.

5   ibid., p. 31.

6   ibid., p. 141.

7   David Bordwell, *Narration in the Fiction Film*, London: Methuen, 1985; Edward Branigan, *Narrative Comprehension and Film*, London: Routledge, 1992; Noël Carroll, *Mystifying Movies: Fads and Fallacies in Contemporary Film Theory*, New York: Columbia University Press, 1988.

8   'The theory I advance attends to the perceptual and cognitive aspects of film viewing. While I do not deny the usefulness of psychoanalytical approaches to the spectator, I see no reason to claim for the unconscious any activities which can be explained on other grounds. In general, current film theory has underestimated the importance of the spectator's conscious and preconscious work. Study of narrative cognition may in fact be a prelude to psychoanalytic inquiry for the same reason that Freud was at pains to show that psychoanalytic theory finds its best application when cognitive explanations fall short'. David Bordwell, *Narration in the Fiction Film*, p. 30.

9   Noël Carroll, 'Cognitivism, Contemporary Film Theory and Method: A Response to Warren Buckland', *Journal of Dramatic Theory and Criticism*, vol VI, 2, Spring 1992, pp. 199-219. Carroll is responding to my review article 'Critique of Poor Reason', *Screen*, 30, 4, 1989, pp. 80-103, a review of his book *Mystifying Movies*.

10 Roger Odin compares his work to Bordwell in 'La sémio-pragmatique du cinéma sans crise, ni désillusion', *Hors Cadre*, 7, 1989, pp. 77-92, esp. pp. 87-88.

TOWARDS A GENERATIVE MODEL OF FILMIC DISCOURSE

DOMINIQUE CHATEAU[1]

Today, it is rare for publications dealing with filmic discourse to ignore the results of the research carried out for over ten years in film semiology. It is by systematically basing its arguments upon elementary scientific principles that, for the first time, allowed significant progress in our understanding of filmic structure, and our re-evaluation of ideas previously expressed in often impressionistic and obscure terms. We find that this change in perspective does not hinder but encourages discussion of new ideas on filmic structure. This is because it is no longer sufficient only to enrich the literature on film with more or less inventive ideas – since the interpretation of film is from now on inseparable from methodological reflection. In other words, the debate moves beyond the 'cinephile' discussion and places itself in the general perspective of research in the human sciences. Like Christian Metz,[2] who has demonstrated the usefulness of adapting to film concepts from European structuralism (although limiting their explanatory range to the corpus of classical narrative films), I attempt here to employ concepts stemming, for the most part, from American linguistics – with the purpose of laying the foundations for a model of the structure of all film, photographic or drawn, narrative or non-narrative, classic or modern.

Preliminary Clarification

For a long time, the concept of film language has been considered a problem, and has now become a supposition of semiology. Beyond the superficial terminological debate, there is all the empirical data to justify the identification of film with signifying systems (or language in the extended sense of the term). In short, film language is nothing less and nothing more that a set of semiological properties of film:

- *nothing less*: instead of presenting itself, as in the past, in obscure or general terms, film language must take the form of a complete and an explicit as possible list of apparently incontestable and universal properties of filmic structure. As a practical consequence of this, there arises the pressing need to ensure that the list will not involve any characteristic which is too distinctive, one that would exclude such and such a class of films from the research domain;

- *nothing more*: it will not be necessary to try and find a more extensive formulation of the concept of filmic language than the one involved in the explanation (or abstract representation) of pre-given empirical data. It is a question of a broad definition that in no way prejudges a form of film that will be captured in all later attempts to construct the internal laws of filmic structure in a conceptual representational system.

More specifically, we can say in conclusion that film semiology is not properly speaking a *theory*, that is to say, a set of ideas about filmic structure, but rather a *discipline*, that is to say, a sphere of knowledge within which can be developed all types of theories supported by different ideas connected to filmic structure, with each theory giving a specific interpretation of the common foundation of film language.

Some Properties of Film Disclosed by a Semiological Analysis
1. The process of communication is discontinuous. The relation established between film maker and spectator/hearer, through a filmic message, is characterised by the absence of direct contact between them. Moreover, there is a division in the two unconnected processes of transmission (recording and projection) which employ numerous intermediaries. Finally, it is impossible for the partners of filmic communication to change roles.[3]

2. The filmic signifiers belong to one of two sensory orders: auditory and visual, abbreviated respectively to AO and VO. Each element that comes within the province of the VO or AO belongs to a set of phenomena which utilize the visual or auditory systems, but differentiate themselves in specific ways to other phenomena related to the VO or the AO. In relation to the VO we can distinguish the image from the graphic marks (written material), and in relation to the AO real sounds from music. These materials of expression, which constitute the signifiers of film, are not in themselves specific. The material of filmic expression is, in reality, a 'specific combination of several materials of expression, not a specific material of expression'.[4]

3. We can distinguish three main types of elements in the visual material of expression: graphic marks, drawn images, and photographic images. Optical recording manifests them respectively in the credit sequence, in cartoon images, and through the filming of fixed or moving objects, using a fixed or moving camera. These three materials enter into the construction of films, either in separate images or together in the same image.

4. The filmic image (abbreviated to FI) is characterised by a particular form that optical recording imposes universally on the visual elements of the material of filmic expression. The FI defines in a (typically rectangular) frame a delimited space inhabited by a certain arrangement of forms (bodies, objects, faces). The animation [*défilement*] of a FI at any moment (i) leaves the framed space fixed or animates it partially or totally, alternates between fixed and moving transformations of space, or varies between them, and (ii) leaves fixed the forms represented in the frame, animates certain movements, or else alternates between fixed and mobile, or again varies between them.

5. A FI is a 'series of states' that projection transforms into a 'temporal continuity in the concreteness of the present'.[5] It can be broken down into fragments, the smallest being the photogram. A FI containing n photograms is divisible into at least n distinct FIs. The number n is theoretically unlimited.

6. The FI or shot is a unit of filmic combination unlimited in number, and is neither discrete, arbitrary, nor pre-established. There is no lexicon of shots. The meaning of shots depends on the objects represented in them, their arrangement, movement, and relations. The number of these objects is indeterminate.

7. Shots can be superimposed, or they can follow one another by overlapping during a determinate lapse of time.

8. Several shots depicting the same space or a different space can appear simultaneously within the frame.

9. The shots can be arranged in linear sequences. We can say that the length of a whole sequence corresponds to the number of shots appearing in it. There is no upper limit to the length of a sequence (we can always add a new shot no matter where it is placed within a given sequence). Clearly, each sequence produced is of finite length.

10. We do not know how to interpret the phrase 'this is an ungrammatical sequence'.

The Form of Filmic Grammar

The notion of grammar has always occupied a central place in the work of film theorists. Nevertheless, for this interest to appear warranted, it has been necessary to await Christian Metz's film theory based on linguistics – which no longer forces film theory to limit itself to fruitless discussions of film in terms of normative grammars of natural languages, but instead submits it to a modern methodological analysis. Linguists are no longer concerned with producing scholarly works that teach speakers to use their native language correctly. Faced with the increased number of these books (most conforming to works of 'correct usage'), the linguist's attention is primarily focused on the properties underlying linguistic phenomena, and develops his work according to concepts which must simulate the capacity of speakers to construct and comprehend phrases in their native language. In relation to film semiology, the preceding list of ten properties constitute the basis of underlying traits upon which can be found the abstract representation of filmic competence.

From this point of view, property 10 is of special interest. Isn't our inability to interpret the notion of an ungrammatical sequence an obstacle to the whole project of filmic grammar? The answer to this question is clear: no. In fact, we only know that the articulation of images (and sounds) can be entrusted to any rule and obey any process of structuration. There should then be no rational ground to oppose the construction of a 'filmic grammar' based on the principles of arithmetic, chess or hydrostatics! Whatever model of description we imagine (no matter which methodology it is based upon), it must simulate the processes compatible to the semiological properties of film and therefore with film language: amongst which appear the absence of a criterion of grammaticality. By this we mean that the processes in question do not impose systematic constraints of correct formation. Among the same semiological properties of film are also to be found some *specific* features of materials of expression, and *specific* necessary conditions affecting the reproduction and manipulation of the signifiers resulting from these conditions; consequently, the processes in question obey certain *specific* laws which are compatible with the semiological nature of film. Thus, to clarify with the aid of list 1-10: film language is defined by physical constraints (separation of image and sound tracks, spatial and temporal limitations imposed on the image in its context, etc.); by the potentialities from the point of view of the signifier (plurality of materials of expression, a more or less high degree of iconic abstraction, etc.); as well as the combined viewpoint – both within images (a mix of visual and sound[6] signifiers juxtaposed in time and space) and between images (sequencing, simultaneity or consecutiveness of images and sounds etc.). The basis of a filmic grammar must be determined from concepts adapted to these constraints and possibilities. In other words, it must be constructed from descriptive laws revealed by the analyst of film language. The development of a formal representation of the structuring strategies that underlie the filmic text has no other foundation. But to carry out this task, it is first of all advisable to know how the concepts constituting filmic grammar correspond to the aim of developing a formal representation of underlying structuring strategies. Christian

Metz's 'grande syntagmatique' is, in this respect, an example we can follow, since it is based upon a justified understanding of filmic grammar.

However, Metz's finding in favour of a structuralist scientific methodology is strongly implicated, not only in this justified understanding of filmic grammar, but more fundamentally in the corpus to which he has limited his research, where 'filmic process' is synonymous with 'process of the filmic representation of narrative'. In fact, if the figures of sequential ordering codified by (or in) the 'grande syntagmatique' conform to the essential super-structural rules of narrative syntax, their number does not exceed the events observed in the corpus of classical narrative films, with the addition of one or two tolerated syntagmatic types (cf. Metz, *Film Language*). In truth, the 'grande syntagmatique' represents prescriptive rules governing the formation and comprehension of filmic segments because they only appear in classical narrative films. Creativity is therefore limited to the 'filling in' of the eight syntagmatic figures and at the same time by an allegiance to a single form of filmic discourse. For me, who looks at the entire class of possible films (historical and logical), the right thing to do is construct a system which allows us to determine the set of possible sequential orderings (real or potential), taking into account the properties of filmic signs and their combination, and the various kinds of super-structural rules open to exploitation. It should be a question of a system of rules of the game (those of film, not chess) governing the formation and comprehension of any filmic sequence, independent of all textual overdetermination. The term 'rules of the game' signifies, in fact, that after having described the semiological conditions of film through filmic language and instead of prescribing image sequences only for a class of specific films, we will be able to forsee by means of a formal calculus an unlimited number of image sequences for each type of super-structural rule employed. In short, the filmic grammar should have as its basis, and at the same time for its standard, the descriptive laws deriving from film language, including all kinds of prescriptive laws which, like the 'grande syntagmatique', specify a practice of historically delimited filmic discourse. In other respects, the filmic grammar can note the transgressions that a code such as the 'grande syntagmatique' has undergone, and characterize these transgressions in terms of subsidary rules, intended either to modify the super-structural rules or to invent new ones ('creativity which changes the rules', according to Chomsky).

Some Problems of Filmic Syntax

The expression 'filmic syntax' is used here in its technical sense. We assume that the formation-comprehension of film obeys the 'rules of the game', in which the role of a filmic grammar is determined by the laws of filmic structure. A model of the structure of film (of filmic grammar) therefore represents an assumption concerning the production and understanding of the filmic message. To use the expression 'filmic syntax', knowing that it can have a technical sense, is already a way to make an assumption concerning filmic structure. In fact, we aim to establish formal principles that govern the construction of a succession of filmic images, of the type: can we combine two shots in any order? Is the co-occurence of images bound by the restrictions of specific selections? Does the construction of sequences obey relational, classificational, transformational processes? etc. Clearly, these considerations will never take into account all meaning (it will be a question, for example, of determining the processes that affect the meaning and those that do not), but they first of all attempt to formally characterise the mechanisms that link meanings to filmic messages. The results obtained must allow us to specify the form of a filmic grammar.

In the wording of property 9 I have implicitly discarded the notion of sequence as a scene or fragment of a story. I have substituted for it the aesthetically neutral mathematical definition: we call a sequence any succession of elements joined in a determinate linear order (the shot is therefore a sequence containing one element). We can form a sequence S from two sequences S1 and S2 by successively lining up all the shots in S1 then all those in S2. Having established this first structural level, we can ask ourselves, like Sol Worth,[7] if a filmic sequence is:

– COMMUTATIVE – that is to say: does $S1S2 = S2S1$? From a general perspective, this cannot be the case, except when there is strict identity between S1 and S2. More precisely, we can show that the necessity of the order S1 then S2, for example, depends on super-structures (either narrative or discursive – for example, if S1 represents x running after y and S2 represents y dead, then the order S1S2 is determined by the narrative structure 'x killed y'). In accordance with property 10, the absence of a criterion of grammaticality, we can conclude that systematic constraints of correct ordering in the formation-comprehension of filmic sequences do not exist, except the constraints imposed by the super-structural rules.

– ASSOCIATIVE – that is to say: does $(S1S2)S3 = S1(S2S3)$? The equality seems real on the strictly visual level: it is possible to 'show' sequences S1 and S2, then the outcome with S3, or again, with the same effect, S2 and S3, then S1 with the outcome. But on the level of meaning the two sequences will not be the same. In general, the meaning of the whole is not equal to the linear sum of the meaning of its parts. From the syntactic point of view, we can establish: 1) the absence in film of a pre-established paradigmatic dimension (classes of substitutable terms) and the absence of the categorisation of shots analogous to those of natural language (noun, verb, adjective, etc.); 2) the existence of distributional schemas governing the regrouping of shots (alternating montage obeying a distribution according to the schema ABAB ...); 3) this paradigmatic *a posteriori* lies on the super-structural level (to take the example in 2, the montage develops the thematic opposition war/peace).

In conclusion, we see that in spite of the absence of a criterion of grammaticality analogous to that governing the language system [*la langue*], filmic structure is characterised, on the one hand, by certain properties of formal structure and, on the other hand, by certain properties dependent on super-structures. By analysing this observation, we can develop a fairly precise representation of the mental processes governing the formation-comprehension of filmic sequences. The following tree-diagram will make the point more comprehensible (for simplicity of exposition it refers to a narrative segment):

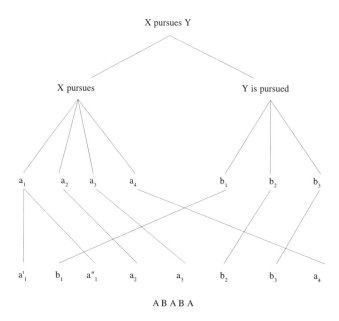

In considering the beginning and end of the diagram, we see that the filmic sequence it concerns (on this level of analysis, there is no need to specify in any more detail the actual filmic representation) has for a structural description the pair:

(X pursuing Y: interweaved ABABA)

In other words, it is a chase scene between two actants, articulated through alternating montage (it alternatively shows the two actants running). Very generally, if we consider the diagram from top to bottom, we can see the successive partitions, and from bottom to top the successive syntheses. In fact, the following three fundamental operations are necessary to the understanding of the proposed sequence:

- *classificational*: the narrative schema 'X pursues Y' is analysed (in the chemical sense of the term) into two sub-schemas, which determine two distribitional classes, A for the pursuers and B for the pursued;
- *transformational*: before it takes its definitive order (the resulting sequence), we have a series of transformations – for example: disjunction of a_1 into a'_1 and a''_2 (cf. property 5), permutations between b_1, a''_1, a_2 and a_3 etc.
- *relational*: the definitive order necessitates a link between a'_1 and b_1, b_1 and a''_1, and a_2 etc. (with the generic constraints: if X runs after Y, we must see Y traverse particular spatial locations before X does).

Remarks on the Textual Analysis of Film

In a celebrated article, Eisenstein recommended 'analysis in close-up' (as opposed to 'in long shot' or 'in medium shot'), which he defines as follows: 'by means of a close analysis, the analyst 'breaks down' the film into its components and identifies its elements, in order to study the whole film exactly as engineers and specialists study a new structural model in their own field'.[8] The 'grande syntagmatique' differs from this programme in that it submits 'by means of a close analysis' a corpus of (classical narrative) films rather than a singular filmic text. In so far as the theoretical model is concerned, it departs from the particular in favour of the general. Moreover, if it is useful to analyse, according to a well-defined order of importance, a film into its component parts (*Adieu Phillipine*, for example), it is not the same as studying the entire structure. In so far as the model of application is concerned, it treats the part at the expense of the whole. To unite the research of Eisenstein and Metz – respectively, textual analysis and the theory of filmic structure – requires a great deal of conceptual integration. We cannot progress any faster than the linguists who, in a discipline supposedly more mature than ours, are groping their way towards the integration of the problems of textual analysis and generative theory.

However, it seems to me that this work is contained in rough outline in the *theoretical* model that I have just developed – in particular, in the notion of a structural description: we can consider representing the structure of a given filmic text by reproducing all the pairs of structural descriptions that correspond with different sized segments found in the film. Would the interlocking between these pairs, similar to the interlocking of the segments, adequately clarify the macro-textual conditions? Film semiology will no doubt respond negatively. In particular, it is necessary to ask oneself about the role of the filmographic and profilmic elements (to use Souriau's terms):[9] respectively, the material characteristics of the images recorded on the film and the different things it reproduces. Another aspect of the question deserves elaboration: from the point of view of natural language, the distinction between a sequence of phrases and a text (spoken or written) and, in the same manner, the distinction between sequence and film (part and whole). The causal connection, established in the narrative, is the first case of this qualitative distinction: it establishes the co-occurence of two shots such as 'Peter seduced John's wife' and 'John challenged Peter to a duel'. There are many narrative or discursive analogical relations, which can come into play in the textual modification of shots and sequences: comparison, opposition, specification, 'thematisation', etc. It will be necessary to study very closely the schemas of 'mise en texte' (according to the German linguist Isenberg).

In the course of the future development of film semiology, we shall continue to employ linguistics. In any case, it will no longer be a question of mechanically applying technical methods, not only because they are open to critical discussion (there are many in linguistics), or even because film is a specific language, but especially because it is not advisable to ignore the profound consequences of theoretical choice which guides us towards the science of language. The contemporary linguistic contribution rests entirely on the axiom according to which spoken language has priority over written language. At first, there is no reason to think that this proposition can assume any role in film theory, even if – there is no need to demonstrate it – the implications largely extend beyond linguistics. Defence of this axiom runs counter to the classical argument of the primacy of Greco-Latin and the languages they helped to form (in so far as they are written). But as John Lyons has noted: 'When the traditional grammarian maintained the principle of the priority of the written language, he was, of course, thinking primarily of the language of literature (rather than, for instance, the language of telegrams, newspaper-headlines or public notices); and he would tend to say that the literary language was the 'noblest' or most 'correct' form of the language'.[10] Now, the majority of film analyses, until recently (except for journalistic criticism, which continues) subjected without discussion filmic structure to schemas of literary thought. On the one hand, this excluded certain types of films (documentaries, non-representational films, etc.); on the other hand, it was revealing a very narrow conception of filmic structure, since it emerged from the aftermath of this 'classical' ideology which established the priority of 'literary language' on written languages of a specific type and written language in general on spoken language. Indeed, we can do what we wish with modern linguistic methods, even falsify them. But, when we claim to respect the spirit as much as the letter, that is to say, the moment when we place film semiology within the great methodological debate of the human sciences, it is advisible to acknowledge the fundamental questioning and the epistemological principles that proceed from them.

(*Translated by Warren Buckland*)

Notes

[1]   This article is a summary of a doctoral thesis 'Problèmes de la théorie sémiologigue du cinéma' defended, in June 1975, at the University of Paris I. [A version of this thesis was subsequently published as *Le cinéma comme langage*, Brussels: AISS - Publications de la Sorbonne, 1987 – trans.]

[2]   Cf. *Film Language: A Semiotics of the Cinema*, trans. Michael Taylor, New York: Oxford University Press, 1974; *Language and Cinema*, trans. Donna Jean Umiker-Sebeok, The Hague: Mouton, 1974; 'L'étude sémiologique du langage cinéma-tographique: à quelle distance en sommes-nous d'une possibilité réelle de formalisation?' *Revue d'Esthétique*, 26, 2-3-4, 1973, pp. 129-143. [reprinted as 'Sémiologie audio-visuelle et linguistique générative' in Metz's *Essais sémiotiques*, Paris: Klincksieck, 1977, pp. 110-28 – trans.]

[3]   Cf. my analysis in 'Propositions pour une théorie du film', *Ça-Cinéma*, 1, 1973, pp. 78-95.

[4]   Metz, *Langage et Cinéma*, p. 25.

[5]   Abraham Moles, *Art et ordinateur*, Tournai: Casterman, 1971, p. 225.

[6]   Concerning the dimension of sound in film, simply touched on here, refer to my article 'Projet pour une sémiologie des relations audio-visuelles dans le film', *Musique en jeu*, 23, 1976.

[7]   Sol Worth, 'The development of a semiotic of film', *Semiotica*, 1969.

[8]   Eisenstein, 'En gros plan', in *Au-delà des étoiles*, Paris: 10/18, p. 266.

[9]   [These are two of Etienne Souriau's seven levels of filmic reality, which are in total: the afilmic, the profilmic, the filmographic, the filmophantic, the diegetic, the spectatorial, and the creational. For a brief discussion of these terms in English, see Edward Lowry, *The Filmology Movement and Film Study in France*, Michigan: UMI Research Press, 1985, pp. 84-86. -trans.]

[10] John Lyons, *Introduction to Theoretical Linguistics*, Cambridge: Cambridge University Press, 1968, p. 42.

THE GRANDE SYNTAGMATIQUE REVISITED

MICHEL COLIN

Introduction

It may seem paradoxical to go back to the grande syntagmatique of narrative film developed by Metz twenty years ago.[1] Much of the literature on film semiology has all too often been limited to simply discussing it, and to listing counter-examples which, contrary to what the authors seemed to think, could never be mistaken for counter-evidence.[2]

The paradox lies in the fact that, although few contemporary texts refer to this syntagmatique, which has now been discarded for no real reason and without having been proved wrong, it is still systematically used as a teaching 'tool'. It is as if a supposedly obsolete 'theory' could retain some value within the context of the teaching of editing codes.

Having frequently been involved in this type of initiation, I was able to observe that these so-called pedagogic virtues of the grande syntagmatique were not self-evident. Listing a range of different types of segments, and examples illustrating them, does not in itself enable you to teach it, to show students, in other words, how to use it as an explicit way of describing certain aspects of film. In order to use the Grande Syntagmatique of narrative film as a teaching tool, one must first explain some of its underlying principles, and attempt to solve the problems encountered in the course of the teaching process.

These two difficulties are indeed related, since, as will be shown later, one's conception of how knowledge is passed on (knowledge, in this case, of certain properties of film editing) depends on how it is represented. Similarly, in the field of linguistics, a normative grammar such as that of Grevisse, is not taught in the same way as a descriptive grammar, such as structural grammar.

It might be said, for instance, in the terminology of Artificial Intelligence, that whereas the former would be explained through a declarative method, a procedural method would be used for the latter.

Both of these two types of representation have advantages and dis-advantages, from a theoretical as well as a pedagogical point of view. Rather than discuss them here – the few points made in chapter 1 [of *Cinéma, télévision, cognition* – that is, 'Film semiology as a cognitive science'] will be sufficient -, I shall attempt to show why the teaching of the Grande Syntagmatique would greatly benefit from a combination of both types of formulation. I shall therefore draw on my experience, particularly of teaching introductory courses to what is known as film 'language', without, however, intending to present anything like a lecture or what is often associated with lectures: a course-book.

I shall, consequently, refrain from any didactic method of argumentation, such as a progression from the simplest to the most complex. Instead, I shall begin with an analysis of how Metz presents his Grande Syntagmatique, particularly in the table drawn in his *Film Language*.[3] Only then will it be possible to identify any theoretical and pedagogical problems, and to consider formulating a certain number of positions.

Preliminary Remarks on the Table of the Grande Syntagmatique (GS)
The GS table corresponds formally to what is known as a tree diagram, linking three types of elements (nodes): a root node, intermediary nodes and terminal nodes (or 'leaves'), all of these nodes being connected together through strings.

In linguistics, trees are used to represent syntagmatic relations. Here, the S node is the initial symbol of derivation, which means that syntagmatic relations lie within the sentence. The intermediary nodes represent grammatical categories, and the 'leaves' stand for the terminal vocabulary (such as the lexicon). As for the branches, they indicate a relation of dominance, which can be paraphrased 'can be rewritten as'. It is worth noticing that in the syntax of natural languages, adjacent branches – those sharing the same node – are connected through the logical operator &. Thus, the rule

$$S \rightarrow NP + VP$$

which reads:

S can be written as NP and VP
will be represented by the tree:

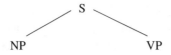

In the case of the GS table, the three types of objects are instantly recognizable: an initial symbol (the autonomous segment), a non-terminal vocabulary: syntagmatic types (syntagmas, non-chronological and chronological syntagmas, narrative, linear and sequences) and a terminal vocabulary: the eight syntagmatic types (autonomous shot, parallel syntagma, bracket syntagma, descriptive syntagma, alternate syntagma, scene, ordinary sequence and episodic sequence). As a tree, the GS will therefore be represented as:

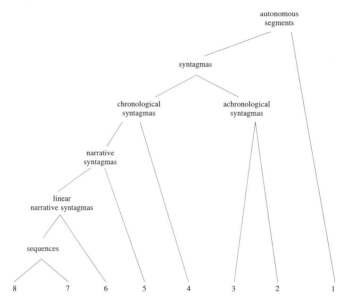

where 1 = autonomous shot, 2 = parallel syntagma, 3 = bracket syntagma, 4 = descriptive syntagma, 5 = alternate syntagma, 6 = scene, 7 = ordinary sequence and 8 = episodic sequence.

In the GS tree,[4] unlike the tree used in syntax, adjacent branches are not linked by the connector &, but by W (or 'disjunctive' connector). As for the branches themselves, they indicate a relation of inclusion (AKO). The latter depends, of course, on the direction in which the tree-diagram is being read, corresponding to what Metz calls an inductive method, starting from the syntagmatic types observed in the film (the terminal nodes):

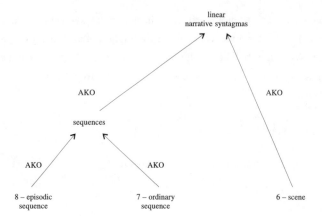

It can be seen that in the GS table, terminal syntagmatic types are in the singular, whereas others are in the plural. This difference can be explained by the distinction between AKO (is a sub-class of) and ISA (is an element of), which does correspond to the different periphrases respectively applied, for instance, to 'sequence' and 'ordinary sequence'. Thus, one would say: 'the ordinary sequence is a sequence' rather than 'ordinary sequences are sequences', and 'a sequence is a linear narrative syntagma' rather than 'the sequence is a linear narrative syntagma'.

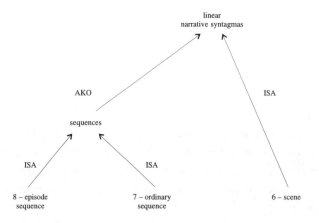

Metz goes on to show another way of reading the tree, corresponding to what he calls the deductive method, starting from the root of the tree and progressing towards the terminal nodes. This second method, however, as has just been shown, cannot be represented by the *same* table, not only because the relationships are different, but also because the nodes represent different objects. Indeed the objects here are not classes and sub-classes; the relationships are not relationships of inclusion, between a whole and its parts. Thus, starting from the root, an autonomous segment can be called an autonomous shot or a syntagma. In other words, the function of such a tree will be to represent the paths between the autonomous segment and the syntagmatic types; the intermediary nodes will then correspond to the properties characterising them: 'autonomous segment' (now in the singular) refers to an object, 'syntagma', 'chronological syntagma', etc. (also in the singular) refer to properties, and 'autonomous shot', 'parallel syntagma' etc., to the syntagmatic types that can be described by these properties. It can then be said, for instance, that an autonomous syntagma which is chronological, narrative, linear and is not a sequence, is a scene. The nodes are then connected by an ISA relationship, but the direction of the string is reversed. By showing the paths towards bracket and parallel syntagmas as continuous lines, and other routes as dotted lines, one can then represent the tree illustrating Metz's deductive method and apply it to the above-named categories as follows:

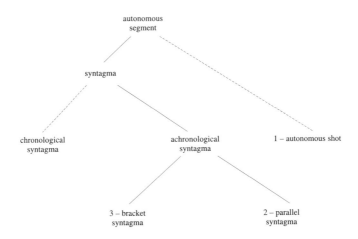

It can be seen that this representation is reminiscent of generative linguistics, which also use the deductive method. The main difference between this and the GS is that in the latter, the branches indicate possible choices (a disjunction), whereas in transformational generative grammar, (TGG), they indicate a concatenation (conjunction). As in the case of syntax, the branches could then mean 'can be rewritten as'. The initial symbol 'autonomous segment', dominating the nodes 'syntagma' and 'autonomous shot', could thus be rewritten as 'syntagma' or 'autonomous shot', which, according to the conventions of TGG, equating -> with 'can be rewritten as', and brackets with the disjunctive 'or', can be formalised by a set of rules of the type:

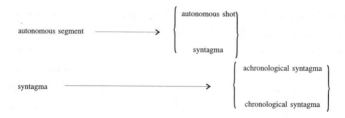

These observations on the formalisation of the GS would be of little interest if they did not raise real problems which are, of course, created by what the table is supposed to represent, rather than by the method of representation. Metz himself draws attention to some of these problems, such as that of the autonomous shot, which includes two completely heterogeneous types: the sequence-shot and the insert.

> It is possible, in particular, that the autonomous shot (Type 1 of my table) is a class rather than a single, terminal type ...; it is the only one of my types having so many sub-types, and this sort of "bulge" may indicate insufficient formalisation of the corresponding point.[5]

Another problem to be confronted when teaching the GS is that of the different approaches taken, depending on whether one interprets the GS table deductively or inductively. One example is Metz's analysis of the beginning of *Adieu Philippine*, in which he identifies two syntagmas: descriptive and ordinary sequence, connected by a cut, then a scene, itself connected by a cut, but a cut for effect this time: this scene precedes an episodic sequence, linked by a dissolve. The first two segments are clearly based on the identification of the two syntagmatic types, whereas the scene is defined on the basis of a cut for effect at the beginning, and a dissolve at the end. This difference of approach is all the more obvious as in the latter segment, the first two shots show a character putting a coin into a juke-box, then the same character in a café, which exactly fits the description of an ordinary sequence. If the method used for the first two segments had been applied to this one, it would have led to the detection of two segments: an ordinary sequence + a scene, where Metz only detects one segment.

It may be said, of course, that two fairly brief shots do not make a segment, but take place at a micro-segmental level, as Bellour would have said.[6] This does, however, raise the problem of what should be considered as an autonomous segment. Moreover, although there is no obligation to choose between the two approaches, it is nevertheless necessary to define the procedures by which they could be used conjointly. A large amount of research, particularly in the field of Artificial Intelligence, points to

MICHEL COLIN

the necessity of articulating what Metz calls the deductive and inductive methods, which might more accurately be called top-down and bottom-up procedures.[7] It may be seen, for instance, that an approach which uses punctuation marks such as the dissolve to identify an autonomous segment, then seeks to define its properties in order to determine its syntagmatic type, goes from the top downwards, although it is basically an inductive approach.

One more implication of the formalisation of the GS through the tree of selection is worth mentioning. Apart from the problem raised by Metz himself, the heterogeneous nature of the autonomous shot, another one can be found in the asymmetry between the branches corresponding respectively to non-chronological and chronological syntagmas. This, of course, reflects the fact that non-chronological syntagmas are far rarer than others in narrative films, which is normal, since a narrative film, by definition, tells a story, implying an order of precedence between events. If, however, one bears in mind what Metz calls the deductive reading of the table, it is impossible to tell the difference between parallel and bracket syntagmas. Both types are merely non-chronological syntagmas (no node helps us to differentiate them). In the case of chronological syntagmas, on the other hand, each node dominates a nonterminal as well as a terminal node, so that there is always a property which helps to distinguish this terminal node from other syntagmas. This difference can be illustrated by the following representation of the GS table in two separate parts:

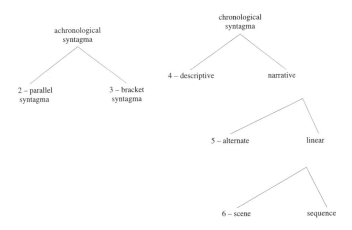

In the above table, only the sequence dominates two terminal nodes: 7 – the ordinary sequence and 8 – the episodic sequence. This is due, of course, to the fact that the ordinary sequence is the dominant syntagma. If, however, we were to limit ourselves to the ordinary sequence, the distinction between scene and sequence would pose a problem, for they would both be linear chronological syntagmas, undistinguishable from each other. Now, these syntagmas are the most deeply embedded in the tree, which shows that they are the two central syntagmas in the grande syntagmatique (and, predictably, the ones occurring most frequently in narrative film).

The Problem of the Autonomous Segment

> In distinguishing between the "shot" and the "sequence," everyday language clearly indicates that there are two things in the cinema (without prejudice to eventual intermediate levels): On the one hand there is the minimum segment, which is the shot ..., and on the other hand the autonomous segment.[8]

The notion of autonomous segment attempts, first and foremost, to reflect an intuitive fact, which characterises film as a visual form of discourse that cannot merely be defined as a succession of shots, just as verbal discourse cannot merely be defined as a succession of sentences.

Film technicians already distinguish, of course, between shots and sequences, in accordance with cutting and editing practices, which obey 'rules' on the ordering of shots, so as to make their mutual spatio-temporal relationships more intelligible. One frequent example illustrating this point is that of the alternating syntagma.[9] This type of segment can only be described by a configuration showing an alternation between shots from series A and series B, following an ABAB... pattern, and a certain type of spatio-temporal relationship: simultaneity between series A and B, but successivity between each shot, which can be represented as follows:

1		3		5		7	: A

	2		4		6		: B

1	2	3	4	5	6	7
A	B	A	B	A	B	A

A and B are simultaneous, but $1 < 2 < 3$,[10] etc. The prototypical example of this type of representation is that of the pursuer/pursued relationship. Interestingly, types of autonomous segment are often illustrated – like grammatical rules – through *ad hoc* examples, as if films did not always provide sufficiently clear examples of certain configurations. Thus, anyone familiar with linguistics will know that it is easier to illustrate the notion of simple sentence through an *ad hoc* phrase such as: 'The boy hits the ball' (Chomsky's example in *Syntactic Structures*), than to find a simple sentence of this type in literature. This does not mean, of course, that such a sentence does not belong among grammatical English sentences.

Similarly, the fact that it is easier to illustrate certain segments through *ad hoc* examples than through film extracts does not mean that these elements are not elements of codification of, for instance, spatio-temporal relationships. It simply means that such types of segment are abstract types, and that their concrete rendering implies a transformation of them. It will of course be necessary to describe in detail this relationship between types and their instances (or, as some would say, between types and tokens). However, we must first determine which status should be given to the notion of autonomous segment. Such a status is, to say the least, a complex one, for this notion refers both to a certain level of segmentation of the discursive surface of the film – a film can be divided into autonomous segments, then into shots – and a level of articulation: the GS can be read as a selection-tree linking types of syntagmatic ordering which are also types of autonomous segments.

This double reading enables us to explain the distinction, apparent in the GS table, between 'autonomous segment', which can be defined as 'syntagma' vs 'autonomous shot', and 'syntagma', which can be defined by syntagmatic types such as 'scene', 'descriptive syntagma', 'bracket syntagma', etc. The very choice of terms such as 'segment' and 'syntagma' is significant. What else can be said about a segment, if not that it results from a segmentation? The syntagma, on the other hand, is, according to linguistics, the product of syntagmatic rules, and therefore a combination of smaller elements.

It can thus be said that the problem with the GS table does not only lie in its double reading, but in the fact that it represents, within a single table, two tables, each with its own initial symbol and representing different approaches. Metz does, incidentally, foresee this problem, by recognising the difficulty of distinguishing between syntagma and autonomous shot, since this distinction is the only one to rest on a single formal criterion: one shot vs several shots.

> The autonomous shot is somehow apt to "contain" all the other varieties of shot.[11]

The status of the autonomous shot is all the more problematic as it includes the insert and the sequence-shot. Now, the association between the insert and other syntagmatic types is difficult to comprehend. An insert, by definition, cannot be substituted for a syntagma – and the sequence-shot is a syntagma; it is, as the name indicates, inserted within a syntagma. Metz does accept the possible existence of two tables, a table of syntagmas and a table of internal combinations within the autonomous shot, which, as can be seen, would then be reduced to the sequence-shot.

According to what was said earlier, it might be better to distinguish between a table of syntagmas and a table of autonomous segments:

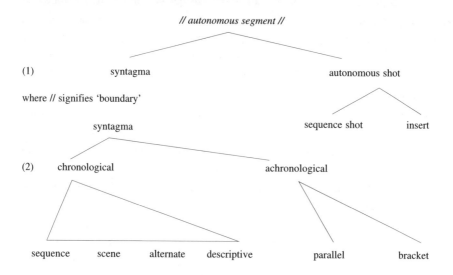

It can be seen that these two diagrams do not merely divide the GS table into two, since in the first one, the symbol 'autonomous segment' is replaced by the sequence '// autonomous segment//'. What this substitution means is that in (1), the rules are contextual ones, which they are not in (2). This, incidentally, makes it impossible to reunite the two diagrams, for (2) would then be embedded in (1) and become contextual.

Diagram (1) can be interpreted as meaning that an autonomous segment can only be defined within a context: the boundaries of the segment. The problem then lies in defining these boundaries. One may think of punctuation, but this is of course not compulsory, and is often superfluous. Moreover, it can appear within a syntagma, such as a sequence, in order to indicate an ellipsis.

Metz defines the autonomous segment according to three criteria: 1) 'major change in the plot', 2) punctuation, and 3) change of syntagmatic type.

The analyst of classical film is therefore entitled to consider as one (single) autonomous segment any passage of the film which is interrupted neither by a major change in the plot, nor by a punctuation sign, nor by the substitution of one syntagmatic type for another.[12]

The main advantage of this definition lies in its formulation. In terms of cognitive theory, it might be called a procedural, rather than declarative, definition. The difficulty, then, is not so much in identifying the properties of an autonomous segment, as in deciding how to proceed in order to identify an autonomous segment. Diagram (1) is therefore of little interest, since it does not in any way represent this algorithmic aspect of the definition of an autonomous segment.

The purpose of this work is not to expand on this algorithm, but simply to present its general philosophy, which enables us to describe in detail how a teaching practice can be based on the GS. Such a practice, after all, consists of a number of procedures. The definition of the autonomous segment can therefore be described as a procedure with the help of representations in the form of parentheses. The beginning of a segment can be compared to the opening of a parenthesis, its end corresponding to the closing of the parenthesis. In the language of algorithms, such a procedure is known as the construction of a 'queue', meaning an 'orderly linear disposition of things'.[13]

The problem is that the notion of a 'major change in the plot' is rather loose. This, again, is an intuitive notion. As for punctuation points, they can unfortunately appear within a syntagma. Should this happen, the presence of punctuation must not result in the closing of the parenthesis labelled as an 'autonomous segment'.

The first of these problems can be solved by resorting to procedures such as those used in the recognition of forms, for instance, and known as 'matching processes', sometimes translated into French as 'filtrage', or filtering. This process can roughly be described as a comparison of each new shot with the previous one.

The filtering process consists in comparing two symbolic expressions: a "data" and a "filter".[14]

The building of 'filters' could be understood as involving the use, in particular, of what Minsky calls 'frames',[15] meaning stereotyped frames of knowledge. When Metz thus justifies the passage from segment 2 to segment 3 in *Adieu Philippine* by the presence of a juke-box in close-up, his analysis may be justified by the fact that the juke-box is seen as belonging to the 'bar' frame, and alien to the 'television studio' frame. In other words, the 'television studio' frame acts as a 'filter', and on the appearance of the 'juke-box' 'data', the latter is identified as alien to the frame in question, and is therefore rejected by the filter.

This procedure, however, does not allow one to distinguish between segment 1 and segment 2. In Metz's opinion, this distinction is actually justified by the appearance of Michel, the main character, which brings us from the descriptive to the narrative level. And yet, both segments belong to the same frame.

If all that has been said so far is correct, it seems necessary to distinguish between 'segmentation' and 'categorisation'. Metz's distinction between segments 1 and 2 thus corresponds to a categorisation (belonging to the table of syntagma), whereas the distinction between 2 and 3 constitutes a 'segmentation' (belonging to the table of autonomous segments).

Within segment 3, as defined by Metz, which can be said to correspond to the scene in which Michel talks to two young girls in a bar, there is an insert, defined by Metz as segment 4, interrupting the conversation and showing Michel sitting in a television studio, doing nothing. According to what was said earlier, the analyst subjecting this insert to the 'filtering' process will identify a change of segment, and close the parenthesis before opening a new one:

sg (   ) sg (

In the next shot, and for the same reasons, he will identify a change of segment and close the parenthesis before opening a new one:

sg (   ) sg (   ) sg (

The problem here, of course, is that this last segment is not a new one, but a return to the first one, which does not correspond to the above-mentioned parenthesis but to:

sg (sg (   )   )

In order to conceive this representation, the analyst must be able to go back to the first parenthesis, after comparing the third sg parenthesis, not with the previous one, but with the first one. This procedure can be called, to borrow the terminology of Artificial Intelligence, a 'cooperative algorithm'.

An algorithm is *cooperative* if it repeatedly adjusts the interpretation of each element to be in greater harmony with its neighbors until global harmony is attained. By "harmony" we mean *constraint satisfaction.* If the interpretation assigned to every element obeys all constraints, then we reached a satisfactory overall interpretation.[16]

This procedure can be seen to solve the problem of the distinction between an insert and a sequence-shot. According to diagram (1), the difference between an insert and a sequence-shot can be explained in configurational terms; the insert corresponds to: (( )), whereas the sequence-shot corresponds to: ( ) ( ). In other words, an insert is *embedded* in a segment, whereas a sequence-shot is *concatenated.*

It can therefore be said that diagram (2) applies to the sequence-shot, but not to the insert, because it only applies to concatenated units. If, moreover, we are to distinguish, along with Metz, between several types of insert, it may be possible, after the configuration of the insert, to examine, by means of an algorithm, the relationships between internal parentheses and context (the content of external parentheses), in order to identify the type of insert, which can be represented by a third diagram of which the 'insert' would be the initial symbol.

Obviously, the problem of the dual function of punctuation: segmentation criterion and categorisation criterion, also implies the use of the notion of cooperative, or relaxation algorithm. This phenomenon is best illustrated by the example of segment 5 in Metz's analysis. This segment, labelled as a 'episodic sequence', opens up with a dissolve: Metz describes it as being composed of three short scenes: 1 – railway station in Paris, 2 – countryside, 3 – airfield.

> The summary effect is emphasized by the internal punctuation of the syntagma: montage of episodes removed from each other in space and in time.[17]

The analyst would therefore identify three segments, and only by recognising a syntagmatic type would he be able to go back and reexamine them as one segment.

The analysis can sometimes be more straightforward. In *Johny Eager* (M. Le Roy, 1942), for instance, there is a segment which starts with the shot of a man coming out of a stationary car; a panoramic shot follows the man from right to left; then a dissolve leads back to the movement of the character. Here, the dissolve is a classic example of ellipsis, since it partly erases the distance covered by the character. According to the 'filtering' principle, the two shots are part of the same segment, since they both belong to the same frame – 'X's itinerary from A to B'. It could be said that in this instance, the analyst does not need to work backwards, for the 'filtering' method recognises no change of segment, which would mean that the consideration of punctuation comes after the filtering process, in case the latter is not conclusive. This phenomenon can be illustrated by an example taken from *The Big Heat* (Fritz Lang, 1953).

The first dissolve takes place when, after her husband's 'suicide', Mrs Duncan phones Mike Lagana, between the dialling and the answer. After this first call, Lagana phones Vince Stone, his accomplice; but this time, there is no dissolve between the dialling and the answer. The telephone can be said to have the ability to connect, within the same space, geographically distant characters.[18] In this sense, it is a frame, which acts as a 'filter' and recognises no change of segment between the dialling and the answer. Yet, in the sense that the two places are disconnected, it could be argued that since there is a change of geographic frame, there is also a change of segment. The presence of punctuation would then cease to be superfluous, and would mean a change of segment; conversely, its absence would mean the absence of change.

The coexistence of two procedures raises the problem of their relationship. Is it better to start by detecting 'punctuation points', or by 'filtering'? The former has the advantage of simplicity and speed, which is good from a teaching point of view, but it is also less reliable, since punctuation can occur within a segment. As, moreover, punctuation is usually considered redundant, it becomes optional, and is often absent from a change of segment.

It can be said, tentatively, that the first method (starting with punctuation points) is best suited to classic films such as *Dodge City* (Michael Curtiz, 1939), and the second one to a film such as *Adieu Philippine*, in which changes of segment usually occur without punctuation.

Syntagmatic Types

It must be said, first of all, that our purpose here is not, as it so often is with our discussions of the GS, to know whether or not Metz's list of syntagmatic types is a comprehensive one, whether it should be shortened or expanded. Our purpose is to determine what properties can help to define syntagmatic types, and what relationships exist between them. In other words, we shall try and find out whether Metz's syntagmatic types can be described by such notions as, for instance, 'narrative', 'descriptive', 'linear' and 'chronological'; and whether the relationships between properties and types are accurately represented by a selection-tree.

Since the autonomous shot has ceased to belong among syntagmatic types, seven of them remain: 1 – parallel syntagma, 2 – bracket syntagma, 3 – descriptive syntagma, 4 – alternate syntagma, 5 – scene, 6 – ordinary sequence and 7 – episodic sequence. 1 and 2 are non-chronological, 4 is chronological but non-narrative, 5 is narrative, but non-linear like 5, 6 and 7. Let us remember that the first obvious problem raised by this representation is due to the unequal length of the paths connecting the root node to the terminal nodes. There is, for instance, no node between the root and 1 and 2, but there are four between the root and 6 and 7. This asymmetry presents no difficulty if the tree is read as representing the parts within a whole – the group of syntagmas – but it raises problems if read as representing the properties helping to identify syntagmatic types.

Once again, contrary to what Metz maintains, the table can only be read in one direction, dividing the class of syntagmas into sub-classes of chronological and non-chronological syntagmas, etc. For it to work in the opposite direction, we would have to be able to say that, given the existence of seven syntagmatic types, each type has one property distinguishing it from the others, which is not true since, for instance, no property allows us to distinguish between 1 and 2. One can, however, wonder whether they could be distinguished by the fact, for instance, that the bracket syntagma is linear, whereas the parallel one is alternating. It then becomes preferable to draw a two-dimensional table, rather than a tree, in order to represent the GS, even as Metz conceived it. One entry would be composed of the seven syntagmatic types, the other of semantic properties:

syntagmas	chronological	narrative	linear
parallel syntagma	−	−	−
bracket syntagma	−	−	+
descriptive syntagma	+	−	+
alternate syntagma	+	+	−
scene	+	+	+
sequence	+	+	+

Some further remarks need to be made at this point. The distinction between ordinary sequence and episodic sequence has been removed, because of what was said in the previous section regarding the example of an episodic sequence in *Adieu Philippine*. This sequence was deducted from a configuration of three consecutive scenes, with the same characters in different locations. We shall come back to this later, but it can already be seen that there remain no properties enabling us to distinguish between scene and sequence (as the table shows).

'Linear narrative' has been replaced with 'linear'. This alteration is of course due to the representation in the form of a table. By representing his table as a tree, Metz is forced to introduce a hierarchy between features, which means that if 'narrative' dominates 'linear', then linear syntagmas are both narrative *and* linear; such a hierarchy is not necessary in the two-dimensional table.

The linear property of the bracket syntagma may seem dubious, for one of its features is a process of reiteration. In the example from *Citizen Kane* quoted by Metz in 'Ponctuation, démarcations dans le film de diégèse',[19] there is, for instance, the reiteration of a close-up on a stage light being turned on and off. This reiteration phenomenon is associated with the frequentative modality of the bracket syntagma.

One question, in any case, is whether the properties being used to identify Metz's syntagmatic types are adequate, and whether the relationships between them can be represented by a tree (whether, especially, there are any hierarchical relationships between the features). The simplest way of starting to answer this question is to go back to the descriptions of Metz's seven syntagmatic types:

> the parallel syntagma contains two or more series, each one having several images, and these series alternate on the screen (ABAB, etc.).[20]

The series in question have no precise link between them, at least on the level of denotation. They have 'a direct symbolic value (scenes of the life of the rich interwoven with scenes of the life of the poor, images of tranquility alternating with images of disturbance, shots of the city and of the country, of the sea and and of wheatfields, and so on)'.[21]

Here, it will be noticed that Metz does not use a verifiable, stated example, as he does when discussing the bracket syntagma, for instance, but *ad hoc* examples which have never been and may never be manifest. This does not impair their value as examples, but it shows how difficult it is to find an example which is only *one* example of parallel syntagma. In other words, it seems that a syntagma can illustrate several types.

A common example of parallel syntagma (much used by Jean Mitry) is the passage from *October* in which shots of a Mencheviks' meeting alternate with shots of harp players.

> These shots are traditionally perceived as non-diegetic metaphors: the metaphorised term (= Mencheviks) belongs to the action, but the metaphorising term (= harps) is alien to the action, and only intervenes in the film because of its symbolic values[22].

For this reason, Mitry prefers the end of Pudovkin's *Mother*.

> Thus, in the final part of *Mother*, the ever-growing wave of strikers and demonstrators, having freed the prisoners, marches on, crushing all obstacles in its way. Pudovkin intersperses these shots with pictures of the Neva[23] triumphantly carrying blocks of ice, as if it had just broken free of its freezing corset. But this is Saint-Petersburg, and the Neva is part of the set. Even better: the demonstrators are walking along the quay and crossing the iron bridge over the river. Both the event and its term of comparison are situated in the same space.[24]

Marie-Claire Ropars[25] reminds us that in an earlier passage from *October*, a character strokes the drawing of a harp on a glass door:

> This is, therefore, also a diegetic metaphor, for both the metaphoriser and the metaphorised have "realistic" references.[26]

In *Mother*, the first shots of the thaw follow prison shots, and are introduced by the notice 'Outside, it is spring'. In other words, the spectator knows, well before he can observe that the thaw takes place in the same space as the demonstration, that they belong to the same temporal field. Indeed, it seems difficult, in this case, to speak of a parallel syntagma as a non-chronological syntagma. To maintain, moreover, that there is no diegetic relationship between the series, is to imply that the relationship of temporal simultaneity cannot, by itself, constitute a diegetic relationship. It could then be argued that, for the relationship of simultaneity to become a diegetic relationship, the two spaces in which the simultaneous events take place must be mutually accessible.

Such a restriction demands a detailed clarification, and a re-examining of the notion of diegesis, which is known to have played a prominent part in film theory after Etienne Souriau. There is now, it seems, a consensus on its definition. The diegesis can be considered as a possible world, meaning, according to Chateau's definition, a 'group of animate or inanimate objects, possessing properties and having *a priori* relationships with one another'.[27] According to this definition, the examples of parallel syntagmas taken from Eisenstein or Pudovkin show relationships between series belonging to a diegesis.

We may wonder, however, if this reference to the notion of possible world does not raise more problems than it solves. One of these problems is that of what is known as the maximality principle. A possible world is a maximum group of propositions.

Such a group is defined by the fact that any proposition from the group can be assigned one of the two degrees of truth: the true or the false. If a third degree – the indeterminate – is admitted, we switch to another type of model: a partial model.[28]

In other words, every true proposition concerning the real world has a true or false equivalent in the possible worlds accessible to it. However,

The modal or hypothetical form of reasoning should not set in motion worlds that are absolutely equal to ours in terms of propositional cardinality.[29]

There are other theories, apart from the one on possible worlds, which are founded on a reasoning on the basis of partial models. One of these is Fauconnier's theory of mental spaces and Kamp's theory on the structures of representation of discourse (SRD).[30] The latter theory is a dynamic model which aims to explain the gradual construction of meaning. Viewed from this angle, the diegesis can be said to be constructed gradually; it is, therefore, not given *a priori*, as Chateau claims.

Our purpose here is not to present the SRD theory, but to give an idea of its principle through one example. If one sees two shots of the same character walking in the same direction, but in two different places, the first shot can be said to correspond to something like 'has walked in P1, comes from Px (source) and is going towards Py (destination)'. As for the second shot, clearly, it corresponds to something like 'has walked in P2', or P2 is different from P1. From the spectator's viewpoint, a single individual cannot be in two places at the same time, unless such a possibility is explicitly mentioned. The spectator, therefore, constructs a chronological relationship between the two shots; the SRD corresponding to the second shot will be embedded in that corresponding to the first shot. P2 then becomes a constant value for PY (P2 is one of the spaces lying in the same direction as the point of destination). This shows that the gradual construction of the diegesis is partly based on the interpretation of anaphoric and co-referential relationships.[31]

As far as the parallel syntagma is concerned, one can now see that it is not necessary to construct such a diegesis in order to understand relationships between series, since they imply no co-referential or anaphoric relationship. When faced with a series of shots of demonstrators, interspersed with shots of melting ice, the spectator finds no instruction there asking him to embed the second space inside the first one, since nothing in there suggests a relationship of inclusion.

It could be objected that in *Mother*, the above-mentioned notice: 'Outside, it is spring', builds a spatial relationship between the prison space and that of the river: the river belongs to the space outside the prison (its space complements that of the prison). The demonstration, which takes place outside the prison, also belongs to that space. Now, the alternation between shots of the prison and shots of the demonstration implies diegetic relationships (and therefore corresponds to an alternate syntagma). It could then be deducted that the thaw represents the spatio-temporal dimension of the demonstration, which is moving towards the prison (it takes place in the spring, by a river). This seems indeed to be an alternate syntagma. This interpretation will be confirmed when Pavel, the hero, crosses the river, jumping over the blocks of ice, to go and join the demonstration.

It may seem, at his point, that this passage confirms previously built (*a priori*) diegetic relationships. This interpretation, however, would be purely static, and would not account for the fact that the spectator knows more about the spatial relationships between the river and the demonstration after seeing Pavel on the river, than when he only sees the two alternating series without any co-referential or anaphoric relationship between them.

In a dynamic partial model, unlike the theory of possible worlds, the reasoning process can be non-monotonous. This means that new pieces of information can result in the shedding of former conclusions. The spectator can initially conclude that the syntagma in *Mother* is a parallel one; then, when seeing Pavel on the ice, reject this conclusion and consider that he is watching an alternate syntagma. In other words, he can initially consider that the river does not belong to the diegesis, and then change his mind.[32]

Consequently, the fact that the river belongs to the same world as the demonstration, since the propositions 'the thaw takes place in the spring, while Pavel is in jail' and 'the demonstration takes place in the spring while Pavel is in jail' are both true, does not mean that they both belong to the same referential universe. In the jargon of the possible world theory, saying that two worlds are temporally simultaneous does not in itself imply that they are mutually accessible. Similarly, to go back to Nef's example,[33] if I meditate 'over what Marie would do if Pierre went on holiday without having to decide, in the world of their holidays, whether Czechoslovakia has been invaded by the USSR', the spectator trying to reconstruct the diegesis, or the spatio-temporal and causal relationships between events, will not have to decide whether all the objects (or events) belonging to the same world also belong to the same diegesis.

Finally, let us remember that the notion of parallel syntagma refers to a syntagmatic type, and that filmic utterances can illustrate several types at the same time, which means, for instance, that the ABAB pattern can illustrate both a parallel and an alternate syntagma. There is, in this case, a semantic interpretation which constructs a diegesis whereby the space to which series B belongs is included in the space to which series A belongs, and implying causal relationships between A and B; and another semantic interpretation, implying no diegetic relationships.

To quote an example taken from television, a report by P. Salviac in the programme Stade 2 about J.P. Rives, the rugby player, showed, in alternation, a series on the Césars awards in which he was taking part, and a second series on the rugby match in which he was to play the next day. This syntagma shows a co-reference between the two series, since they are both about the same person in different situations. This particular alternation, however, as the reporter himself remarks, aims to present the contrast between the player's social and night life, and his (more serious) sporting activities on Sunday afternoons, two types of activities normally considered incompatible. This discourse displays two syntagmatic types: a parallel one, corresponding to a non-diegetic reading of the type: 'rugby (or, more generally, "serious sporting activities") and a night life are incompatible' and an alternate one: 'In less than 24 hours, J.P. Rives can take part in two events: the Césars awards and a rugby match'.

This last example also shows us that the parallel syntagma, like the *bracket syntagma*, with which Metz associates it, is not so much defined by the feature + non-chronological, as by the feature + generic. In fact, an example such as that of Stade 2, even when read as non-diegetic, implies the interpretation of a chronological relationship: 'It is unusual to play rugby (to practice a sport at top level) after a night of celebrations'. The difference between the two readings may well be, rather, a difference between the *generic* ('one doesn't go out the evening before a rugby match') and the *specific* ('a certain person went out one evening before playing rugby the next day').

The generic nature of the denotation, in the bracket syntagma, is made very clear in Metz's definition: a bracket syntagma is a

> series of very brief scenes representing occurences that the film gives as typical examples of the same order of reality, without in any way chronologically locating them in relation to each other in order to emphasize their presumed kinship within a category of facts.[34]

Metz does, in fact, specify that

> Thus, among the nonchronological syntagmas, it is the presence or absence of a systematic alternating of images in interwoven series that allows us to distinguish between the parallel syntagma and the bracket syntagma (presence equals parallel syntagma; absence equals bracket syntagma).[35]

There is, therefore, no reason why the bracket syntagma should be defined by the absence of chronological relationships, especially as Metz himself quotes the frequentative syntagma, which would be perfectly illustrated by the above-mentioned example from *Citizen Kane*, as a sub-type of it. This example, which shows a repetition of previous shots of rehearsals, performances and critical reviews, can be considered as chronological. For instance, the consecutive shots of newspaper headlines represents the consecutive critical reviews following consecutive performances.

> In the bracket syntagma it is frequently the case that different successive evocations are strung together through effects (dissolves, wipes, pan shots, and, less commonly, fades).[36]

This list could also include certain formal properties which enable us to identify the bracket syntagma: superimpositions and 'unconventional' framing, such as 'oblique' framing. A good example of this can be found in *Dodge City*. The first general shot of a street teeming with people, over which appears a superimposition of a caption identifying the town as 'Dodge City', and describing it as a place that 'got rich on the cattle trade', and in which 'the only law is the rule of the toughest' ('of money and violence'), is followed by a series of very brief shots linked together by dissolves or split screens showing scenes of street fighting, gambling (with close-ups of the roulette wheel), lynching (hangings), and the closing of the sheriff's office. Some shots are also repeated, such as the street-fighting shot, which can be interpreted as representing the frequentative element, and oblique close-ups on the fronts of the 'saloon' and cabaret buildings.

This bracket syntagma can be semantically described as a description of *a* lawless town. The indefinite article must not be read 'specifically' but 'generically'. As Metz remarks, this type of configuration is 'a kind of filmic equivalent to conceptualization',[37] meaning, in this case, the notion of a town 'without law and order'.

In natural languages, the determiners can be notoriously ambiguous in certain contexts. Thus, in 'Arthur wants to buy a moped', 'a' can refer to a specific moped, the one that Arthur has just seen at the local shop, or to the fact that the coveted object belongs to the moped group. In the latter case, the extension may be meaningless, for Arthur might conceivably be looking for a moped with a turbo engine, only to discover that there is no such thing.

Much has been written on this sort of problem,[38] and we shall not dwell on it here. Let us simply remember that this type of ambiguity depends on the context (the presence of the modal verb 'to want'). In the case of the bracket syntagma, however, what enables us to recognise it, and thus perceive the reference as a generic one, is not the conceptual content of the shots, but the presence of a number of formal properties, such as visual effects or unconventional framing.

It could thus be argued that punctuation is a compulsory component of the bracket syntagma, constituting what could be called a 'modal' context. Metz actually points out that these visual effects aim to make the spectator treat the segment 'as a whole, and that he must not attempt to link the short partial scenes directly to the rest of the narrative' (Metz, 1974: 127). Interestingly, the disappearance of visual effects instantly puts an end to the generic reading, in favour of specific reading.[39] The syntagma then ceases to be considered as a bracket syntagma, and becomes a *descriptive* syntagma.

Another example of this phenomenon can be found in another film by Michael Curtiz: *Virginia City* (1940). The film opens up on a series of battle shots, showing the two camps attacking alternately (the Northerners from left to right, the Southerners from right to left). This segment only contains cuts, but two obliquely framed shots of two soldiers: A steep downward shot of a Southerner, and a steep upward shot of a Northerner. This segment can be seen to have one thing in common with the bracket syntagma in *Dodge City*: unconventional framing. But it differs from it by the absence of any visual effects. In *Virginia City*, however, the generic reading, although not ruled out (largely because of the unconventional framing) seems to give way to a specific reading.[40] In other words, the semantic interpretation of the segment will be 'description of a specific battle in the American Civil War', rather than 'generic description of a battle'.

Another example proving that the absence of any formal markings results in a specific reading (that in the absence of any visual effects and unconventional framing techniques, the syntagma is classified as a descriptive, rather than a bracket syntagma) can be found in Metz's description of *Adieu Philippine*.

> The film begins with a rapid succession of contrasting shots representing partial views of a television studio set on which we see musicians, cameramen, and technicians moving around. The ordinary sequence is, in this case, the only type of sequence that might be confused with the bracket syntagma. But the actors, who are, purposely, barely characterised, are picked up and abandoned by the camera in such as way that their activity is never organised into a true consecutiveness. Their actions are not followed in their vectoral unfolding, but are merely choosen as representative of a certain reality: work in a television studio.[41]

We may well ask ourselves whether this segment is not a descriptive, rather than a bracket syntagma.

> In the descriptive syntagma, the only intelligible relation of coexistence between the objects successively shown by the images is a relation of *spatial* coexistence.
>
> This in no way implies that the descriptive syntagma can only be applied to *motionless* objects or persons. A descriptive syntagma may very well cover an action, provided that it is an action whose only intelligible internal relationship is one of spatial parallelism... . Example: a flock of sheep being herded (views of the sheep, the shepherd, the sheepdog, etc.).[42]

Metz could just as easily have quoted the beginning of *Adieu Philippine*: the recording of a television programme on a jazz band (shots of the musicians, cameramen, technicians, etc.).

It may be seen that the possibility of confusion between the bracket and descriptive syntagmas implies that, unlike the parallel syntagma, the bracket syntagma is diegetic.[43] The problem raised by Metz's table concerning the chronological/non-chronological distinction, which prevented any representation of the feature differentiating the bracket syntagma from the parallel syntagma, has thus been solved. The tree representation has become homogeneous: each node is the starting point of two strings, one leading to a lower node, the other to a terminal node:

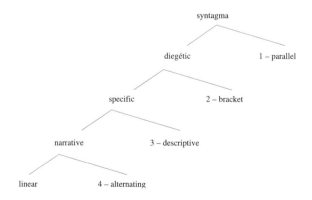

According to Metz's description, the second segment of *Adieu Philippine* is an ordinary sequence. Yet, no punctuation or 'major change in the plot', apart from the introduction of the 'hero', comes between the first two segments, which explains Metz's view that the first segment may be confused with an ordinary sequence; this would then mean that there is only one segement (an ordinary sequence) including the first two.

This description suggests that the distinction between *descriptive* and narrative depends on the absence or presence of what is intuitively defined as a 'hero'. Thus, a succession of shots of the type: general shot of a house, medium shot of the front door, indoor shot (corridor), indoor shot of a room with a table, chairs, perhaps people eating, will be classified as a descriptive syntagma. But if, given the same shots, the first one shows a 'character' walking towards the house; if in the second shot, we recognise the same person ringing the door-bell, then going inside; and if we then see this character entering the dining-room, we will call this a narrative syntagma (an ordinary sequence). Basically, it can be said that the passage does not aim to describe a spatial frame (a house), but to narrate an 'action': a character going somewhere.

To borrow Strawson's terminology,[44] it can be said that the distinction between 'narrative' and 'descriptive' does not depend on the identification of individuals, but on their *reidentification*. According to Strawson, the reidentification is a passage from the 'person' to the 'individual', occurring when two people are identified as being the same individual in two different situations. In the jargon of modal logic, this is a 'cross-world identification'. A certain situation can thus be defined, following the example of Barwise and Perry, as implying a type of situation and a localisation.

> Formally, we define a *constituent sequence* to be a sequence $y = < r, x1, ...,$ $xn >$, where r is an n-rary relation and $x1, ..., xn$ are objects. *A situation-type* is an extensional relation between constituent sequences $< r, x1, ..., xn >$ and 0 or 1, that is a set of pairs $< x, i >$ where y is a constituent sequence and i is 0 or 1.[45]

Such 'realities' as 'television work' or 'a town without law and order' correspond to this definition of 'types of situation'. In other words, the bracket syntagma can also be considered as being descriptive; it does not then describe a specific situation, but a type of situation. In the case of the descriptive syntagma, the situation is specific, and therefore localised in the diegesis ('connected to the rest of the narrative', as Metz would say), which is not true of a type of situation.

A bracket syntagma can, however, be narrative without being descriptive. Thus, the example from *Citizen Kane*, showing a repetition of shots of Susan in different situations (in rehearsal, on stage, for instance), corresponds to a narrative syntagma. It can then be considered as a narration of a typical succession of events.

Within narrative syntagmas,

> there are two divisions: the syntagma may interweave several distinct
> temporal progressions, or, on the contrary, it may consist of a single
> succession, encompassing all of the images. Thus, the alternate narrative
> syntagma (or alternate syntagma) is distinguished from the various sorts of
> linear narrative syntagma.[46]

A frequently quoted example of this type is, of course, the chase pattern: a shot of the
pursuer, then a shot of the pursued, again a shot of the pursuer, etc. Let us simply
remember that, according to Burch, this example corresponds to what he calls a
successive syntagma, in which:

> It is made clear that the time of the second shot is linked to that of the first
> shot by a relationship of posteriority, and that the two spaces are relatively
> close; in other words, that the succession of the two images on screen must
> be read as signifying the diegetic succession "more or less close".[47]

The alternate syntagma is therefore defined as signifying that 'the two events are
diegetically *simultaneous* and *distant* in space'.[48]

As for the successive syntagma, the prototype of which is the chase, it can be
argued, on the basis of Barwise and Perry's theory, that the alternation takes place
within *one* event, for the pursuers and pursued are part of the constituent sequence
representing this type of event: a chase. A chase implies a relationship between two
arguments, and the alternation between their respective value. Moreover, the spaces in
which the pursuers and pursued are moving belong to the same spatio-temporal
location. This space is, indeed, mobile (as in the ordinary sequence), but it is the same
space. It can be seen that the alternation usually occurs between identical spaces, or that
there are at least some points of intersection between the spaces denoted by the shots.
Thus, if the first shot shows the person being pursued, and the second shot shows the
pursuer, there will probably be at least one point of intersection between the fields
covered by these two shots, and we shall probably accept that the pursuer crosses that
same space that the person he is pursuing has just crossed.

In the alternate syntagma, the alternation takes place between at least two
events, which implies at least two locations. One of the classic examples of this is, of
course, the end of *Birth of a Nation*, in which the attack on a cabin and the ride of the Ku
Klux Klan are the two alternating events, which implies two locations: that of the riders
(a mobile space) and that of the cabin.

Within *linear narrative syntagmas* (i.e., a single succession linking together all the acts seen in the images), a new criterion lets us make yet another distinction: Succession may be *continuous* (without break or ellipsis), or discontinuous (jumps).[49]

The first case corresponds to what Metz calls the *scene*; the second one, to what he calls the *sequence*. The term 'scene' relates to three types of parameter: 'spatial' (the scene implies a spatial frame similar to that of a stage), 'narratological' ('an unbroken spatio-temporal field') and 'filmic'.

> The signifier is fragmentary in the scene – a number of shots, all of them only partial "profiles" (*Abschattungen*) – but the signified is unified and continuous.[50]

In other words, the 'scene' is defined here as a succession of shots indicating a spatial *frame*, within which takes place a *continuous* and coherent *pattern* of events.[51]

It can be deducted from this that Metz's sequence is not only opposed to the scene in that it indicates a partial discontinuity, but in that it denotes no spatial frame.

> The sequence is based on the unity of a more complex action (although it is still single, contrary to what occurs, for example, in the parallel syntagma or in the bracket syntagma), an action that "skips" those portions of itself it intends to leave out and that is therefore apt to unfold in several different locations (unlike the scene). A typical example is the sequence of escape (in which there is an approximate unity of place, but one that is essential rather than literal: that is, the "escape location," that paradoxical unit, the mobile locus).[52]

The fact that the scene and the sequence are opposed by two distinct parameters raises a few problems. As Odile Bächler points out,[53] 'temporal hiatuses' can occur in a spatial frame, just as temporal continuity can be perceived in a mobile space. It must be remembered that any joints within a movement imply a 'hiatus', but that the latter is not perceived as such by the spectator. In other words, the feeling that a movement is continuous implies that any change of shot occurring within that movement skips part of it. Thus, in the example analysed by Colin[54] of a barrel floating down a river, filmed in several shots (*The Adventure of Dollie*, D.W. Griffith), should the hiatuses be considered as being simply linked to joints within the movement, and the river be interpreted as the spatial frame for the scene?

The simplest solution seems to be to consider, as we did earlier, the scene and the sequence as mainly distinguishable from each other by their representation of space. In the scene, space is constructed as a topological frame, so that 'each point has a range of environments'.[55] In the sequence, space is constructed by the movement of an object, in the sense that the object 'can follow a certain trajectory within space'.[56]

This could lead us to argue that Burch's successive syntagma is a sequence, and is not to be treated as a particular syntagmatic type, any more than the shot-reverse-shot technique, corresponding to the alternation between fields within a spatial framework (within the scene), is to be treated as a syntagmatic type.

Interestingly, the typical example of the sequence is the escape, whereas the typical example of the successive syntagma was the chase; the escape can indeed be considered as being part of the chase: the person being pursued escapes from the pursuer. The only difference is that, in the escape as an active structure, the subject is the pursued person, whereas in the chase, which has the same structure, the subject is the pursuer. 'Marie escapes from Arthur' therefore implies that 'Arthur chases Marie'.

Among sequences, Metz proposes a distinction between the ordinary sequence and the *episodic sequence*.

> Definition: the sequence brings together a number of very brief scenes, which are usually separated from each other by optical devices (dissolves, etc.), and which succeed each other in chronological order.[57]

This last property is in fact considered as the feature distinguishing the episodic sequence from the bracket syntagma, for they are similar in every other respect, with their brief shots, the absence of any 'syntagmatic development' and the presence of visual effects. Metz's example tends to reinforce this possible confusion.

> In Orson Welles's *Citizen Kane* (1941), the sequence portraying the gradual deterioration of the relationship between the hero and his first wife shows a chronological series of quick allusions to dinners shared by the couple in an atmosphere that is decreasingly affectionate; the scenes, treated in a succession of pan shots, are connected over intervening periods of months.[58]

The example, taken from *Adieu Philippine*, of 'short scenes' linked together by cuts for effect, representing different moments during the Sunday spent by Michel with the two young girls (segment 5 in Metz's description), is more difficult to confuse with a bracket syntagma. The difference between these two examples lies in the fact that the syntagma is read as generic in *Citizen Kane*, but as specific in *Adieu Philippine*; the events represented here are diegetically specific, they take place on the Sunday following the conversation in the café, and are therefore temporalised within the diegesis. In *Citizen Kane*, it is not the meals but the marital decline which is temporalised. The chronological relationship appears to be a feature of this decline (a decline implies a temporal succession); therefore, it does not allow us to prevent its interpretation as a bracket syntagma.

In fact, the example from *Adieu Philippine* is a good illustration of one of the features of the sequence: it does not occur in one place only; there is, therefore, an itinerary. We may wonder, however, whether it does not constitute what could be called 'episodic scenes', meaning 'a number of brief sketches separated by visual effects', implying a pattern of events within a fixed spatial frame. A restaurant scene, called as such from a narrative point of view, could conceivably be composed of a succession of brief scenes dissolving into one another, showing the characters entering the restaurant, ordering the meal, eating, and leaving. Similarly, segment 29 of *Adieu Philippine*, showing the preparation of an advertising film, could be considered an 'episodic sequence', since:

> A number of punctuational devices (dissolves) and a reading of the images themselves (weariness of the actors in the little film) lead us to understand that the shooting has occupied a much longer stretch of time than what we experience on the screen.[59]

Another example, which would traditionally be considered as a sequence and could be treated as an episodic scene, can be found in *The Great Singer* (Robert Siodmak, 1949). The film opens with three series of shots taken on a train, connected by dissolves, and showing the same characters. As O. Bächler shows on the subject of the stage coach in a western, shots taken inside a vehicle can be treated as constituting a scene, inasmuch as the vehicle acts like a fixed spatial frame: it is not the coach, but the scenery which is in motion. In this respect, the beginning of *Dodge City* is quite remarkable: Dodge and his companions are sitting on a train, looking at a horse-driven coach through the window; here, the window frame acts like the fixed frame of a screen, within which an object (a coach) is moving.

Having chosen the type of space being constructed as the principal criterion distinguishing between scene and sequence, we may deem it unnecessary to retain the scene and the episodic sequence as 'autonomous' syntagmatic types. Let us remember that, unlike other syntagmas, they are necessarily constructed from several segments, hence the presence of visual effects. These syntagmatic types might then be thought to be derived from others. In, for instance, the episodic sequence from *Adieu Philippine*, there is a concatenation of scenes (Metz calls them 'sketches'). What, then, distinguishes this type of syntagma from the one in *East Side, West Side* (M. Le Roy), in which a dissolve separates the beginning of the meal (characters sitting down at the table) from after-dinner activities (games of chess, dancing), and which has been treated as two syntagmas (two scenes), if not one, purely intuitive criterion: in the first instance, there is no 'syntagmatic development'.

One cannot pretend to give an explicit definition of this intuitive criterion. Such an explanation would probably rely on notions of 'script' and 'shot'.[60] A sequence or an episodic scene might be considered as referring only to 'the main concept-ualizations' of 'scripts' and 'shots'. Thus, a scene referring to the 'restaurant' script through shots of someone entering a restaurant, then ordering a meal, and finally leaving the restaurant, would be an episodic scene.

These descriptions of syntagmatic types could be summarized by recalling Chomsky's rules of lexical sub-categorization.[61] In the same way as terminal syntactic categories such as N, Adj, V, can be rewritten as CS (complex symbol), in the GS, 'syntagma' can be considered as a CS, meaning a group of features: +/- diegetic, +/- specific, +/- linear, etc. This would result in:

parallel syntagma	→	< −diegetic, −linear >
bracket syntagma	→	< +diegetic, −specific >
descriptive syntagma	→	< +diegetic, +specific, −narrative, +linear >
alternate syntagma	→	< +diegetic, +specific, +narrative, +linear >
scene	→	< +diegetic, +specific, +narrative, +inclusive >
sequence	→	< +diegetic, +specific, +narrative, +linear, −inclusive >

The above rules need some further explanations. The introduction of the feature <inclusive> enables us to distinguish between scene and sequence, so that the table of syntagmatic types can be represented by a tree similar to the one constructed by Metz, except for the fact that it would be homogeneous, each node dominating respectively a nonterminal and a terminal node. This tree can be replaced by a parenthetic representation:

(syntagma (parallel) (diegetic (bracket) (specific (descriptive) (narrative (alternate) (linear (sequence) (inclusive (scene)))))))

This <inclusive> feature means that the scene shows relationships of inclusion between the spaces. In the language of the theory of models, it could be said that the semantic 'frame' is composed of a number of spatio-temporal intervals, connected by the two relationships of <(precedence) and INCLUDED (inclusion), which can be rewritten as:

< I, <, INCLUDED >

Conversely, it could be argued that the sequence, given the importance of the construction of space as an itinerary, is a structure of points connected only by a relationship of precedence:

< P, < >.

Chomsky distinguishes between two aspects of sub-categorization: what Lakoff[62] would call grammatical sub-categorization (G), and lexical sub-categorization (L); the lexical insertion itself consists of the substitution of a lexical item to a CS, as long as the L features of this item are identical to the G features of CS. Among Chomsky's rules on the sub-categorization of N, one finds:

(I) N	→	<+N, +/–animate, +/–common>
(II) <common>	→	<+/–countable>
(III) <-countable>	→	+/–abstract –animate
(IV) <+animate>	→	<+/–human>

On the basis of this formalism, one could propose the following rules on the sub-categorization of syntagmas in the GS:

(1) syntagma	→	<+/–syntagma, +/–diegetic>
(2) <+syntagma>	→	<+/–linear>
(3) <+diegetic>	→	<+/–specific, +/–narrative, +/-inclusive>

It must be pointed out that 'should one require, as a formal condition, that these rules be represented by a tree-diagram', this would be impossible.[63]

The sub-categorization <+/-syntagmatic> is, of course, intended to explain the fact that a syntagma (as Metz understands it) can consist of several shots or a sequence shot. Rule (2), therefore, seems justified, for it means that only syntagmas with the feature + syntagma can be non-linear.

The fact that these rules cannot be represented by a tree diagram, unlike Metz's syntagmatic types, show how important it is to show the difference between what Metz would call a deductive and inductive reading. With the help of such rules, one can easily see that it is possible to deduce many more types than are represented in the table, for instance: a syntagma <+syntagma, +diegetic, -specific, -linear>, corresponds neither to the parallel syntagma (it is diegetic), nor to the alternate syntagma (it is not specific), although it has the same property as those two types (-linear). This, therefore, solves the problem of knowing how comprehensive the GS is, since it predicts the possibility of as yet undetected types. This, however, does not mean that everything is possible. The rules assume that certain types are impossible, for instance <-syntagma, -linear>.

Let us remember that the rules on linguistic sub-categorization distinguish between three sub-groups of features: phonological, syntactical and semantic features. On this basis, as far as the GS syntagmas are concerned, it could be argued that there are 'configurational' features, such as <optical effects> or <short shots>, which are, as we saw earlier, necessary to the sub-categorization, for instance, of the bracket syntagma.

Segmentation/Categorization

It is time that we raised the problem of the relationship between the determination of autonomous segments and that of syntagmatic types. As was shown earlier, the terms 'segment' and 'syntagma' presuppose different approaches: respectively, a segmentation approach and a categorization approach. In Chomsky's terminology, the first approach would correspond to what he calls the hypothesis of structural independence; the second approach, to that of structural dependence. Chomsky illustrates this distinction through the example of pairs of declarative and interrogative sentences – like:

The man is here – Is the man here?
The man will leave – Will the man leave?

These two hypotheses are capable of explaining this infinite class of pairs:
H1: Process the declarative sentence from beginning to end (from left to right), word by word, until you encounter the first occurrence of the words

"is," "will," etc.; transfer this occurrence to the beginning (to the left), thereby forming the corresponding interrogative sentence.

H2: Proceed as in H1, but choose the first occurrence of "is," "will," etc. following the first nominal syntagma of the declarative sentence.

H1 will be called a "rule independent from the structure" and H2 a "rule dependent on the structure". Thus, H1 requires an analysis of the declarative sentence as a simple sequence of words, whereas H2 requires, as well as an analysis of successive words, an analysis in terms of abstract syntagmas such as "nominal syntagma". Syntagmas are abstract, in the sense that their boundaries and their labelling are not, as a rule, indicated physically; they are mental constructions.[64]

In Chomsky's view, these two hypotheses are clearly opposed, and the second one is more adequate than the first. It can easily be shown that if the declarative sentence resembles something like: 'The man who is brown is here', the analysis proposed in H1 will result in: 'Is the man who brown is here?' as an interrogative sentence, whereas H2 will analyse 'The man who is brown' as a nominal syntagma, and result in the following grammatical interrogative sentence: 'Is the man who is brown here?'.

It could, of course, be argued that film semiology must choose betwen these two hypotheses, and base its descriptions on either segmentation or categorization, but it could also be said, as in 'computational' linguistics, that the two approaches should be integrated. From the point of view of film analysis, the dual approach enables one to explain the non- necessary coincidence between autonomous segments and syntagmas. *Touch of Evil* (Orson Welles, 1957) is a good example of this. The film is famous for, amongst other things, the initial sequence-shot of two and a half minutes, which starts with a close-up of a bomb and ends with its explosion.

If one considers the sequence-shot as an autonomous segment, the first autonomous segment in *Touch of Evil* starts with the close-up on the bomb being set, and ends with the medium shot of the hero (Vargas) kissing his young wife, raising his head and looking towards the left of the off-screen space, then suddenly hearing an explosion (off). The following shot represents the explosion itself. The relationship between the sequence-shot and the next shot corresponds to a relationship between shots within a scene: it is characterized by temporal continuity and by a link, in the forms of the hero's glance. From what was said on the difference between segment and syntagma, it can be inferred that the sequence-shot is an autonomous segment, and that the syntagma includes this segment and the next shot, which could be represented parenthetically in the following way:

```
( (    )  ( )  (    )  )
sg s   sg sg s  s    s sg
```

It can be said, more simply, that the second segment starts before the end of the first syntagma: the first shot in segment 2 is the last in what can, for the time being, be considered as the first syntagma.

```
(        (shot) .........
        sg2    s1
```

This configuration corresponds to the one I analysed at the beginning of *Last Train from Gun Hill*,[65] and called 'straight dislocation', or 'thematisation'. It has a textual function, inasmuch as it carries a change in emphasis: it tranforms the shot in question into the element which will later be seen as playing the most important part in the development of the discourse.

Since categorization defines syntagmatic boundaries which do not necessarily correspond to segment boundaries, we may wonder whether a syntagmatic boundary might not appear within a sequence-shot. This possibility is in fact self-evident, since it is possible for a whole film to consist of one sequence-shot, which does not mean that it will only contain one syntagma. In *Touch of Evil*, for instance, the camera follows the car, inside which the bomb has been placed; then, still moving towards the left, lets the car disappear off-screen and follows the movement of two characters (Vargas and his young wife). If one applies Metz's criterion from his description of *Adieu Philippine*, which introduces a new syntagma on the appearance of the main character, one has to admit that the introduction of new characters by the camera corresponds to a change of syntagma.

Again, the fact that new characters are introduced by a movement of the camera from right to left is interesting from a textual point of view; for it is a significant form of the right-left movement introducing and emphasizing a new theme.[66] Interestingly, the same movement here serves as an accompaniment, then becomes 'dramatic'. It can also be seen that the categorization of this syntagma does not imply the end of the previous one. The beginning of *Touch of Evil* could therefore be represented as follows:

```
< (sequence-shot (  sequence-shot > < shot )  )  (   shot...
sg s1            s2                  sg sg   s2 s1 s3
```

The end of the sequence-shot and the beginning of the next segment again remind us of the beginning of *Last Train from Gun Hill*, which also displays a permutation of the relationship:

> Looking (Agent, Object):
> <-   A   O
> instead of
> O   <-   A

If my previous analyses are correct, the explosion shot can be considered as a theme belonging to S1 and S2, and as the theme of S3, which results in the following categorization:

> (sequence-shot (sequence-shot (shot)) shot...
> s1   s2   s3   s2 s1

On the basis of the description of *Touch of Evil*, it can be said that syntagmas are not necessarily concatenated. In fact, the configuration:

> (X (Y))
> s   s   s s

corresponds to the following tree diagram:

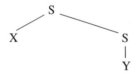

The second node S is therefore dominated by the first one. This is indeed called a righthand branching. The other configurations can be envisaged: self-embedding: (X (S) Y), lefthand branching, even if one considers that, here as in verbal languages, the righthand branching is dominant. What really matters here is, of course, the recursive feature.

Categorization thus enables us to define the notion of syntagma otherwise than as a type of autonomous segment, since the recursive feature allows the introduction of an in-depth representation. Segmentation does not allow any such construction; it can only define the film as a succession of segments. Parenthetically, this difference can be represented as follows:

```
(      )    (      )    (      ) ...
sg     sg   sg     sg   sg     sg


(  X   (  Y  (  Z   )       )       )
s      s     s      s       s       s
```

The beginning of *Touch of Evil* is a good illustration of this difference. Segmentation results in something like:

```
(  sequence-shot  )    (  syntagma  ) ...
sg                     sg  sg            sg
```

Categorization would result in:

```
(  sequence  (sequence  (scene   )   )   )
s            s          s        s   s   s
```

The first sequence would correspond to the itinerary of the car, the second to that of the two characters as far as the customs office. The scene would correspond to the explosion, meaning the dialogue between the two characters and the customs officer, then between the customs officer and the two characters in the car, the shot of the two characters kissing, followed by the explosion itself. This last shot is also the first one in the next syntagma, which can be considered as a sequence corresponding to the itinerary of the hero towards the site of the explosion. The beginning can thus be represented as follows:

```
( sequence-shot ( sequence-shot ( sequence-shot + shot  )   )   )
sq               sq               sc                         sc sq sq

( syntagma-shot  )
sq               sq
```

in which sq = sequence and sc = scene.

If we try to represent the relationship between segmentation and categorization, we end up with:

```
//  (  p-s  (  p-s  (  p-s  +  //  (  sh  )  )  )  +  syntagma )
sg1 sq        sq       sc        sg2 sq   sc sq sq       sq    //
```

THE GRANDE SYNTAGMATIQUE REVISITED

It could thus be argued that segmentation plays a dual part. It initially acts as a preliminary step in the categorization process. Categorization can, indeed, be seen as following segmentation. Since, however, segment boundaries do not always coincide with syntagmatic boundaries, segmentation enables us to analyse more clearly what could be called the 'prosodic' structure of the film.

Conclusion

The moment has now come to summarize the main points developed in the previous pages. First of all, let us remember that this study is driven by a pedagogic motive, since it attempts to solve the problems raised by the teaching of the GS, as a method of description of the image track in the film. Our purpose, therefore, was not to explain the spectator's competence, by analysing, for instance, the rules of semantic interpretation of filmic utterances. According to Chomsky, an explanatory theory is characterized by a description of rules, rather than of data; it is grammar, rather than the language system, which is the subject of generative grammar.

It thus seems quite reasonable to use segmentation as a starting point when teaching the GS. This, however, does not imply that spectatorial competence proceeds in the same way. It is even conceivable that an explicit theory on this competence would not have to distinguish between these two procedures.

We could summarize the segmentation procedure by saying that it seeks to discover segment boundaries. Let us remember that Metz proposes three criteria: 1) a major change in the plot; 2) punctuation; 3) a change of syntagmatic type. Because of the distinction between segmentation and categorization, it may seem unnecessary to keep the third criterion among the criteria used in the definition of segments.

The first two criteria do not, however, enable us to justify the segmentation that was applied to the beginning of *Touch of Evil*. Here the change of segment is not due to punctuation (there is a cut), or to a major change in the plot, since the glance provides a link, a temporal and spatial continuity, but to the passage from a sequence-shot to a syntagma. In relation to the pattern representing the types of autonomous segment, from an autonomous shot to a syntagma. In other words, the change is of a configurational nature.

Because of the distinction between categorization and segmentation, it is therefore necessary to distinguish between a configurational change and a change of syntagmatic type. Thus, in the sequence-shot from *Touch of Evil*, the passage from the sequence to the scene is a change of syntagmatic type, but without a configurational change. Similarly, in Metz's analysis of the beginning of *Adieu Philippine*, the passage from the descriptive to the narrative syntagma is a change of syntagmatic type, but not a configurational change.

It will, of course, be necessary to give detailed explanations of the types of configuration appearing in the film. Among syntagmas, for instance, we shall distinguish between syntagmas in which the shot boundaries are cuts, and those with boundaries in the form of visual effects. In *Dodge City*, for instance, the bracket syntagma ends on a dissolve and the next shots, contrary to the preceding ones, are connected by cuts; this is not only a change of syntagmatic type, but also a configurational change. In fact, in the light of what was previously said about the bracket syntagma, it is not surprising that it should act as a configurational, as well as a syntagmatic type.

It will be noticed, in the case of this last example, that music plays a part in segmentation, since the change of segment is accompanied by a change of musical theme. In other words, extra-diegetic music, as it is called, can be considered as a configurational feature. The explanation of the different types of configuration can, indeed, be expected to use some features common to music and cinema: balance between the respective length of segments, rhythm, etc.

In other words, although this study does not concentrate on sound, there is no reason, contrary to what is commonly thought, why the GS should not take acoustic information into account, despite the fact that Metz defined the GS as only relevant to the image track. One can indeed conceive the GS as a system of explicit procedures and rules which enable us, on the basis of visual and acoustic information, to describe filmic discourse by means of segmentation and categorization procedures.

Thus, the definition of a number of consecutive shots as a 'scene' is an explicit indication that this configuration is the image of a spatio-temporal frame and structure of events. The existence of a dialogue, or, as in *Touch of Evil*, the fact that the sound of the explosion starts on the first shot and continues into the next one, illustrate this image. In this sense, there is no reason to distinguish between 'image track' and 'sound track', since the GS can be considered as an explicit analysis of syntagmatic relationships between the mental images constructed by the spectator on the basis of the visual and acoustic information provided by the film.

Even if the main purpose of the GS is descriptive adequacy, which makes it interesting from a pedagogic viewpoint, it still raises the problem of what an explanatory theory of filmic discourse might consist of. Inasmuch as it explains rules and procedures, the GS cannot escape the problem of their explanatory adequacy from the point of view of 'spectatorial' competence.

Description and explanation have often been opposed, in the name of the induction/deduction opposition. This amounts to forgetting that an explanatory theory is just as empirical as a descriptive theory, and is just as concerned with descriptive adequacy. It could be said that what characterizes an explanatory theory is the necessity of describing data by representing them as rules. It would seem, therefore, that the changes brought to the GS improve its descriptive, as well as its explanatory adequacy.

(*Translated by Claudine Tourniaire*)

Notes

1. The first version of the grande syntagmatigue was published in the issue *Communications*, 8, in 1966.
2. 'No theory can be proved wrong by an unprocessed datum; it can only be proved wrong by a fact, meaning a datum (or data) processed by an alternative theory', Jean-Claude Milner, 'La Constitution du Fait en Linguistique', *Histoire et Linguistique*, Paris: Editions de la Maison des Sciences de l'Homme, 1984, p. 177.
3. Christian Metz, *Film Language: A Semiotics of the Cinema*, trans. Michael Taylor, New York: Oxford University Press, 1974, p. 146.
4. Metz's GS table corresponds to what is known as a tree of selection.
5. Metz, *Film Language*, p. 133 (footnote).
6. Raymond Bellour, *L'Analyse du Film*, Paris: Albatros.
7. Another distinction, often used in AI, illustrates these two types of reading: that between forward chaining and backward chaining. Forward chaining is based on the following modus ponens: from 'P' and 'P implies Q', one deducts 'Q'. Backward chaining is a mode of reasoning guided by the goal to be reached.
8. Metz, *Film Language*, pp. 123-24.
9. Metz, *Film Language*; Noël Burch, 'Passion, Poursuite: la Linéarisation', *Communications*, 38, 1983, pp. 30-50.
10. < means, of course: 'chronologically anterior to'.
11. Metz, *Film Language*, p. 133 (footnote).
12. Metz, *Essais sur la Signification au Cinéma*, tome 2, Paris: Klincksieck, 1972, p. 129.
13. Patrick Henri Winston & Berthold Horn, *LISP*, Reading Mass.: Addison Wesley, 1981, p. 118.
14. Roger Voyer, *Moteurs de systèmes experts*, Paris: Eyrolles, 1987, p. 118.
15. Marvin Minsky, 'A Framework for Representing Knowledge', in: Patrick Winston (ed.), *The Psychology of Computer Vision*, New York: McGraw Hill, 1975.
16. Eugène Charniak & Drew McDermott, *Introduction to Artificial Intelligence*, Reading Mass.: Addison Wesley, 1985, p. 132.

[17] Metz, *Film Language*, p. 153.

[18] The fact that the first telephone call, unlike the second one, contains no fade, is interesting in the context of textual analysis: it can be interpreted as meaning that in the first case, the characters belong to different spaces (social spaces especially), whereas they belong to the same space in the second instance.

[19] Metz, 'Ponctuation, démarcations dans le film de diégèse', in *Essais sur la Signification au Cinéma*, tome 2, Paris: Klincksieck, 1972.

[20] Metz, *Film Language*, p. 127.

[21] ibid., p. 125.

[22] Christian Metz, *Psychoanalysis and Cinema: The Imaginary Signifier*, London: Macmillan, 1982, p. 230.

[23] Myrial Tsikounas (in a personal communication) spotted a mistake in Mitry's description: the river is not the Neva, but the Volga, since the action does not take place in St Petersburg but in Nijni-Novgorod, now known as Gorki. This, of course, changes nothing to the present analysis.

[24] Jean Mitry, *Esthétique et Psychologie du Cinéma*, tome 1 Paris: Editions Universitaires, 1963, p. 371.

[25] Marie-Claire Ropars, 'Fonction de la Métaphore dans *Octobre* d'Eisenstein', *Littérature*, 11 , 1973, pp. 109-128.

[26] Metz, *Psychoanalysis and Cinema*, p. 230.

[27] Dominique Chateau, 'La Semantique du Récit', *Semiotica*, 18, 3, 1976 (Chateau's emphasis).

[28] Frédéric Nef, 'La Constitution des Théories de la Référence', *DRLAV, Revue de Linguistique*, 31, p. 133.

[29] ibid.

[30] Gilles Fauconnier, *Les Espaces Mentaux*, Paris: Minuit, 1984; Hans Kamp, 'Evénements, Représentations Discursive et Référence Temporelle', *Languages*, 64, 1981, pp. 39-64.

[31] See Michel Colin, 'Interprétation sémantique et représentations spatiales dans la bande image', *DRLAV, Revue de Linguistique*, 1986, pp. 359-76.

[32] The notion of partial model implies naturally that all spectators do not necessarily share the same information about the film. Thus, a spectator from the USSR will know more about the places being filmed than a western spectator, and may immediately realise that the film and the prison belong to the same space. This does not prevent the interpretation of the syntagma as a parallel syntagma, for nothing indicates the presence of a diegetic relationship, of a constituent sequence, between these places which belong to the same profilmic referent. Nothing indicates that the

spectator, from the very beginning, and because of what he knows already, will assume, from the proximity of the river to the jail, that the prisoner is planning to escape from the jail by walking over the ice, which would correspond to an alternate syntagma.

[33] See footnote 28.

[34] Metz, *Film Language*, p. 126.

[35] ibid., p. 127.

[36] ibid., p. 126.

[37] ibid.

[38] One example of this is issue No 57 of *Langue Française* (1983).

[39] This may need qualifying to a certain extent, for it only seems to apply to fiction films. Many examples of bracket syntagmas without visual effects could be found in documentaries, or in news bulletins and current affairs programmes.

[40] Reducing the opposition between descriptive and bracket syntagma, as regards the question of reference in the GS of the image track, and introducing it as the only opposition between the specific and the generic, is far too simplistic. We know that other oppositions appear in natural languages, from the point of view of reference: namely between attribute and referential, transparent and opaque. This last opposition, made famous by Quine, enables one to distinguish between contexts in which Leibnitz's principle, which stipulates that two co-referential entities can be substituted without altering the degree of truth of the proposition, is preserved, from those in which it is not. Thus, 'the director of *Bande à part* directed *Les Carabiniers*' contains the same degree of truth as 'Godard directed *Les Carabiniers*'. It is therefore a transparent context.

It could thus be argued that the difference between bracket and descriptive syntagma also depends on this opposition. The bracket syntagma could then be considered as constituting an opaque context in the film, which would explain, incidentally, the presence of visual effects, the function of which is then to clarify this opaque aspect of the reference in the syntagma.

Galmiche reminds us that, according to Quine, expressions appearing in opaque contexts are considered as 'not purely referential'. Examples of this type of configuration could be found in the opening credits of television series such as *Starsky and Hutch* or *The A Team*, consisting of several brief shots connected by cuts, representing extracts from the series. These opening credits can be defined as bracket syntagmas in which the shots do not refer to the events in the diegesis, but to the narrative itself (to the discourse); they are quotations.

[41] Metz, *Film Language*, p. 150.

[42] ibid., pp. 127-28.

[43] Concerning the distinction between opaque and transparent, it can be argued that the bracket syntagma, inasmuch as it depends on an opaque context, causes utterances with a transparent reference to the diegesis to be read non-diegetically, which is why, in this case, the shots have previously been uttered (or will reoccur) in the film, in a transparent context. This does not, of course, apply to the parallel syntagma.

[44] Paul Strawson, *Individuals*, London: Methuen, 1959.

[45] Jon Barwise and John Perry, *Situations and Attitudes*, Cambridge, Mass.: MIT Press, 1983, p. 53.

[46] Metz, *Film Language*, p. 128.

[47] Noël Burch, 'Passion, Poursuite', p. 47.

[48] ibid.

[49] Metz, *Film Language*, p. 129.

[50] ibid., p. 130.

[51] The notion of event is, of course, rather vague. An event can always be considered as divisible into smaller events. A chase, for instance, can always be said to consist of two events: A and B's respective actions; if it is a car chase, it could be said that A, by driving a car, is the agent of several actions which are events (turning the wheel, changing gears, braking etc.). How the structure of the event is constructed also depends on the viewpoint (the topic). Thus, A chases B is a structure defined from A's viewpoint, for from B's viewpoint, it would be B runs away from A. Basically, however, despite these different aspects, the spectator's reasonings on what he sees in a film inevitably imply the notion of event.

This question can be illustrated by an example from Metz's description of *Adieu Philippine*. It is syntagma 12, characterized as an alternate syntagma, filmed 'Inside the screening room' where 'We see alternately the room itself (with the two girls, Pachala, and the client) and the screen on which the rushes of an unsuccessful commerical are flickering by', *Film Language*, p. 156. Inasmuch as there is a spatial frame (the projection studio), this could be considered as a scene in which the pattern of events would correspond to 'S looks at O', in which S = the two girls, Pachala and the customer and O = the rushes; the alternation would then correspond to the shot-reverse-shot characteristic of the scene. What motivates the characterization of the syntagma as an alternate syntagma is that the projection of the rushes is constructed as an event with its own location (namely the screen); the alternation then takes place betwen two structures of events: 'S looks at O' and 'X projects O'. What distinguishes this example from the ones usually quoted is that the second event is not concatenated to the first event (this is not an alternation between event A *and* event B, but embedded (included) within it.

[52] Metz, *Film Language*, p. 132.

[53] Odile Bächler, *La Diligence et l'espace dans le western américain*, mémoire de doctorat, Université de Paris III, 1985.

[54] Michel Colin, 'Coréférence dans *The Adventures of Dollie*', in: Jean Mollet (ed.), *D.W. Griffith*, Paris: L'Harmattan, 1984, pp. 273-282.

[55] Dieter Wunderlich, 'Langage et espace', *DLRAV, Revue de Linguistique*, 27, 1982, p. 65.

[56] ibid., p. 66.

[57] Metz, *Film Language*, p. 130.

[58] ibid., p. 131.

[59] ibid., p. 162.

[60] Roger Schank and Robert Abelson, *Scripts, Plans, Goals, and Understanding*, Hillside: Lawrence Erlbaum Associates, 1977.

[61] Noam Chomsky, *Aspects of the Theory of Syntax*, Cambridge, Mass.: MIT Press, 1965.

[62] George Lakoff, *Irregularity in Syntax*, New York: Holt, Reinhart, and Winston, 1971.

[63] Chomsky, *Aspects*.

[64] Chomsky, and Jean Piaget, *Théories du Langage, Théories de l'Apprentissage*, Paris: Le Seuil, 1979.

[65] Michel Colin, 'La Dislocation', in: Jacques Aumont and Jean Louis-Leutrat (eds.), *Théorie du Film*, Paris: Albatros, 1980, pp. 73-91.

[66] Michel Colin, *Langue, Film, Discours*, Paris: Klincksieck, 1985.

FILM SEMIOLOGY AS
A COGNITIVE SCIENCE

MICHEL COLIN

Introduction

If the role of film semiology is, according to Metz's definition in *Langage et cinéma*, to understand what understanding a film means, it must, as Winograd would say,[1] determine what previous knowledge someone needs to have in order to understand filmic 'language', and how such knowledge is processed by the mind so that it can be used.

The theoretical framework of such an approach corresponds to what is commonly known as cognitive science.

> Cognitive science includes elements of psychology, computer science, linguistics, philosophy and education, but it is more than the intersection of these disciplines. Their integration has produced a new set of tools for dealing with a broad range of questions.[2]

This field owes much of its development to Artificial Intelligence (AI), which is 'the study of mental faculties through the use of computational models'.[3] Indeed,

> the fundamental working assumption, or 'central dogma' of AI is this: what the brain does may be thought of at some level as a kind of computation.[4]

This 'computational' model of human 'cognition' can of course be questioned; the most famous criticism comes from Dreyfus.[5] It can be argued, for instance, that the simulation of a mental process through a computational model does not prove that the psychological process itself functions in the same way. Braunstein, for instance, shows that human vision can be different from a machine's perception.[6]

> It will be seen that, depending on what the machine is being asked to do, it can be reasonable not to expect any of the cognitive plausibility which 'cognitive sciences' aim to achieve. To admit this is the same as admitting that so-called 'intelligent' systems devised in AI do not necessarily claim to be

models of human 'cognition'; and that this is as legitimate as it is common in practice.[7]

Research in AI, the cognitive adequacy of which could only be measured with reference to a semiological and psychological theory, can be suggestive. In other words, even if the role of AI is to produce computer programmes capable of carrying out human tasks – which does not mean that they do this in the same way as a human being –

> the design of computational systems has also a theoretical side, which is often called *cognitive science*. The same concept of programmes and data that serves as a framework for building and understanding computer programmes can be applied to the understanding of any system carrying out a process that can be understood as the rule governed manipulation of symbols.[8]

The purpose of this study, therefore, is not to ask what an automatic recognition of filmic codes (a computer simulation of filmic perception) might consist of, but to show how the afore-mentioned cognitive science can serve as a stimulating theoretical framework for what is commonly called a semiological approach to film. Interestingly, both fields share the same research areas.

> Within most scientific disciplines there are several distinct areas of research, each with its own specific interests, research techniques, and terminology. In AI these specializations include research on language, vision systems, and problem solving.[9]

There is no need to insist on the fact that film semiology is concerned with problems of vision and language; only the third field can seem unrelated to the semiological approach. It is, however, reasonable to consider that the interpretation of semantic phenomena, such as spatio-temporal relationships or co-reference, imply the solving of problems. Thus, it can be argued that the understanding of the shot-reverse shot implies a solution to the problem of determining the position of the characters within the diegetic space on the basis of the filmic configuration (alternation between two shots). More generally, it could be said that the codes postulated by the semiological approach are an explanation of the knowledge necessary to the solving of the problems raised by the interpretation of filmic configurations. For instance, a code such as the grande syntagmatique of narrative film[10] can be considered to represent the knowledge that the spectator needs in order to solve the problems of spatio-temporal relationships within the image track.

We can already conclude, from the above remarks, that the interpretation of certain semantic phenomena, considered as solutions to problems, implies a representation of knowledge:

> in AI, a representation of knowledge is a combination of data structures and interpretative procedures that, if used in the right way in a programme, will lead to 'knowledgeable' behaviour. Work on knowledge representation in AI has involved the design of several classes of data structures for storing information in computer programmes, as well as the development of procedures that allow 'intelligent' manipulation of these data structures to make inferences.[11]

If film semiology can be considered as a 'cognitive science', its place among cognitive sciences, and especially psychology (namely psychology of perception) and linguistics, is still to be determined. Before answering this question, however, it will be necessary to summarize the main characteristics of forms representations of knowledge in AI.

Representations of Knowledge. A Few Preliminaries.
The goals of AI systems can be described in terms of cognitive tasks like recognising objects, answering questions, and manipulating robotic devices. But, the actual use of the knowledge in these programmes involves three stages: (a) acquiring more knowledge, (b) retrieving facts from the knowledge base relevant to the problem at hand, and (c) reasoning about the facts in search of a solution.[12]

(a) The problem of acquisition can be considered as the problem of relating new knowledge to already acquired knowledge.

> AI systems often classify a new data structure before it is added to the data base, so that it can be retrieved later when it is relevant.[13]

In the case of the film spectator, the problem, of course, is the nature of this distinction between given and new knowledge. The latter is bound to vary from one spectator to another. What matters here is the distinction itself, the fact that the understanding of the filmic message cannot be limited to the recognition of previously interiorized data. This may seem pointless. Yet, most film theories adopting a semiological approach seem to consider that the spectator only understands what he already knows. Roger Odin's position is typical of this: according to him, the spectator is endowed with an 'encyclopedic competence', meaning 'a vast pool of knowledge structured into sub-categories or 'worlds', into which he can delve simultaneously in order to attribute meaning to the film'.[14] In order to clarify this distinction between acquired knowledge and new knowledge, we must identify the acquisition mechanisms: which types of reasoning enable the spectator to understand situations or events that he does not know?

(b) 'Determining what knowledge is relevant to a given problem becomes crucial when the system "knows" many different things'.[15] In order to do this, it is of course necessary to determine how memory succeeds in organising the data.

> The fundamental ideas about retrieval that have been developed in AI systems might be termed *linking* and *lumping*. If it is known that one data structure is going to entail another in an expected reasoning task, an explicit link is put between the two; if several data structures are typically going to be used together, they are grouped into a larger structure.[16]

The two main types of formalism used in the representation of these relationships are *semantic networks* and *frames*.

Semantic networks are composed of *nodes* connected by *arcs*. The nodes represent objects, concepts or situations belonging to the relevant field, and the arcs represent the relationships between them. A simple example of this can be a sentence like: 'ravens are birds', which can be represented by two nodes: 'ravens' and 'birds', connected by an arc:

If one wishes to express the fact that a bird has wings, the arc is labelled 'has-part':

In order to represent situations or actions, 'each node can have a set of outgoing arcs,

MICHEL COLIN

called a case frame which specifies the various arguments to the situation predicate'.[17] As in the example 'Clyde has a nest' (in which Clyde is a raven):

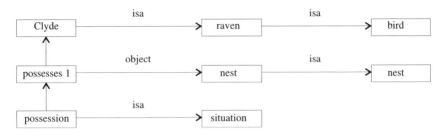

It can be seen that this type of notation enables us to explain 'the apprehension of relationships between objects, or at least their most factual relationships'.[18] It can indeed be argued that recognising a raven, for instance, in a picture, implies the recognition of a bird from the fact that the animal in the picture has wings. Representation through semantic networks actually makes use of notions developed in structural semantics: it also raises the problem of semantic primitives. This problem has often been discussed, and remains largely unsolved. Let us simply remark that all systems of semantic representation inevitably entail a primitive vocabulary including notions such as 'state' versus 'action', 'situation' versus 'event', cases like 'agent', 'object', 'instrument', 'recipient', etc., abstract predicates such as 'cause', or predicates that McCawley calls 'creators of worlds', such as the one named MBUILD (mental building) by Schank and Abelson, this list being far from exhaustive.[19]

Frames serve to express the properties necessary to the knowledge of an object, a concept, or a situation.[20] A *frame* can be represented as a list associating properties and values. For instance, someone called Henri can be represented as a *frame* (frame: Henri) consisting of a list of properties like: sex, height, weight, hobbies, job, associated to values like: male, 1m75, 75 kgs, jogging, skiing, teacher. This example could then be represented as follows:

> Henri (sex (value (male))
> (height (value (175))
> (weight (value (75))
> (hobbies (value (jogging) (skiing))
> (job (value (teacher))))

One of the most important aspects of the notion of *frame* is the notion of value by *default*, 'which suggests a value for the slot in the absence of contradictory evidence'.[21]

A logic admitting values by default is called non-monotonous,[22] for it is founded on the notion of plausibility or probability, rather than on the notion of the true as opposed to the false, which defines what is known as a monotonous logic. This notion of default enables one to explain, for instance, why the spectator can recognise a chair with a leg missing, the number of legs (4) being a value by default.

(c) The third aspect implied by a cognitive process such as the understanding of a film is the process of reasoning about data, the main types of which are:

Formal reasoning, of which the most typical example is mathematical logic;

Procedural reasoning, which 'uses simulation to answer questions and solves problems';[23]

Reasoning by analogy which 'seems to be a very natural mode of thought for a human'.[24]

Thus, if someone does not know that nightingales fly, but knows that ravens do, he could deduct it by analogy: 'Nightingales are like ravens (they have wings); as I know that wings enable ravens to fly, nightingales also fly';

Reasoning by generalization and abstraction is also a natural mode of reasoning for humans. 'This capability may be at the core of human learning'.[25]

The meta-level of reasoning implies a level of meta-knowledge, of knowledge about what we know, 'in particular about the extent of your knowledge and about the importance of certain facts'.[26]

It is fairly easy to show why these different types of reasoning are considered to be capable of explaining how a film is understood. One simple example will serve this purpose: that of televised broadcasts of sport events. The advantage of this type of audio-visual message is, of course, that it allows a fairly easy definition of what understanding can consist of. This understanding basically implies the identification of the goals of actions within the framework of the rules of the game.[27] Thus, a race is defined by the goal 'arriving first (or in the shortest space of time) at a given point'; football is defined by the goal 'putting the ball into a specific place as many times as possible, respecting rules such as not touching the ball with one's hands, not hitting the opponent, etc'. The Georgian film *L'Hirondelle*, which tells the story of the creation of the first

Soviet football team at the beginning of the century, is a good example of this. At the start of the film, the hero sees a number of players on the field, running after a ball that they try to control with their feet and score goals. The hero, watching the scene, and totally ignorant of the game, asks his neighbour why they play with their feet and not with their hands.

A preliminary knowledge of these rules, however, is not necessary to an understanding of the broadcast. Let us suppose, for instance, that a spectator knows about football (soccer) but not rugby. It is conceivable that reasoning by analogy (similarity of the spatial context, existence of two teams, specific places where the ball is to be sent, arithmetic inequality of the score distinguishing the winner from the loser) should enable the spectator to understand a rugby match; on this basis, he will be able to integrate new information about rugby: the ball is usually played with the hands, a goal is scored by throwing the ball over a horizontal pole and not under it as in football; points are scored by holding the ball, which is oval, on the ground behind the goal line, points are not counted in the same way as in football, etc. This whole set of rules can in fact be constructed by generalization:[28] if, every time that the spectator sees a player holding the ball down behind the goal line, he notices that the team gets 4 points, he will conclude that this action (scoring a try) is worth 4 points, whereas the kick following this action, if the balls goes in, is only worth 2 points; yet when the kick follows the referee's whistle, and not a try, it scores 3 points. Finally, this example implies a level of meta-knowledge on the importance, amongst other things, of certain facts in the context of field sports opposing two teams. One caricatural example of this is that getting the ball matters more than getting a bottle of water, even if one happens to see a player quenching his thirst, an action that can have important consequences on his future ability to seize the ball. On the whole, this meta-level of reasoning is likely to be crucial in the understanding of the audio-visual message, in that it allows the spectator to select the information necessary to the understanding of the meaning.

Among the necessary knowledge, there is, of course, what is known as 'filmic language'. It allows the spectator, for instance, to conclude that if a long shot is followed by a close-up on part of the scene, the latter is more important than the rest; in this case, there is what is called a 'putting into focus' accompanied by right dislocation (or rhematisation).

Inasmuch as this type of operation occurs in natural languages, as, for instance, in French, in *Paul l'a lu, le livre*, we may ask ourselves whether this knowledge of 'filmic language' is a specific one, or whether the spectator applies his 'linguistic' knowledge to filmic configurations, largely through the use of reasoning by analogy.

More generally, the problem here is that of the modularity of the representations of knowledge.

> One characteristic that is often used to compare representation schemes is *modularity*, which refers to the ability to add, modify, or delete individual data structures more or less independently of the remainder of the database.[29]

There is no doubt that modularity presents many advantages from the point of view of AI, as in the case of the implantation of AI software, since it permits a modification of local data without modifying the whole. This notion of modularity can be illustrated by Pitrat's example: if a file of cooking recipes is organised in a modular way, each recipe must be independent of others:

> Referring to another recipe constitutes a breach of modularity.[30]

> Winograd suggests that no system is completely modular – in all systems there is some degree of interaction between the data structures that form the knowledge base.[31]

If this is the case, one can only talk of a greater of lesser degree of modularity.

This question of modularity is linked to the question of how representations of knowledge are put forward. In other words, there is a link between modularity and declarative vs procedural representations.

> I say that knowledge is presented in a declarative form if we do not, at the same time, give an indication of when it will have to be used, or how to apply it if one decides to do so. On the other hand, it is presented in a procedural form if we also have indications on how it can be processed, and what is to be done before and after.[32]

For instance, 'a common noun is preceded by a determiner' is declarative, but 'if one encounters a noun, one checks whether or not it is preceded by an article and one then verifies whether it is a common noun' is a procedural representation.

Our purpose here is not, of course, to try and determine the advantages and disadvantages of these two types of representation. Let us merely remember that procedural representations try and account for human reasoning, and especially reasoning by default. However, procedural representations are less modular than declarative representations, since by implying information on context, they result in an inevitable inter-action between different fields.

A quick glance at film semiology is enough to show that its representations take on a declarative form, the best example being that of the grande syntagmatique of narrative film, since the different syntagmas are defined in terms of properties (espe-cially temporal properties). Thus, narrative syntagmas are defined as 'syntagmas in which the temporal relationship between the objects seen in the images contains ele-ments of consecutiveness'.[33] Much has already been written about this 'Metzian' syntagmatique, and it has been abundantly criticised. We shall refrain from any obsolete additions to this material. Let us, rather, try and conceive a representation of the data examined in the grande syntagmatique, on the basis of the various points which have just been developed.

Spatial Relationships in the Image Track
Metz's grande syntagmatique defines the various syntagmas according to temporal, rather than spatial, relationships, as is shown by the distinction between chronological and non-chronological syntagmas. This under-estimation of spatial relationships may seem surprising, since film, being a succession of images, can be considered as a suc-cession of spaces. Moreover, the image itself can be defined as the projection of a three-dimensional space onto a two-dimensional space.

It has already been shown[34] that the difference between scene and sequence, for instance, does not depend so much on the difference between temporal continuity and a hiatus, as on that between a spatial *frame* and an *itinerary*. If, indeed, during a live broadcast on formula 1 motor-racing, a car goes out to the right of the shot, then reap-pears in the next shot from the left, there is a hiatus, but it is a spatial, not temporal hiatus; in a live broadcast, the temporal intervals represented by each shot are adjacent (filmic time = diegetic time). However, it is possible that the spaces being represented do not exactly coincide. There is, therefore, a hiatus in the itinerary of the car. The car could, for instance, disappear round a bend, then reappear out of the bend, while its itinerary round the actual bend remains invisible. But the combination of the two shots corresponds to the time it took the car to go round the bend, so there has been no tempo-ral ellipsis. The sequence could then be defined as being constructed around objects covering a certain distance, whereas the scene would be constructed topologically: 'for each point, there are several environments'.[35]

Consequently, it has already be argued that the semantic interpretation of the image track implies the interpretation of spatial relationships between shots, which could follow the model of the 'general space planner'[36] described as follows by Barr & Feigenbaum:[37]

Work on the general space planner addressed the task of arranging things in a space subject to given constraints that must be satisfied. A simple problem is following:

given the space   and the objects

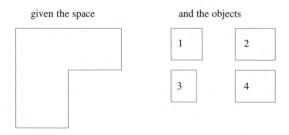

and the constraints:

      (3) must be adjacent to (4)

      (2) must be adjacent to (3)

      (1) must be visible from (3)

      (1) must not be adjacent to the others.

one solution is:

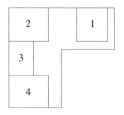

The way in which this type of representation could be used in film can be illustrated by an example from *The Barefoot Contessa* (J.L. Mankiewicz): at the beginning of the film, four characters: K. Edwards, O. Muldoon, Myrna and H. Dawes (the narrator[38]) sit down at a table in a cabaret, where M. Vargas is to perform. The narrator's 'voice off' introduces the characters over close-ups on each of them; a conversation follows, with a succession of shots and reverse-shots that never show all four characters together. It can then be assumed that the spectator goes through the mental process of reconstructing the spatial relationships between the characters on the basis of successive shots of each one. The space in question can be represented by a quadrilateral figure inside which a circle is inserted, representing a round table inside a rectangular room.

The spectator must therefore place the characters around this table. The constraints are to be deducted from the factual relationships between the characters. Thus, if Dawes looks towards the right as he speaks, and Edwards answers looking towards the left in the reverse-shot, then Dawes and Edwards are facing each other. Several solutions are then possible, one of which can be:

If Edwards turns to his right as he speaks, then he is not speaking to Dawes, but to someone on his left. The next shot (representing Myrna) will represent the character occupying that place, the fourth place being occupied by Muldoon. The four characters could then be interpreted as having the following type of spatial relationship:

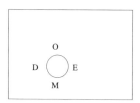

It can be argued that this is not the only possible representation within the above-mentioned constraints. The following representation could be just as valid:

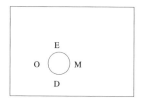

When asked to solve this problem, it is interesting to see that students do not all offer the same solution. However, all solutions do have one thing in common: Dawes is distinguished as sitting on the left of the field, facing the other three characters; what varies are the respective positions of Edwards, usually, but not always facing Dawes, Myrna and Muldoon. We could thus end up with:

E

D   M

O

or:

M

D   E

O

It can be concluded from this that the main constraint is: 'placing the four characters in such a way that Dawes faces the other three', and that constraints such as 'Muldoon is facing Myrna' or 'Myrna is sitting to the left of Edwards' are therefore discarded. Interestingly, this spatial construction is characterized by a left/right lateralization, implying that the spatial construction assumes an implicit viewpoint according to which Dawes is sitting on the left. A representation placing O on the left and D at the bottom will therefore never occur, since O would be on the left, although that would be closer to reality than the other two representations.

Moreover, the table itself must be accommodated within the space of the cabaret. As this scene is interpreted as showing four characters entering a cabaret and sitting at a table, a first constraint is of course the necessity for the table to be inside the cabaret. Here again, however, many solutions can be found that would meet this constraint. Another constraint would result from the characters' travelling from right to left as they enter. This also allows several interpretations, independently of the viewpoint adopted. In other words, the entrance could be placed at the very top, with the table in front, which would mean that the viewpoint is on the right; but the spectator seems to place the entrance in the top right corner, which implies that in our representation, the viewpoint is at the bottom, as follows:

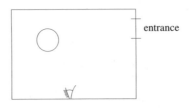

    MICHEL COLIN

It can be seen that if representations are dependent on a viewpoint, the number of possible representations decreases.[39] If all of the above-mentioned constraints are taken into account, the position of the characters can be represented as follows:

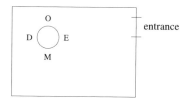

This type of model shows that the interpretation of spatial relationships in film should not necessarily be considered as implying the construction of a complete, biunivocal image of the scene in the spectator's mind. Indeed, the greater or lesser degree of completeness of the representation depends on the number of constraints and on their more or less restrictive character. In the present example of *The Barefoot Contessa*, the entrance of the four characters in question is preceded by close-ups on spectators, all of them looking in the same direction: in this case, the constraint dictates that these spectators are seated facing the stage in a cabaret, but no constraint regulates their mutual relationships. If, for instance, there are three shots of three different spectators looking in the same direction, this can be represented in one of the following ways:

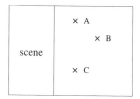

or:

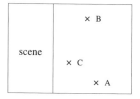

but also in many other ways.

The example from *The Barefoot Contessa* naturally corresponds to what Metz defines as a scene, since from the point of view of temporal relationships, there is a succession and continuity between shots and, from the spatial point of view, the space in question is a frame. In the case of what Metz calls the sequence, which can be defined in terms of the notion of itinerary, 'an itinerary can be represented as the projection of a temporal interval (orientated) into space'.[40] To go back to the example given by Metz in *Adieu Philippine*, (J. Rozier), in which a character, Michel, leaves the studio to go and fetch an ear-phone in the production van (second segment of the film), the space in question can be represented by a vector on which the studio (starting point) and the production van (point of arrival) can be situated:

It will be noticed that in televised broadcasts of cycling races along roads, which are evidently based on the notion of itinerary (since the winner of a race is the one who covers a certain distance faster than other competitors), this itinerary is represented by a vector showing the points of departure and arrival, as well as the distance. Moreover, when one or several competitors 'break away', racing ahead of the main body of racers, this advantage is represented by a vector showing the time needed for the main body of racers to reach the point where the leading racers were:

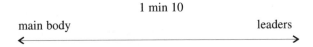

The vector represents the distance covered by the leaders when the main body of racers reaches the point at which the chronometer was started. The time does not correspond to the time needed to cover this distance, but to the time needed to reach the point where the leaders were when the chronometer was started. If this point corresponding to the starting of the chronometer is called 0, the time indicated on the vector corresponds to the interval of time between situation 1, in which the leaders are at 0, and situation 2, in which the main body of racers is at 0. The representation then being used corresponds to a projection of the S1, S2 interval onto the space of the straight line representing the spatial relationships: being in front, being behind. Of course, since A is ahead of B, then B is behind A; a double arrow can then be used:[41]

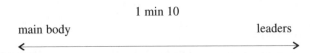

Let us remember that according to the theory of graphs, 'an itinerary is any sequence of adjacent arcs'.[42] It is possible to construct itineraries within a spatial frame. In *The*

Barefoot Contessa, for instance, the door through which the characters enter is visible before the table at which they will sit, but cannot be seen any longer when they sit down. In other words, the relationship between the entrance and the table inside the cabaret is constructed on the basis of the itinerary of the four characters:

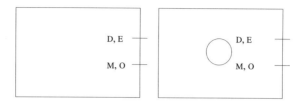

When Muldoon goes out to the left of the frame, the spectator understands that he does not go out by the same door through which he came in. Again, it is Muldoon's itinerary which enables us to situate a door in the wall opposite the door through which the characters have come in:

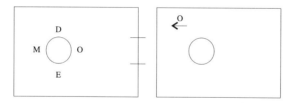

However, when Muldoon comes back into the field, the door is to the right and not to the left of the frame, and the character moves from right to left, in the same direction as when the four characters came in and when Muldoon went out; the spectator then understands that there has been a 180° change in viewpoint.

In other words, contrary to popular belief, the infringement of the 180° rule according to which if two characters, for instance, are facing each other, the camera must not cross the imaginary line between them

is not only more common than is generally thought, but is interpreted without any difficulty by the spectator. It can indeed be seen that in the scene in which the four characters
are sitting around the table, this rule is infringed if D and E do not permute whereas O
and M do so:

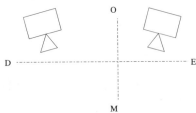

This ability of the spectator's can easily be predicted with the help of this model. Given
the spatial frame and the constraints, one of which could be the fact that the door cannot
have moved, the only (or at least most likely) solution to the problem raised by
Muldoon entering the field from the right after leaving it on the left, is to assume that
Muldoon enters through the same door through which he went out, and that the camera
has infringed the so-called 180° rule.

It can of course be argued that the spectator has recognised a number of
recurrent elements in both shots, which enable him to assume that the door through
which Muldoon comes in is the same as the one through which he went out and not the
same as the one through which the four characters came in. Such a comparison, however, implies the memorization of a far greater number of data[43] than is necessary for the
model inspired by the *general space planner*.

One final remark must be made. The explanation of the interpretation of
spatial relationships between shots on the basis of the *general space planner* can just as
easily take on a declarative form as a procedural form. The declarative formulation is
what has just been used, but a procedural formulation is not difficult to imagine. For
instance, instead of saying that if A looks to the right and B to the left, A and B are
facing each other, one could simply say: follow the characters' eyes. If A looks to the
right, find out whether, in the next shot, B looks to the left. If he does, position B opposite A, etc.

It is, of course, impossible to spell out all the rules and procedures explaining in detail the semantic interpretation of spatial relationships between shots. Let us
mention just a few:

inclusion: the space of one of the shots is included in the space of the other;

adjacency: the spaces denoted by the two shots are contiguous. This relationship can provide a basis for relationships of the type: being opposite, next to, in front of, behind;

prolongation: 'The prolongation of two wholes is the reunion of their common parts'.[44] It can therefore be said that two shots are in a relationship of prolongation when they are not adjacent but can be connected by an itinerary.

These last two relationships enable us, amongst other things, to explain the distinction made by Burch between successive and alternate syntagmas:[45] in the former, where, according to Burch, the two spaces are 'fairly close', they can be called adjacent, whereas in the latter, in which the spaces are 'remote', there is a prolongation. In the parallel syntagma, on the other hand, there is no adjacency or prolongation.

The interpretation of these spatial relationships naturally implies relationships of co-reference. 'There is a relationship of co-reference between two referential units A and B when they happen to share the same co-reference'.[46] This relationship therefore implies a process of connection between two referential entities. They can be identical, or be connected by a relationship of transformation. One usually recognises three elementary transformations, which can be combined: translation, in-depth translation and rotation.[47] A co-reference can also occur without any such correspondence: a flashback, for instance, can show a co-reference between a baby and an old man.

Film Semiology and Cognitive Sciences
It may be remembered that Saussure defined semiology as a branch of social psychology. He also chose to use the term 'semiology' as a way of distinguishing it from semantics, which, at that time, consisted of the study of changes of meaning. Things have changed, of course, since the death of Ferdinand de Saussure; semantics, as a subject, is no longer concerned with the diachronic study of the signified; linguistics, like semiology, is more based on cognitive psychology than on social psychology. Chomsky considers linguistics as a branch of psychology, and Lyons has abandoned the term 'semiology' in favour of that of 'semantics'.[48]

According to Winograd, structural linguistics is based on the development of discovery procedures, for which chemistry provides the scientific model. As for generative linguistics, its model is to be found in mathematics:

generative linguistics views language as a mathematical object and builds theories that are very much like sets of axioms and reference rules in mathematics. A sentence is grammatical if there is some *derivation* that demonstrates that its structure is in accord with a set of rules, much as a proof demonstrates the truth of a mathematical sentence.[49]

This form of semiology corresponds to what Winograd calls a 'computational' paradigm. This new 'paradigm' shows many similarities with the 'generative' paradigm.

> From a greater distance, they may be seen as two variants of a single 'cognitive' paradigm, which is based on the following principles:
> The proper domain of study is the structure of the knowledge possessed by an individual who uses a language.
> This knowledge can be understood as formal rules concerning structures of symbols.[50]

The main differences between these two concepts are:

> In the computational paradigm, the structure of language is derived from the structures of the processes of comprehension and production.[51]

Because of the distinction between competence and performance in the generative concept, 'the structure of a person's linguistic competence is characterized independently of any process by which it is manifested'.[52]

This question of the link between mental and linguistic faculties has already been the focus of debates between AI specialists, generative linguists, and psychologists; especially the debate between Chomsky and Piaget.[53] As far as film semiology is concerned, the problem is then knowing whether the homologies between linguistic and filmic structures depend on linguistic faculties, or derive from the fact that language and film call for the same mental faculties. The latter hypothesis is not, of course, incompatible with the generative approach. Indeed, it could be argued that generative semiology would bring no relevant answer to this question.[54]

Seen from the 'computational' angle, the problem disappears altogether. One could even conceivably replace the label 'semiology' with that of 'cognitive semantics of film', since the latter implies the same conceptual structures as language. 'There is a *single* level of mental representation, *conceptual structure*, at which linguistic, sensory, and motor information are compatible'.[55] The role of semantics is then to describe the rules affecting the correspondance between syntactic and conceptual structures, and the rules affecting the correct formation of concepts. This link between conceptual structures and syntactic structures can be conceived in two ways.

> First, conceptual structure could be a further level beyond semantic structure, related to it by a rule component called *pragmatics*, that specifies the relation of linguistic meaning to discourse and to extra-linguistic setting.[56]

This is the theory put forward by Katz and Fodor, amongst others, and was therefore prevalent in the field of generative and transformational grammar, until the time of Jackendoff.[57] 'Alternatively, semantic structures could be simply a subset of conceptual structures – just those conceptual structures that happen to be verbally expressible'.[58] This was the theory advocated by Chomsky, particularly in and after his *Reflections on Language*, and by many researchers in the field of AI. The first theory would of course be justified by the existence of primitives and/or combination principles particular to language, in other words 'distinct from those appropriate to the communication of visual information to the linguistic system'.[59] This inevitably raises problems in film semiology, for it implies a distinction, especially when interpreting visual data semantically, between the respective importance of linguistic structures and of the visual system.

This theory corresponds to the position defended by some psychologists in favour of 'double coding', according to whom 'visual information and verbal information are functionally independent but interrelated'.[60] It could thus be argued that although the understanding of an image does imply its categorization, the latter can vary depending on whether it is of a linguistic or visual nature, since the same image, for instance, would not be described in the same way by spectators speaking different languages. Needless to say, observations of this kind prove nothing, since they are equally compatible with the second theory, according to which semantic structures can be, and so are, verbalized differently depending on the language spoken, amongst other factors. Besides, it could be said that the recognition of forms in AI implies visual primitives enabling us to construct a 3-D representation of a scene, by detecting, for instance, the edges through changes in luminous intensity, then by determining surfaces from changes in texture and volumetric primitives (cylinder, axis, and so on), as well as a semantic base capable of interpreting these representations.[61] There is no reason, however, to consider this semantic base as a specifically linguistic level of representation; it can correspond to a set of frames representing linguistic (a frame has a name) and visual data. Any correspondence between semantic and visual representation implies the existence of redundant elements. Jackendoff's hypothesis on the existence of a single level of mental representation therefore seems to be the simplest and most adequate as regards the interpretation of the filmic message. Only linguists, at any rate, can attempt to solve this problem.

This arguably pointless question has at least served to present us with a clearer picture of what part film semiology can play in relation to linguistics and perception psychology: it must describe the rules governing the links between the visual representations of 3-D scenes and conceptual structures. As for the theory of perception, it seeks to reveal the mechanisms which enable us to explain how, for instance, the spectator recognises a 3-D scene on the basis of the perception of 2-D images. Our purpose is not, of course, to erect rigid barriers between the theory of perception, semiology and linguistics. Film semiology, like semantics, creates links between formal structures (syntax) and conceptual structures; they are differentiated by syntactic structures.[62] Various studies carried out on the recognition of forms, especially those by K.S. Fu,[63] aptly demonstrate that these structures are just as relevant to the theory of perception as to semiology. It could be argued that the theory of perception concerns itself mainly with the description of what Barrow & Tenenbaum call the intrinsic image,[64] whereas semiology concentrates mostly on describing the scene. From the point of view of film semiology, this description largely implies the analysis of the links between shots.[65]

Conclusion

The present hypothesis presents film semiology – defined by Metz, in *Langage et cinéma*, as an explicit theory on the spectator's understanding of a film – as being closely related to cognitive sciences, namely linguistics and psychology. It is therefore possible to show, on the basis of certain concepts and systems of data representation (among which the *general space planner*), how the mental construction of diegetic space in film can be explained.

Although the aim of film semiology is similar to that of the theory of perception and semantics, film semiology, as a study of the links between audiovisual configurations and conceptual structures, can nevertheless be considered as a cognitive science in its own right.

This essay could not possibly claim to offer more than a rough sketch of problematic issues, the results of which are still unpredictable, as well as dependent on the development of experimental procedures.[66] Thus, the interpretation of relationships raises the problem of the size of the working memory,[67] illustrated by *backtracking* phenomena, for instance. The spectator only retains a certain quantity of information within what is known as the *buffer* (short term) *memory*; he must also have access to information stored within his *long term* memory, whenever necessary.

Film semiology is now over twenty years old. Its demise has been announced for quite some time, often by its once most ardent supporters. The only aim of this text is to show that it has indeed become a subject, complete with reinterpretations and unsolved problems, which are proof of its vitality. [last paragraph omitted]

(Translated by Claudine Tourniaire)

Notes

[1] Terry Winograd, *Language as a Cognitive Process*, Reading, Mass.: Addison-Wesley, 1983.

[2] Daniel Bobrow, and Allan Collins (eds), *Representation and Understanding*, New York: Academic Press, 1975, pp. ix-x.

[3] Eugene Charniak and Drew MacDermott, *Introduction to Artificial Intelligence*, Reading, Mass.: Addison-Wesley, 1985, p. 5.

[4] ibid., p. 6.

[5] H. Dreyfus, *What Computers Can't Do: A Critique of Artificial Reason*, New York: Harper and Row, 1979.

[6] Myron Braunstein, 'Contrasts between human and machine vision: should technology recapitulate Philogeny?', Hope Beck and A. Rosenfeld (eds), *Human and Machine Vision*, New York: Academic Press, 1983.

[7] Danièle Clément, 'Syntaxe et compétence, syntaxe et performance, syntaxe cognitive?', *DLRAV. Revue de Linguistique*, 33, 1985, p. 76.

[8] Terry Winograd, *Language as a Cognitive Process*, Reading, Mass.: Addison-Wesley, p. 2.

[9] Aaron Barr and Edward Feigenbaum, *The Handbook of Artificial Intelligence*, vol. 1, California: William Kaufman, 1981, p. 7.

[10] Christian Metz, *Film Language: A Semiotics of the Cinema*, trans. Michael Taylor, New York: Oxford University Press, 1974, pp. 108-146.

[11] Barr & Feigenbaum, *The Handbook of Artificial Intelligence*, p. 143.

[12] ibid., p. 145.

[13] ibid.

[14] Roger Odin, *L'Analyse sémiologique des films*, mémoire doctorat d'état, Paris: Ecole de Hautes Etudes en Sciences Sociales, miméo, 1982, pp. 152-53.

[15] Barr & Feigenbaum, p. 146.

[16] ibid.

[17] ibid., p. 183.

18   Christian Metz, *Essais sémiotiques*, Paris: Klincksieck, 1977, p. 35.

19   Schank, Roger, and Robert Abelson, *Scripts, Plans, Goals, and Understanding*, Hillside: Lawrence Erlbaum, 1977.

20   There is a particular type of *frame*, implying events, called a *script* (Roger Schank and Robert Abelson, *Scripts, Plans, Goals, and Understanding*, Hillside: Lawrence Erlbaum, 1977). On the notion of *frame*, as applied especially to the perceptive recognition of objects, see Marvin Minsky, 'A framework for representing knowledge', P. Winston (ed.), *The Psychology of Computer Vision*, New York: McGraw Hill, 1975.

21   Barr & Feigenbaum, p. 218.

22   On non-monotonous logic, see Drew MacDermott and Jon Doyle, 'Non-monotonic logic, I', *Artificial Intelligence*, 13, 1980, 1-2, pp. 41-72.

23   ibid., p. 146.

24   ibid.

25   ibid., p. 147.

26   ibid.

27   For a more detailed analysis of this point, see chapter 3 of Michel Colin *Cinéma, Télévision, Cognition*, Nancy: Presses Universitaires de Nancy, 1992.

28   Schank and Abelson differentiate between specific knowledge of sequences of events, and general knowledge, through the notions of script and *shot*.

29   Barr & Feigenbaum, p. 149.

30   Jacques Pitrat, *Textes, ordinateurs et compréhension*, Paris: Eyrolles, 1985, p. 48.

31   Barr & Feigenbaum, 1981, p. 150. [Barr & Feigenbaum refer to Winograd's 'Five lectures on artificial intelligence', AI memo 246, AI laboratory, Stanford University (also published in A. Zampolli (ed.), *Linguistic Structures Processing*, Amsterdam: North Holland Publishing Co., 1977, pp. 399-520).]

32   Pitrat, *Textes, ordinateurs et compréhension*, p. 52.

33   Metz, *Film Language*, p. 128.

34   Michel Colin, 'Interpétation semantique et relations spatailes dans la bande-image', *DLRAV. Revue de Linguistique*, 34-35, 1986, pp. 359-76; Odile Bächler, *La diligence et l'espace dans le western américain*, mémoire de doctorat, Université de Paris III, 1985.

35   Dieter Wunderlich, 'Langue et espace', *DLRAV. Revue de Linguistique*, 27, 1982, p. 65.

36   C.M. Eastman, 'Representations for space planning', *Communication for the Association for Computing Machinery*, 13, 1970, pp. 242-50; and 'Automated space planning', *Artificial Intelligence*, 4, 1973, pp. 41-64.

37   Barr & Feigenbaum, 1981, p. 202.

[38] Letters E (Edwards), O (Oscar Muldoon); M (Myrna) and D (Dawes) will be used in order to refer to the characters.

[39] This does not contradict the fact that the semantic interpretation of the diegetic space implies a mental construction independent from the viewpoint. In fact, even if a frame implies a viewpoint, the links betwen this and the different shots imply that the latter are interpreted independently of the viewpoint from which they were filmed. On the contrary, they are transformationally linked to the viewpoint from which the frame was constructed.

[40] Wunderlich, 'Langue et espace', p. 66.

[41] For a more developed analysis of this point, see chapter 3 of *Cinéma, télévision, cognition*.

[42] Pierre Goujon, *Mathématiques de base pour linguistes*, Paris: Hermann, 1975, p. 98.

[43] On the problems raised by the automatic analysis of consecutive images, see Thomas Huang (ed.), *Image Sequence Analysis*, New York: Springer Verlag, 1981.

[44] Marcel Boll, *Manuel de logique scientifique*, Paris: Dunod, 1948, p. 33.

[45] Noël Burch, 'Passion, poursuite: la linéarisation', *Communications*, 38, 1983, pp. 30-50.

[46] Jean-Claude Milner, *Ordres et raisons de langue*, Paris: Le Seuil, 1982, p. 32. This link is especially crucial to the distinction between alternate and parallel syntagmas. To quote once more the famous example from the end of *Mother*, by Pudovkin, showing an alternation between shots of a workers' demonstration and shots of the ice thawing on the river: when the hero, whose space was a direct prolongation of that of the demonstration (he has just escaped from jail, and his mother takes part in the demonstration), appears on the ice, the syntagma is interpreted as being an alternate one. The relationship of prolongation is therefore, unlike the relationship of adjacency, a transitive one (if A = B and B = C, then A = C).

[47] On this point, see Shimon Ullman, *The Interpretation of Visual Motion*, Cambridge, Mass.: MIT Press, 1979.

[48] John Lyons, *Semantics*, Cambridge: Cambridge University Press, 1977.

[49] Terry Winograd, *Language as a Cognitive Process*, p. 12.

[50] ibid., p. 20.

[51] ibid., p. 21.

[52] ibid.

[53] Noam Chomsky and Jean Piaget, *Théories du langage, théories de l'apprentissage*, Paris: Le Seuil, 1979. Two participants in this debate were S. Papert, a specialist in AI and author of the theory of perceptions, and Fodor, author of *Modularity of Mind*, Cambridge, Mass.: MIT Press, 1980.

[54] See Colin, 'Propositions pour une recherche expérimentale en sémiologie du cinéma', *Communications*, 38, 1983, pp. 239-255.

[55] Ray Jackendoff, *Semantics and Cognition*, Cambridge, Mass.: MIT Press, 1983, p. 17.

[56] ibid., pp. 19-20.

[57] Jerrold Katz and Jerry Fodor, 'The structure of a semantic theory', *The Structure of Language*, New Jersey: Prentice-Hall, 1964; Jackendoff, *Semantic Interpretation in Generative Grammar*, Cambridge, Mass.: MIT Press, 1972.

[58] Jackendoff, *Semantics and Cognition*, 1983, p. 20.

[59] ibid.

[60] J. Donnay, *Upplantation audio-visuelle en communication orale*, Doctorat, Universite de Liège, miméo., 1981.

[61] There is a fair amount of literature on computerized vision. We shall simply mention the famous volume by David Marr, *Vision*, Cambridge, Mass.: MIT Press, 1982.

[62] Michel Colin, 'Syntaxe et sémantique dans le message filmique', *Iris*, 1, 1983, pp. 83-100.

[63] K.S. Fu, *Syntactic Pattern Recognition and Applications*, New Jersey: Prentice Hall, 1982.

[64] H. Barrow and J.M. Tenenbaum, 'Recovering intrinsic scene characteristics from images', A. Hanson and E. Riseman (eds), *Computer Vision Systems*, New York: Academic Press, 1978. For Marr, the intrinsic image corresponds to the image 2-D 1/2, which 'makes explicit the orientation and rough depth of the visible surfaces, and contours of discontinuities in these quantities in a viewer-centered coordinate frame' *Vision*, Cambridge, Mass.: MIT Press, 1982, p. 37.

[65] Michel Colin, *Langue, film, discours*, Paris: Klincksieck, 1985.

[66] See Colin, 'Propositions pour une recherche expérimentale en sémiologie du cinéma', *Communications*, 38, 1983, pp. 239-55.

[67] Guy Denhière (ed.), *Il était une fois... Compréhension et souvenirs de récits*, Presses Universitaires de Lille, 1984.

SECTION 2

FILM AND ENUNCIATION REVISITED

INTRODUCTION

WARREN BUCKLAND AND JAN SIMONS

Enunciation: An Ambiguous Concept

Already from the outset, it was never very clear what was actually meant by the concept of enunciation. In their *Analytical Dictionary*, A.J. Greimas and J. Courtés point out that the concept actually has two different definitions.[1] It is conceived either as a non-linguistic, referential structure underlying linguistic communication, or as a linguistic concept, logically presupposed by the existence of the 'utterance'. In the first definition, the term 'enunciation' comes close to the notion of 'speech act', and refers to how the meaning of an utterance depends on the circumstances under which it is produced (by whom, to whom, referring to what or whom, and with what communicative intention, at what time and at what place?). Conceived this way, enunciation is an instance that mediates between a linguistic expression and the non-linguistic context in which it is uttered, that is, an instance of *communication*.

However, Greimas and Courtés only accept the second definition, in which the enunciation is a linguistic instance, the passage from the virtual and abstract language system (*langue*) to the actual and concrete utterances in which a language manifests itself (discourse). Since this logical instance allows for the transformation of the virtual language system into actual discourse, it can be considered as the 'discursive competence', necessary for the production of linguistic utterances. In this view the enunciation is a purely linguistic instance, and has to be clearly distinguished from the (non-linguistic) communication. The concept of enunciation thus refers to an abstract, transcendental subject, logically presupposed by the very existence of an utterance itself, while the concept of communication refers to concrete, individual subjects who produce linguistic utterances to communicate particular messages with particular purposes and in particular circumstances to other particular subjects.

But, as Metz himself stresses, a third, slightly different conception of enunciation has emerged, in which the enunciation is closely tied to the notion of *subjectivity*, that is, to the emergence of the subject within discourse. This emergence of the subject is a symptom of the problem of, as well as the problem with, enunciation.

Enunciation and Film

Curiously enough, one of the most fundamental paradoxes that was logically introduced with the concept of enunciation has hardly ever been mentioned. If on the one
hand the notion of 'enunciation' is supposed to mediate between a *langue* and the concrete utterances of a language, and if on the other hand the cinema is indeed, as Metz
has put it, a *langage sans langue*, the question immediately arises, what is it the concept
has to mediate? It is quite legitimate, of course, to consider films as 'signifying systems', comparable in many respects to languages: they are usually not randomly arranged strings of images and sounds, and meanings ascribed to films are generally not
idiosyncratic interpretations of individual spectators but normally meet a large degree
of interpersonal agreement. In the history of film some fundamental, stable and pervasive norms of filmic construction and comprehension can be observed, which not only
allow spectators to comprehend canonic instances of a particular mode, but also to comprehend innovative forms and stylistic devices they could not possibly have encountered before, etc.

Metz briefly discussed a number of stable norms of filmic comprehension in
his paper 'Story/Discourse (A note on two kinds of voyeurism)'.[2] Metz transferred to
film Emile Benveniste's distinction between enunciation and the utterance and, within
the utterance, the distinction between *histoire* and *discours*. More specifically, he transferred Benveniste's two forms of utterance (*discours* and *histoire*) to a psychoanalytical
theory of vision. He identified exhibitionism with *discours* and voyeurism with
histoire. The exhibitionist knows that s/he is being looked at and acknowledges the look
of the spectator, just as *discours* acknowledges the speaker and hearer of the utterance
(through its manifestation of deictic terms), whereas the object of the voyeur's gaze
does not know that s/he is being watched. The voyeur's look is secretive, concealed,
like the marks of the speaker and hearer in *histoire*. Metz argued that classical narrative
film is primarily voyeuristic – hence *histoire*, for it conceals its own discursive markers
(here, the spectator's look), an activity other post-structural film theorists identified
with film's ideological function, and feminists with film's patriarchal function (for the
look is traditionally conceived as masculine, etc).

Metz therefore employed the linguistic theory of enunciation to develop a
rigorous post-structural theory of spectatorship in the cinema. Francesco Casetti, on the
other hand, has remained within the framework of linguistics, and has taken to its logical conclusions the discussion of filmic discourse within the context of the linguistic
theory of deixis. The aims of Casetti's theory of filmic enunciation (as represented in his
book, *Dentro lo sguardo*, and his essay 'Face to Face', anthologized here) has been
clearly summed up by Giuliana Muscio and Roberto Zemingnan, in their introduction
to the work of Casetti:

[Casetti's] interrogations concern three issues: How does the film take into account the spectator? How does it "anticipate" him/her? How does it direct him/her? The book develops three fundamental principles: that the film signals the *presence* of the spectator; that it assigns a *position* to him/her; that it makes him follow an *itinerary*.[3]

To achieve his aims, Casetti employs the pronouns of verbal language, since pronouns are deictic terms that grammaticalize within the utterance itself particular points of its context (specifically, the enunicator and addressee). He then establishes formulas of four basic types of shots/looks: (1) So-called objective shots: I (enunciator) and YOU (addressee), we watch IT (the utterance, character, film); (2) Interpellations: I and HE, we watch YOU; (3) So-called subjective shots: YOU and HE see what I show YOU; (4) Unreal objective shots: As if YOU were I.

In his essay 'The Impersonal Enunciation, or the Site of Film', Christian Metz responds to Casetti's formulas. Metz points out that it is quite odd that the spectator of a film, posited as a *you*, should find in front of him/her an *I* in such an impersonal (and even immaterial) object as a film. And indeed, how could a film, and for that matter, *any kind of text* posssibly 'say' *I*? As Metz himself says, the general feeling, when reading a book, is 'If it speaks, it means someone is speaking', that is, it is not the book, nor the 'text' that is in the book, but some human agency who the reader supposes to have written the text or told the story who 'speaks', and maybe even refers to him or herself with the personal pronoun 'I'. Objects like books, strings of letters and words, series of images and sounds, patterns of colours and lines only become 'texts' or symbols when they are understood as produced or used by some person to communicate some meaning to other persons, that is, when some *intentionality* is imposed upon them, and it is hard to see why this should be different for film (an issue François Jost raises in his papers collected here).

But Metz argues exactly in the opposite direction. He differs from Casetti in refusing to discuss filmic enunciation in terms of deictic expressions like personal pronouns, because the film constitutes an *impersonal* activity. It is precisely this characterization of film as impersonal enunciation that has created controversy and discussion around Metz's paper. Rather than the concept of deixis to characterize filmic enunciation, Metz employs the concepts of reflexivity, metalanguage and anaphora, to argue that

cinematic enunciation is always enunciation on film. Reflexive, rather than deictic, it does not give us any information about the outside of the text, but about a text that carries in itself its source and its destination.

Such a formulation is controversial because it ignores the way external supports (enunciator and addressee) are grammaticalized in the filmic text, and instead develops a purely immanent theory of filmic enunciation.

In his two papers in this section, François Jost takes a serious look at the notion of intentionality in film and TV images. In 'The Authorized Narrative' he begins by asking 'Where does one draw the line between truth and falsehood, mistakes and paralepses?', which he approaches through a discussion of *Une belle fille comme moi* (Truffaut, 1972). Jost concentrates on the cognitive discrepancies in the film, which he attributes to a narrative authority (rather than considering them to be careless mistakes). Jost recognises that the meaning of such discrepancies are underdetermined by the film itself, since they depend on the addressee's judgements (particularly about the narrative authority's intention).

Jost then turns his attention to TV images, to news reports on the Rumanian revolution and the Gulf war. He argues that comprehension of these images is dependent on the TV viewer's ability to identify 'the communicative intention relevant to [their] reception'. Among his examples, he refers to news images of an Iraqi mosque destroyed during the Gulf war. The meaning of these images is dependent upon the TV viewer's recognition of the communicative intention of the narrative authority: whereas a Western journalist's intention could be read as that of keeping the viewer informed about American military action, the intention of an Iraqi would be to urge the viewer to condemn the aggression.

Jost offers several other examples in his second paper, 'The Polyphonic Film and the Spectator'. Here he makes clear an important point arising from his previous paper – that he is first of all interested in understanding the diversity of readings images provoke, rather than in attempting to fix one particular reading. He also makes the important point that marks of enunciation only have a functional, rather than an ontological, status (that is, they are not autonomous, pre-existing entities in texts but constitute one potential function of all textual features).

Finally, In "Enunciation': From Code to Interpretation', Jan Simons also stresses the non-ontological status of marks of filmic enunciation, and begins to work through the consequences of this argument, the most far reaching one being that this characterization of filmic enunciation brings to an end its usefulness as a concept in film theory. This then gives Simons the opportunity to develop a generative and cognitive semantics of film, drawing in particular from the recent works of Gilles Fauconnier, George Lakoff, Mark Johnson, Ray Jackendoff, and Ronald Langacker.

Indeed, the introduction of the work of the above linguists and cognitive scientists into film studies opens up new vistas of research, which perhaps could be designated as a transition from mind to body.

Notes

1   A.J. Greimas and J. Courtés, *Semiotics and Language: An Analytical Dictionary*, Bloomington: Indiana University Press, 1982, pp. 103-4.

2   The English translation is published in Metz's *Psychoanalysis and Cinema: The Imaginary Signifier*, trans. Ben Brewster et. al., London: Macmillan Press, 1982, pp. 89-98.

3   Giuliana Muscio and Roberto Zemingnan, 'Francesco Casetti and Italian Film Semiotics', *Cinema Journal*, 30, 2, 1991, pp. 32-33.

FACE TO FACE

Francesco Casetti

One often examines the figure of the spectator from this common fact: there is someone who watches the film. But this obvious point is not very helpful: the problem of all discourse addressed to others is not so much that of being heard than of being listened to. In the same way, what is important for the filmic text is not so much that of being seen by somebody than making itself visible to somebody: in fact this is important for the filmic text (more than for the film, a term designating an inert object, precisely a roll of film), that is, for a reality that fixes its own fundamental axes of reference, and which therefore straightaway presupposes what it will encounter by opening in itself a space ready to receive whomever it is addressed to.

The following pages attempt to describe this space, guided by the conviction that the look which, in the cinema auditorium, captures on screen the contours of a world, is not a supplementary element but the necessary complement of the game: a signpost, or entrance, into a scene. In sum, it is a look that adds itself to the other looks constituting and residing in the world that gives itself to be seen. But we must not exclude the fact that, in the actual experience of watching a film, expectations are denied: at the moment when the circle is closed (for example, in the instant a role encounters a body), processes different from those the text had sought to highlight can emerge. But once again, it is 'being seen' that undergoes a disruption and not 'making itself visible': to present itself, to propose itself, to give itself to be seen, all these strategies can easily be inscribed with their own fate – with their own design – even the unpredictable.[1]

***

We shall first of all examine the openings of two films. The first is the beginning, in sequence shot, of *Riso Amaro* (Giuseppe de Santis, 1949): a man in close-up facing the camera lists a number of facts on rice farming in Northern Italy. A phrase ('This is Radio Turin') and a backwards travelling shot reveal an announcer who, from the roof of a train carriage, is recounting live the arrival of rice planters in a marshalling yard. A panoramic shot shows a large part of the station with the coming and going of rice planters among the tracks, while the voice of the announcer, now off-screen, interviews a young woman. The camera continues to crane downwards until it frames in medium long shot two men talking. Through their dialogue, we come to understand that they are two policemen pursuing a wanted man.

The second opening to be analysed is the first shot of *The King of Marvin Gardens* (Bob Rafelson, 1972). A man in close-up, staring at the camera, tells a story from his childhood. The narration continues, punctuated with long pauses, half-way between confession and the exploration of memory. A slow backwards travelling shot, some gestures of the man towards off-screen space and an intermittent red light allow us to discover that we are in the studio of a radio station. What the man recounted in the first person is probably a story intended to hold the attention of the listeners.

What characterizes these two openings and links them to each other appears clear: both characters directly address the spectator; they look and speak directly from the screen, as if they wanted to invite us to participate in the action. In other words, both openings aim to *interpellate* the spectator: they implicate him by claiming to recognise him and by insisting that he recognise himself as its immediate interlocutor. Here, this interpellation takes place through looks and speech addressed directly to the camera, as if it were made by the intermediary of an exhortative intertitle or a metanarrative announcement likewise addressed to those following the narrative but not to those who live within it.[2] In other words, the interpellation works here by taking risks, since this procedure is traditionally considered to be a process of unmasking and a transgression of an interdiction.

We shall first of all consider interpellation as a process of unmasking. In fact, whatever the reasons determining them, the look and speech directed at the camera reveal what is usually hidden, the camera and the work accompanying it. Both look and speech equally impose an opening on the only space irredeemably other, a unique off-screen space that cannot be transformed into on-screen space – the auditorium facing the screen. They thus effect a rupture in the texture of the fiction by the emergence of a metalinguistic consciousness – 'we are at the cinema' – which, in unveiling the game, destroys it.[3] In this sense it constitutes a point where the film no longer follows convention.

Secondly, these two procedures of interpellation transgress an interdiction because they reveal a concealed foundation that must remain concealed. Because they illegitimately attempt to invade a space that must remain separate and because they destroy the frame that must remain intact, the look and speech directed at the camera are perceived as an infringement of an orthodoxy, an attack on the 'correct' functioning of filmic representation and filmic narrative. Consequently, it does not seem that interpellation is suitable in the 'normal' progression of filmic communication. Nonetheless – and here the problems are multiplied – this interdiction does not manifest itself in a resolute manner. For example, it varies according to the *form* interpellation takes: thus recourse to the look at the camera demands more caution than an intertitle or a voice-off addressing the spectator to inform, solicit or exhort him.[4] In the same way, this interdiction varies according to *where* interpellation is manifest. In terms of genres, it is usually forbidden to look at the spectator in an adventure film, although comedies and musicals allow it to a greater extent.[5] In terms of systems, if the look at the camera is prohibited in fiction films, it is not in educational films and home movies.[6] Finally, in terms of the medium itself, if, in cinema, looking at the camera is prohibited, in television this is not usually the case.[7] All these observations show us that in certain situations, this interdiction actually changes into an obligation: for example, when it is necessary to assure the spectator that he is really the addressee of what he sees and hears on screen, or when its use is more important than the risks involved.

We are therefore faced with an enigma: we have two segments of film that interpellate the spectator in the most direct way possible, and we discover that the mechanisms they employ infringe an interdiction; then, that this interdiction only functions when it wants to. At the moment we notice explicit ties between screen and auditorium, we rightly perceive that these explicit ties pose a problem, in fact a double problem. To resolve these questions and to begin the research we have proposed, it is necessary to recognise that our remarks at the beginning, which refer to common knowledge, are insufficient. To understand if, when and why interpellation of the spectator takes place, or under what conditions the spectator is assigned a space of action, it is not sufficient to refer to a work (that of the camera) or a space (the auditorium) the film attempts to exclude, or to a character (who sees and hears) the film attempts to conceal. On the contrary, it is necessary to refer to a more complex domain, that of *filmic enunciation*, in looking for a principle of explanation.[8]

But what is filmic enunciation? By this term, we mean the conversion of a language system [*langue*] into discourse; that is to say, the passage from a set of simple virtual units[9] to a concrete and localised object. In other words, enunciation is the fact of using the expressive possibilities offered by cinema to give body and substance to a film.[10] We must underline the fact that this gesture (which has something inaugural about it although it does not represent an 'origin' in the proper sense of the term) fixes the coordinates of filmic discourse and directly adapts them to its requirements: enunciation constitutes the base from which the characters, the places and the times of film are articulated. It is the zero point (the 'I-here-now', in other words, the *who*, the *where*, and the *when*) from which the different roles of the game are distributed (the characters, reflecting the *who* of enunciation, can be structured in I/you/he; the places, reflecting the *where*, in the here/there/elsewhere; time, reflecting the *when*, in the now/before and after/in the past). Whatever the operative choices may be, the existence and parameters of the referential functioning of discourse is dependent, in a strict sense, on enunciation.[11]

We can examine the various processes, previously only sketched out, by following the profile of the characters: maybe because it is a question of an essential node, given that the overall process seems to involve and engage especially the subjectivity of an 'auteur', or maybe because it is in this space that the fate of the spectator is played out. First of all, we can say that enunciation and, with it, what we can designate as its subject, never present themselves as such. Enunciation (whether we consider it as an instance of mediation that assures the *passage* from a virtual instance to a realisation, or indeed as a linguistic act that assures the *production* of discourse[12]) only gives itself to be seen in the utterance that presupposes it ('in the utterance' – that is to say, in the film or sequence, or in the framing[13]). The subject of enunciation, whether we reduce it to a simple operation – the actualization of a process – or to any empirical entity – which actualizes the process – can only be identified through traces in the film. In sum, enunciation, which initiates the game, has a profound effect, but remains off-screen, behind the scenes.[14]

In exchanges, there is *always* something in the utterance that denounces the activity of enunciation and, in this sense, attests to its presence.[15] The trace of the subject of enunciation never abandons the film: we perceive it in the look that establishes and organises what is shown, in the perspective that delimits and arranges on-screen space, and in the position from which we follow what is before our eyes;[16] in a word, in the *point of view* from where we observe things – that is to say, in what, in a film, we cannot miss and that *at the same time* determines the coordinates and the angle of view. But to move on: this point of view, which marks the affirmation of the subject of enunciation in the utterance and which refers back to the inaugural gesture – conversion, passage, actualization, mastery – can be traced back to the camera's location during filming or, on the contrary, to the ideal and hypothetical position in which those who watch the scene projected on screen are placed. Consequently, this point of view can be traced back to two things, not one. But, even before returning to a camera or an ideal eye, such an alternative is deeply rooted: from the moment enunciation manifests its own utterance as displaced object (directing it towards a different point from where it was constituted), the utterance establishes within itself a gesture of actualization and a point of destination. Otherwise, it takes form at the moment enunciation is invested in a modality, thanks to which we can distinguish a 'let the image be' from a 'let the image be made to be', which corresponds, *grosso modo*, to the act of seeing and the act of showing. In any case, it is important to note that we find ourselves immediately before a division – a double polarity, a double activity – which leads the subject of enunciation to split up into *enunciation* and *addressee*:[17] the point of view will then fall within the province of one, then the other, thus distinguishing between the two superimposed movements, in which the film on the one hand is constructed, and on the other gives itself to be seen. Here we shall attempt to determine more precisely the second, that is to say the destination of the utterance and also the moment when interpretation is assigned.

But first of all, to proceed with our argument. The subjects of enunciation can furnish a direct guide to the film as discourse or, if one wishes, as text.[18] In certain cases when the coordinates that situate a film openly give themselves to be seen, we come to locate not only a general acknowledgement of the existence of the enunciator, but equally its manifest incorporation in the utterance. This is when deictics appear: although we generally doubt the capacity of a film to refer to its enunciative situation, it always delegates part of itself to this aim; for example, the credits at the beginning or ending of a film, to which we can add the numerous technical traces which, in the very body of the film, betray the work of sound and image recording, whether as voluntary inclusions or involuntary residues.[19] We can also note the reproduction of the gestures of enunciation as much as the gestures of the utterance. For example, the fundamental gestures of actualization and destination are either translated in the text by an intermixing of intentions and aims, with the effect of activating the discourse, or are translated by an emphasis on the points of origin and destination, with the effect of structuring a certain linearity.[20] Finally, we can describe the large domain of figurative processes, as well as thematisation, through which enunciation disguises itself or slips into the elements inhabiting the film (it suffices to think of all those things that are equivalent to a linguistic operation: omniscient looks, voyeurs and spies, phantoms and doubles, actions that motivate camera movements, camera movements miming human movements, etc.).

At every stage of this process, the subjects of enunciation seem to seek grounds for development as if, beginning from a reality where they can be identified through only a few traces, they wanted to become objects treated entirely separately in the film.[21]

The framework thus becomes richer and more complicated, but it is only by taking into account this complexity that we can differentiate the operations and analyse them. My aim now is therefore to specify, next to the common fragments of the process, specific traces and issues. The first thing to note is that, if the process we have spoken of is accomplished, it builds up a correspondence or intimacy between the two terms we began with: in fact we have an utterance that, before taking in hand anything else, explores again its own enunciation (enunciative utterance), explaining its operations and mechanisms just as we have an enunciation that attempts to show itself for what it is in the utterance whose foundation it constitutes (uttered enunciation). Although there always exists between the two terms an insurmountable gap – what appears from enunciation is nevertheless always and only an utterance – it is as if the first term had completely slipped into the second.

But things can again be organised differently; sometimes because the process has not been fully realised: in this case, the signs of enunciation remain suspended, and the discourse continues without accounting for the gesture that constitutes it (except that its very formation attests to the process that gives it its existence and uniformity); and sometimes because the process has been carried too far: in this case, the signs of enunciation remain invisible, the narrative having completely reabsorbed and returned them to its own logic, making them an element of its own set-up. The film then finds itself preserving a secret, either because of a presupposition that remains silent, or because a sign is disguised in an excessive way.

In every case, this leads to a result very different to those we have previously seen: the utterance no longer accounts for itself, but is preoccupied only with its own contents (utterative text); enunciation no longer seeks to be part of the action but retreats in an orderly manner behind the scenes ('evasive' enunciation).[22] We can find a correspondence to these developments if we reflect on the different treatments the addressee has undergone: it suffices to set out, on one side, certain appeals to the spectator – for example, in propaganda films – which manifest the existence and requirement of an addressee, and on the other hand, the majority of narrative films, which are either not preoccupied with revealing their own coordinates, but concentrate instead on the story they are in the process of presenting, or with playing on the 'film within a film' theme to reduce the addressee to a character in the story.

Such a division evokes other oppositions. We are not thinking so much of the Platonic distinction between *diegesis* and *mimesis*, or of James' distinction between *telling* and *showing* (opposing a page of authorial intrusion to a page directly reflecting reality), than to the distinction, which has wider scope, between discourse and story, or the distinction between commentary and narrative,[23] which oppose an utterance offering up its own parameters of reference (the *who*, the *where*, and the *when* of its gesture of departure) and an utterance acting as if it was outside any determined place; in sum, speech that foregrounds its own status as enunciation, and speech that has no need or desire to show its enunciation. It is not a question here of analysing the degree of correspondence between these pairs and those we previously evoked:[24] they confirm for us that, not only can the results we attain be very diverse, but also that it is from these articulations that we can measure the effective importance of each of the elements of enunciation.

We shall again consider the case of the addressee: its presence can be grasped in an absolute form when a film makes explicit reference to itself or when, on the contrary, it radically attempts to avoid the question of self-reference (resulting in the option for 'pure' commentary or 'pure' narrative), or perhaps – which is more frequent – it is grasped through conflict, when different forms in the same film clash (there is then an alternation between commentary and narrative[25]).

Whatever the results attained and the measures employed, there are permanent marks accompanying the filmic text all along its development, threads that run through its texture. Explicitly or implicitly, the addressee is precisely one of these marks, one of these threads. It constitutes a *role*, a term that underlines the addressee's active aspect, either in the sense of its capacity to act on the text, or its capacity to take charge of what acts on the text. On this *role* will be grafted a *body*, in an encounter that constitutes the point of departure of what is usually called an act of communication.[26]

We shall close this long parenthesis on enunciation and return to the problem we started with: two opening filmic sequences (where a character looks directly at the spectator, an interpellation that functions as if the character wants to involve the spectator in the action on screen, capturing him in the film), and the taboos that reveal themselves in diverse and capricious ways in order to block this appeal. But maybe we already have the instruments to unravel this problem. In fact, in relation to the previously defined framework, the look at the camera and, more generally, interpellation, present themselves as a case of uttered enunciation: not only can the coordinates that locate a film in relation to its enunciation be inscribed in the text, but they can also become explicit signs. In particular, designation is manifest in the gesture of addressing someone, and the person who is addressed becomes a real destination.

In the two sequences, the addressee attains a kind of fullness: he is affirmed and placed within the film, without dissimulating his own identity. The spectator's own traces are arranged where one can clearly distinguish them on the organising line of a look that goes beyond the screen and into the auditorium. At the same time, these two film sequences are characterized by commentary, not by narrative: as if, wanting to go through again the successive stages of the dialogue – the decisive moments where the *who, when* and *where* of enunciation are programmatically reviewed – they put their cards on the table straight away, and adopted the grammatical status of *I* and the *you*.

Nevertheless, with a change of shot and the new point of view which results, such a characterization very quickly appears provisional, not because of the impossibility of cinema to follow certain processes to the end,[27] but because the process chosen by these two films will be abandoned very quickly for another. This is foreseeable from the beginning, from the moment the two men in close-up deliver their narrative to the camera: public or private, reportage or recollection, these speeches already admit a moment of hesitation, obliging us to verify whether what is said relates to the film or concerns something else.[28] The suspicion is reinforced when we perceive that the two men speak on the radio: in discovering that it is not a question of their own filmic enunciation but another form of enunciation, we are inclined to demand who is the real addressee of what is said. The question is no longer only 'whose story is it?' but equally 'Am I the real addressee?' Finally, slight displacements transform hesitation into certainty. Glances aside tend to reduce the non-diegetic off-screen space to a diegetic space (a zone that can be traversed by characters and therefore filmed). In the first example, the camera movement ends on the opposite field of vision, but it is not the complement to the field of vision at the beginning,[29] since it consists of two characters (the two policemen) in medium long shot already entirely integrated into the fiction. In the second example, the camera movement ends on a long shot, which widens the close-up at the beginning and created an atmosphere totally characterized by the narrative (the radio station).

From this moment onwards, the signs of enunciation operate silently: each element will serve to comport a story. The form imposed will be that of a pure narrative. But the look and speech directed at the camera will not have been in vain: not a single reverse shot will show to whom the characters addressed themselves, and we can always count on the existence of someone who lives, even without a precise delineation of him – a point of view, the sign of an addressee. This moment is, from then onwards, impossible to efface, and we can refer to it throughout the film, *a free zone* reserved for an encounter with the spectator who, in the auditorium, witnesses the events on screen, who guarantees a possible conjunction.

The lesson of these two opening sequences appears clear: 'I'm telling the story to *you*' they seem to say, assuming the function of what usually introduces a discourse: *a dedication.* 'I'm telling the story to *you*', they appear to say, but immediately add: 'To you who exists only by my acknowledgement, an observation point on the limits of the narrative, a tacit promise of an effective encounter'. This is because the opening sequences have the advantage of thoroughly knowing the rules of the game. They know that it is enunciation that fixes the coordinates of a film (and the *you* that emerges owes its own coherence to these openings). They know that it is the utterance that receives the traces of enunciation, up to the point of making the place one of its own guidelines (and the *you* can accede to a privileged position: the dedication dominates the whole of the text that is dedicated). They know that it is the rhythm of a narrative that effaces the traces of enunciation in the utterance (and the *you* is always ready to become a character: a dedication assumes the role of a first chapter). But they also know that it is always a definite point that gives itself to be seen: revealed or submerged, overt or covert, it is the place of the affirmation and location of an addressee, the space in which a role will attach itself to a body, and define the behaviour and profile of what we call the *spectator*.

It now remains for us to confront the second problem, the taboo that seems to affect interpellation, at least in some of its forms. The framework we have traced, in addition to revealing the dynamics of the phenomenona, also reveals its relations and causes. We have said that enunciation makes explicit, *for* and *in* the utterance, a distribution of elements that foreshadow and reflect the actual conditions of the experience of communication. We therefore see articulated those characters, spaces and times that constitute the reality in which the film is based and in relation to which it operates. This results in hypotheses that one must conform to, traces that indicate the unfolding of the action, and parameters that must be obeyed.

Each utterance fixes its own context in relation to enunciation,[30] and this context must be respected[31] if we want the discourse to function as it should function. It is in relation to this definition, with the interlocutors face to face and with their respective roles and effects, that we can then analyse the interdiction against the look at the camera. With reference to our two examples, we can ask why the look at the camera here gives the impression of being an unusual gesture (we simply need to note the tension created by this glance), without, nevertheless, appearing as an irremediable break with orthodoxy. The answer is almost self-evident. In fact, in the dynamics between enunciation and utterance, we can consider as an interdiction either anything that contradicts the setting or fails to protect it adequately. The look at the camera is an interdiction when it is not *appropriate* to the context.[32] It is an interdiction, for example, in adventure films, which maintain the narrative in its objective form: a regime of absolute fiction, a transparent diegesis obtained at the expense of the effacement of marks of enunciation. But the interdiction is lifted in the musical, which is criss-crossed by forms of commentary: the fictional regime frequently shows metadiscursive components (films within films, theatre within films etc.) that render possible, and almost inevitable, the overt and determinate presence of signs of enunciation (even if, very often, these signs are figurative, and therefore very quickly reabsorbed into the narrative).[33]

In our two examples, we have an intermediary situation: the context characterizing these films tends to exclude interpellation. But if it does appear, it is because it is placed in a marginal position (at the beginning of a film, sheltered under the credits: uttered enunciation *par excellence*[34]), and because it can be returned to narrative, slipped into the diegesis. From this, we conclude that these two looks are unnatural but are, at the same time, legitimate: they have been rendered appropriate for a small price and manage to function well by means of their mode of intervention. Their advantage is that they represent what usually operates in silence – the trace of the addressee; a momentary spectacle, which will, however, make its presence felt throughout the film.

This capacity to discover mechanisms and actions that are usually concealed makes the look at the camera undoubtedly an exemplary case. But it is not a question of an isolated case: the die in not cast once and for all, since the game can unfold in different ways. If the addressee finds in this or other forms of interpellation a type of fullness and an often surprising efficacy, that does not suggest that it exhausts the range of possibilities. On the contrary, from the establishment of a point of view, there exist numerous ways of indicating the movement, not just of the production of discourse, but of its interpellation. Throughout the film, and from film to film, numerous methods follow and compete with one another to suggest a second person (*you*). We shall examine one in particular, taking again and expanding the lines of investigation already traced above.

***

We will work with a new example, the opening sequence of *The Kid From Spain* (Leo McCarey, 1932). The passage begins with a little girl waking up. She turns towards the camera and begins to recite a rhyme. We are in a dormitory, inhabited by a group of girls. In turn, they look at the camera as well as each other, continuing to recite the rhyme, transforming it into a song. A geometric dance begins, following the rhythm of the music, which moves from the dormitory up a spiral staircase and towards a swimming pool. A high angle shot frames the bodies in the water, which form a totally abstract pattern. Outside the swimming pool, close to a toboggan, the girls dry themselves and change behind translucent screens. When the camera tries to by-pass this obstacle, the girls flee, casting glances at the camera. Then the headmistress enters and calls for silence.[35]

This passage takes advantage of its position at the beginning of the film (before the narrative properly begins). At the same time, it makes use of the freedom that characterizes this genre (the musical), the period (the first years of sound cinema) and the choreographer (Busby Berkeley) to invent surprising forms.

To understand what is presented, let us take again the moment when point of view is established. As we have said, the relation between a look and a scene allows us to appraise at the same time the enunciator, addressee and the discourse they control; that is to say, a group of three elements that correspond to, respectively, the gesture of actualization thanks to which one sees, the gesture of destination that gives itself to be seen, and the thing (or the character) that is seen. In fact, if we want to establish indicative identities, we have an *I*, a *you* and a *he* (character or thing).

As for the nature of the elements in the triangle, it is a question of abstract categories that indicate a fundamental articulation, not of the present reality, but of the filmic text:[36] the *you* posited by a look at the camera, for example, does not refer to any body in particular but rather to the fact that the film gives itself to be seen. These are traces that refer to the constitutive mechanisms of the filmic text, the spaces that only enunciation has opened, but which, in opening, it has rendered free at all times. (The possibility of a *you* does not even exist so long as we find ourselves in the realm of the cinema, peopled only by pure virtual units:[37] we commit ourselves to this course by placing ourselves in the field of film, of something born from the transformation of a language system [*langue*] into discourse; but discourse, precisely by its intrinsic nature, guarantees that a course of this type would always be present[38]).

Although the enunciator and addressee are concerned with the look, and the utterance corresponds to scenic space, there is no look without a scene nor a scene without a look:[39] the point of view unites the point from where one looks, the point through which one shows and the point that one sees.[40] What plays a determining role is not the presence – in itself obligatory – of such or such an element, but the *form* of the relation it establishes with the others and, in consequence, *the position* it assumes in the whole.

From these observations, we can establish a typology of recurrent propositions in a film clarifying the various perspectives open to the addressee.

The first case we shall examine is that of a fundamental equilibrium between the elements. The opening sequence from *The Kid From Spain* is a good example, with its eye-level framing which aims to immediately establish the facts, as if it wanted to grasp the essentials of the action without revealing the work of observation and examination, of which the action is the object. More precisely, we are thinking of the moments when we see the girls looking and talking to one another but without our being able to see their actual gaze: the enunciator and addressee are thus placed on a level of perfect equality, supported by a point of view that only allows to be seen what cannot be concealed: the utterance. Opposite a *he* that shows itself for what it is, there is an *I* and a *you* that are present but which do not make their presence explicit. In particular, the addressee must assume the position of a witness: he is the one who is led to look, and therefore who is permitted to look, but without this mandate being made explicit and without this task (of looking) intervening in the events.[41] If he wishes to declare his presence, he can do so, but off-screen, in another story in which he will this time become the protagonist. Classical film 'grammars'[42] have listed this case under the broad label of objective framing. They also speak of anonymous shots (*nobody's shots*), meaning that the look belongs to nobody. But this 'nobody', we repeat, signifies that the possibilities are open to all.[43]

The second case is that of interpellation in its different forms. In the passage from *The Kid From Spain*, we find it when the girls look directly at the camera. Here we have a rupture in the equilibrium between the elements: both the enunciator and addressee establish themselves in the utterance, but in an unequal way and in an utterance that releases something from one of them – as if he were the enunciator of the film, a character in the film interpellates the one who is addressed. We have someone who is led to look and indeed who can look without being seen. An *I* (who looks and sees) coincides with a *he* (who is seen but at the same time looks at he (the spectator) who is led to look), whereas a *you* (who is meant to be looked at and is looked at, but is not seen) enters in the game without assuming any precise form.[44] The enunciator is represented in a character, who depends on a question of action (the act of looking) and a question of framing (reaching the spectator), effecting a slippage from the level of enunciation to the level of the utterance.[45] As for the addressee, he shows himself for what he is: nothing other than a point of view. This is why the utterance releases something from the enunciator: it shows what is presupposed.

These dynamics also intervene when, from the silhouettes of the girls undressing behind the translucent screens, the camera creates confusion when it attempts to surprise them in the act. In this variation, the *I* instead of slipping towards the *he* of a character, shifts to become the *he* of the whole utterance. The screen within a screen (the translucent screens) and the shadows in the play of shadows (the silhouettes) aim to reunite metalanguage,[46] designation and interpellation in a structure that can be expressed in the following terms: 'this is for you/it is a film/that is me'.[47] The girls who, in the following shot, turn towards the camera and glance at it with mischievous anger will bring about the confirmation of this syncretism.

But let us move on to the addressee. For each of the two variants examined here, he assumes the classic position of the *aside*: a type of reappropriation of the theatrical usage, where the author often speaks to the audience through the intermediary of a character.[48] Here also, we have someone who *participates* in the game, while set *aside*. Traditional film 'grammars' are very rarely concerned with this case, either because it recovers an interdiction, or because it is usually referred to as a 'subjective shot'.

The 'subjective shot' has, on the contrary, a very different meaning. When faced with a structure that has two stages, to which syntactically correspond two shots or two different moments of the same shot,[49] we translate the first moment (the one where we see a character who looks) as 'I look and make the spectator look') and the second moment (the one where we see through the eyes of a character) as 'I make him look at what I make you look at'). We therefore have a series[50] that goes from 'You and I see him' to 'You and he see what I show you'. The result is that the conjunction is no longer developed between the character and the enunciator, but between the character and the addressee. The final configuration no longer says 'You and I look at him' as in the 'objective view', nor even 'He and I look at you' as in interpellation, but 'I make you and him look'. This third subdivision, where the enunciator assumes the position of a *character*, is not directly found in *The Kid From Spain*: it could exist if the camera movements that attempt to surprise the girls undressing behind the screens was followed by a reverse shot attributing this mischievous look to someone. But this process is entirely customary in the cinema. Moreover, it has given rise to extreme practices[51] and to very particular aesthetic propositions.[52]

On the other hand, a fourth case is illustrated in *The Kid From Spain*, in which the high angle shot, showing the girls in the swimming pool, creates a completely abstract image. It is, apparently, an 'objective shot': 'I look at something and I make you look at something'. But the wayward nature of this angle (we pass from an eye level shot to a high angle shot perpendicular to the horizon) disrupts the image's equilibrium. The activity of the enunciator and addressee are foregrounded; they impose themselves in an obvious way at the limit of spectacle. Such an emphasis has a specific implication: due to the strangeness of the result, not only do we return to the opening presupposition – 'there is someone who looks' – but we also determine the meaning of a relation – 'if you see, it is thanks to me'. This is where the syncretism between addressee and enunciator arises: that one thinks like ... . We experience the sensation of being detached from any contingency, of dominating the shot, fabricating reality, and sharing the omnipotence of the camera. In conclusion, next to the 'as if *he* were *I*' of interpellation and the 'as if *he* were *you*' of the 'subjective scene', we now have 'as if *you* were *I*': the addressee renounces his own competence in order to slide into the other. He confines himself to a pure faculty of seeing, to a look without a determinate place. Traditional film 'grammars' have sometimes reserved for these shots the term 'unreal objective shots': we could keep this term if it reflected, not only the impossibility of finding a character to whom we can attribute this shot,[53] but also if it designated the impossibility of a scene being presented without the look of the enunciator and addressee.

**

The four cases discussed here outline four canonical configurations, which lead the addressee to assume respectively the posture of the witness (a confirmed *you* opposite a confirmed *I*: the 'objective shot'), the spectator set aside (a *you* installed opposite an *I* combined with a *he*: interpellation), the character (a *you* combined with a *he* opposite a confirmed *I*: the 'subjective shot'), and the camera (a *you* combined with an *I*: the 'unreal objective shot'). These four configurations demonstrate that 'dynamic' relations exist between the elements from which they are made. We have alluded to these dynamic relations in speaking of degrees of emergence or forms of incidence, but we would have been able to approach them more directly if we had considered issues such as the distribution of knowledge in the filmic text. We would have thus perceived that, in the 'subjective shot', the addressee knows as much as the character, whereas in interpellation, the addressee knows less than the character;[54] who, at this moment, knows as much as the enunciator can claim to, and so on. Briefly, each of the four cases reveals a series of relations that strongly resist revision. To look and to see can be related to terms such as *to wish* and *to know*, so that the opposition 'to make (the image) *vs* to have (the image) made' not only gives rise to a neutral observation and to a neutral exposition but also to pairs such as 'to wish to make *vs* to wish to have made', 'to know how to make *vs* to know how to have made', 'to make known *vs* to have made known', etc.

But over and above any modal investment, these configurations are in a position to suggest the last word on the mechanisms through which the subject emerges. Let us return to interpellation: it is clear that the *you* appears only because it responds to the appeal of the *I*. And yet, it is a question of a very paradoxical *I*, if it slides into a *he* that looks ahead without necessarily seeing anything, given that he is addressing the non-filmic field whose contours can never be shown. There is therefore he who is seen but whose look leads nowhere: the enunciator, at the moment he attempts a figurativization in the utterance, discovers the possibility of emptiness, the blank space, a point of suspension.

We now pass to the 'subjective shot'. Here the *he* slides into the *you*, and both see what is shown to them. Things only appear because someone shows them, and not because a will intervenes to discover them. Therefore, opposite an enunciator who acts as absolute arbiter, the addressee cannot delude himself regarding his own ability to manoeuvre. The sensation of being there, inscribed in the limits of a scene, within a world that has been addressed to him, is contrasted with the certainty that each presence has already been decided.

Comparison between the two cases is then easy: in interpellation, the enunciator, although seeming to put the game in place, admits to a look not connected to an effect; in the 'subjective shot', the addressee, who seems directly involved in the game, nonetheless admits to a look deprived of intention. Consequently, the limits of those who are the pivots of the two configurations are fixed. The points of syncretism, respectively the *we* and the *you*, strengthen the explicit link between enunciation and utterance, but they are also the black hole where the potentiality of vision is cancelled out. Another consequence is that we are offered a number of useful ideas on the alternation, within the filmic text, between subjectivity and subjection on the edges of the frame and outside it: there is between finding and losing oneself only a very narrow margin.[55] A final consequence is that we can complete a diagram that we had started to construct: in comparing the two situations, we note that, in interpellation, we do not make a character look (he looks at you, but he does not see), and that in the 'subjective shot' he does not see (he sees what is shown to him). This signifies that what appears on the screen, the utterance, the *he*, reveals two distinct forms. After the pair (enunciator and addressee), and the triangle (enunciator, addressee and character), we now have a square, consisting of four terms. It is on this that the essential parameters are fixed, the roles distributed, that opposes people to things, subjects to anti-subjects.[56] With this we complete the fundamental articulation for which the look was our point of departure.

(*Translated by Warren Buckland with Guy Austin*)

Notes

[1] Is it not an unpredictable event that is condensed in the *punctum* that Roland Barthes speaks of with regard to photography? Cf. Barthes, *Camera Lucida*, trans. Richard Howard, London: Jonathan Cape, 1982.

[2] Moreover, we are thinking of the exhortations used for political ends in propaganda films, as well as intertitles of the type 'ten years later' in numerous narrative films.

[3] Among the numerous contributions on this theme, principally in the 1970s, we shall note Pascal Bonitzer, 'Les deux regards', *Cahiers du Cinéma*, no. 275, 1977, and Jean-Paul Simon, 'Les signes et leur maître', *Ça Cinéma*, no. 9, 1976, both of which centre on an analysis of the look. This theme, or similar themes, is equally tackled from a psychoanalytical perspective; see Christian Metz, *Psychoanalysis and Cinema: The Imaginary Signifier*, trans. Ben Brewster et. al., London: Macmillan, 1982. Finally, recall André Bazin's reflections on the screen as frame and window.

4   A less direct interpellation is also evident in designation: the 'here is' is always 'here is for you'. Cf. Simon, 'Référence et désignation: notes sur la deixis cinématographique', *Regards sur la sémiologie contemporaine*, CIERC. Universitie de Saint-Etienne, 1977, pp. 53-62.

5   For film musicals, cf. Jim Collins, 'Toward Defining a Matrix of the Musical Comedy: The Place of the Spectator Within the Textual Mechanisms', in Rick Altman, ed., *Genre: The Musical*, London: RKP/BFI, 1981, pp. 134-46; for film comedies, cf. Simon, *Le Filmique et Le Comique*, Paris: Albatros, 1979.

6   For home movies, cf. Roger Odin, 'Rhétorique de film de famille', *Revue d'Esthétique*, 1/2, 1979, pp. 340-73.

7   For looks directed at the camera in television, cf. Francesco Casetti, L. Lumbelli, M. Wolf, 'Étude sur quelques règles du genre télévisuel', *Ricerche sulla communicazione*, 1980 and 1981.

8   The enunciation we speak of here, to explain what other mechanisms cannot explain, must in our opinion be conceptualised within a *theory of the filmic text*: in particular, it constitutes a key concept in defining the pragmatic component of this theory. Cf. Casetti, 'Le texte du film', in Jacques Aumont and Jean-Louis Leutrat, eds., *Théorie du film*, Paris: Albatros, 1980. An important contribution to the relation between enunciation and text is developed through an analysis of filmic temporality by Gianfranco Bettetini in *Tempo de senso*, Milano: Bompiani, 1979.

9   For a long time it has been discussed if and when this set of virtual units constitutes a *langue* in the proper sense of the term, that is to say, a complete and stable system. Cf. Emilio Garroni, *Progetto di semiotica*, Bari: Laterza, 1972, and Christian Metz, *Language and Cinema*, trans. Donna-Jean Umiker-Sebeok, 1974. If, here, we have brought the two terms [cinema and *langue*] together, it is because cinema, understood as a reserve of signs, procedures and constructions that we can reduce to a set of formal structures (opposed to film as a realised discourse), constitutes an abstract level comparable to *langue*. But may be the best thing to say is that cinema represents the space of a competence, from which the realized film is performance [in Chomsky's sense of these terms – trans.]: cf. Casetti, 'Le texte du film', op. cit.

10 Cf. Emile Benveniste, *Problems in General Linguistics*, trans. Mary Elizabeth Meek, Coral Gables: University of Miami Press, 1971. In particular, we will often refer to the definition of enunciation as the putting of *langue* into operation by an individual act of usage.

11 There is already a number of contributions that have confronted the problem of filmic enunciation, or which have used this notion to guide their analyses. We shall mention the already cited interventions of Benveniste, Casetti, Collins, Odin and

Simon; see also, Nick Browne, 'The Spectator in the Text: The Rhetoric of *Stagecoach*', *Film Quarterly*, XXIX, 2, 1975-76, and M. Buscema, 'L'enunciazione visiva', *Filmcritica*, no. 300, 1979, 'L'enunciazione visiva II', *Filmcritica*, nos. 307-307, 1980.

12 For these two meanings of enunciation, see A.J. Greimas and J. Courtès, *Semiotics and Language: An Analytical Dictionary*, Bloomington: Indiana Univeristy Press, 1982, pp. 103-105.

13 We use the term 'utterance' [*énoncé*] to designate any unit on the level of discursive realisation: image, sequence, film etc. This extension is equally justifiable by the absence of a term that: a) defines in an homogeneous way the relative units of different 'size' (sign/phrase/discourse, etc.); b) distinctively defining the units referring to empirical or referential entities, and units referring to theoretical entities (discourse/ text). The construction of a terminology to speak of cinema and film is one of the tasks we shall attend to again.

14 We can think of directly tackling enunciation from a sociological approach, which will analyse it as a *mode of production* of the utterance (unlike the semiotic approach, which analyses it as an immanent *rule of production* of the product). But if this divide between these domains suggests a differentiation between the objects of analysis (we can say: the material production of meaning *vs* its construction), it also indicates a sliding of the notion of enunciation outside the semiotic field – which is, on the contrary, the very one where we would like to keep it.

15 It is certainly a question of a paradoxical presence, but one that cannot be neutralized nor transformed into its opposite. In fact, the non-immediacy of the subject of enunciation in the utterance cannot really be called an *absence* – a term employed by Bettetini and Simon in the texts already cited – because the word 'absence' signifies either effacement of presence (and this is not the case, given that its presence is in any case felt), or a momentarily lack (and this is not the case anymore, seeing that there is no real possibility of a return). For these reasons, I prefer to continue to speak of presence – although a *deferred* presence; that is to say, the subject of enunciation is there, but is displaced: it is precisely in the utterance (where it cannot be the subject of *enunciation*) rather than being in the enunciation (where it is, however, the subject). The example of a letter, sent and delivered, rather than stolen or lost, gives a good idea of it.

16 See the very good analysis of the relation between look and view in Browne, op. cit.

17 The pair enunciator/addressee [*énonciateur/énonciataire*] is defined by Greimas and Courtès, op. cit. p. 105. [Here, I have decided to differ from the translators of Greimas' and Courtès' dictionary and translate *énonciataire* as 'addressee' – trans.]

[18] We understand the opposition between *discourse* and *text* as a fundamental opposition between an empirical object and a theoretical object, or a concrete fact and a principle of explanation. Although we can say that *discourse* always presents an addressee, however much importance it assumes, it is the text that must account for this presence and explain it, even when it operates in silence.

[19] Doubts on the importance of a shot of the enunciation in a film has been put by Metz in 'Story/Discourse (A Note on Two Types of Voyeurism)', *Psychoanalysis and Cinema*, op. cit.

[20] In this sense, the 'communicative dynamics' such as 'rheme' and 'theme', studied in the cinema by Michel Colin, must find its roots in the enunciative process before finding them in the conflict or in the meeting between the partners of communication. [See chapter VIII of Colin's *Langue, Film, Discours*, Paris: Klincksieck, 1985, pp. 163-92 – trans.]

[21] In speaking of the stages of exploration, and further on of a trajectory, we do not want to return to a 'genetic' model of enunciation: the path suggested here, going from the simple to the complex, sets out to order the description of facts, and not to represent the relations in a 'realist way'. All that does not prevent us from thinking of the different *levels* in the construction of filmic discourse (here we are inspired by Greimas); in this sense, the stages must be considered like the steps of a staircase rather than the successive phases of a linear 'becoming'.

[22] For the difference between enunciative and utterative [*énonciatif* and *énoncif*], and a definition of uttered enunciation [*l'énonciation énoncée*], cf. Greimas and Courtès, op. cit. [The reader is referred to several entries in the dictionary (and I follow the translators of the dictionary); see the entries 'utterance', pp. 362-64 and 'enunciation' pp. 103-106 – trans.] Nonetheless, I give the term a wider meaning: by always returning to a compound enunciation, we increase the possibilities of giving an account of it.

[23] The two pairs, deriving respectively from Benveniste and Weinrich, have been commented on and used in film theory, the first by Simon, *Le Filmique et le comique*, op. cit. (but equally by Metz in *Psychoanalysis and Cinema*, op. cit.), the second by Bettetini, *Tempo del senso*, op. cit.

[24] The impression is that, whereas in verbal language discourse and story are distinguished by the use of different forms (cf. Benveniste, *Problems in General Linguistics*, op. cit.), in film they are only distinguished by the presence or absence of certain specific marks. This implies a reflection and a deepening of relations between this pair (discourse and story) and the preceding pair (enunciative utterance and utterative text). A possible solution – and I owe this proposition to Isabella

Pezzini – can consist of considering the pair enunciative/ utterative as indicative of two different moments in the construction of the utterance, and the pair discourse/ story as indicative of two differently realised forms (two 'genres').

25 On the types of superimposition between narrative and commentary, see the important reflections and precise analysis by Bettetini, *Tempo del senso*, op. cit.

26 The relation between role and body finds an essential reference point in Umberto Eco, *Lector in Fabula*, Milano: Bompiani, 1979 where, on the one hand, the notion of *model reader* designates either the course of the reader in the text, or the readings made of the text (but the two aspects must be considered, given that we return with one to 'abstract' reality, the other to an empirical or statistical reality: the two aspects must therefore be envisaged even if they are superimposed), and where, on the other hand, the notion of empirical reader is added to that of the model reader, to designate a point of an actual, individual interpretation, and maybe an idiosyncratic interpretation. Other essential indications of the relation between role and body can be found in Cesare Segre, 'Contribution to the Semiotics of Theatre', *Poetics Today*, 1, 3, 1980, where the relation between the external *I* of the text and the internal *I* of the text refer to an interesting typology of forms and modes of communication.

27 We have frequently thought that transparent narrative cinema, where the traces of enunciation do not seem to hold an important place, was 'the' cinema. On the restructuring processes that today span the cinema and lead us to adopt new linguistic models, see Casetti, 'Fuori del cinema', *Ikon*, 112, 1978 (as well as the huge literatre on the avant-garde and experimental cinema).

28 In the two narratives addressed to the camera, there is a very precise intertextual relation. In the first case, a relation to neorealist practices opens the film with a voice-off, giving the historical coordinates of the narrative that will unfold (cf. *Paisà*, Roberto Rossellini, 1946); in the second case, a relation to TV journalism and TV talk-shows.

29 It is not, therefore, a question of a reverse shot.

30 For several definitions of the notion of context in the cinema, cf. Casetti, 'Cenni d'intesa', *Communicazioni sociali*, 314, 1981.

31 It can either be a question of obedience to presupposed rules by the act of communication, or of a negotiation made in the course of communication. In relation to the way these two types of interaction between the partners of communication gives space to these two different models, cf. Marina Sbisà and P. Fabbri, 'Models for a Pragmatic Analysis', *Working Papers*, Centro Internazionale di semiotica e linguistica, Università di Urbino, no. 91, February 1980.

32 For the distinction between actualization, grammaticality, and appropriateness, see Casetti, 'Le texte du film', op. cit.

33 For the superimposition between commentary and narrative, particularly in the musical film, cf. Bettetini, *Tempo del senso*, op. cit. (which is also useful for relativising a distinction we have made too sharply here).

34 Even if the *incipit* constitutes, in other respects, a 'dynamic' textual position. Cf. Casetti, Lumbelli, Wolf, 'Indigine ...' op. cit.

35 In the description of this sequence, we have not noted the editing, camera movements, framings etc. that are irrelevant to the way we use this example.

36 The Greimassian notion of 'actant' fits these abstract categories.

37 Here we take the term 'cinema' in the sense of 'cinematic language' and not in the sense of a 'group of films' [where 'cinema' exists *within* the filmic and designates what is specifically filmic – trans.]: cf. Metz, *Language and Cinema*, op. cit. chapter 2.

38 It must of course be a question of filmic discourse, or better, of a filmic text, and not a coherent, non-delimitable and non-communicable set of images and sounds (but the status of the *text* can also be guaranteed pragmatically: an avant-garde film, which contradicts the nature of textuality, becomes a text when it is projected in the conditions that require it 'to be followed'). For these issues, see Casetti, 'Le texte du film', op. cit.

39 The pair look/scene can also be substituted for the pair look/seen – which we shall do in the following pages (cf. Browne, op. cit.), on condition that it disregards the 'intentional' dimension that the term 'look' implies.

40 The phrase 'point of view' helps us out, since it unites *point* (which calls attention to the place of looking) and *view* (which calls attention to the effects and contents of the look).

41 Cf. the notion of 'tangential receiver' in G. Nencioni, 'Parlato-parlato, parlato-scritti, parlato-recitato', in *Strumenti Critica*, no. 29, 1976.

42 For example, R. May, *Il Linguaggio del film*, Milano: Poligono, 1947.

43 Can't the addresse have the look, or can't he watch? This can happen by the suppression of the scene (moments of darkness) or by the arrangement of a scene in a way that something escapes the point of view (is off-screen, irremediable, etc.). But even in these precise cases, as long as there is a filmic text that establishes in itself or in the context a destination, we shall have the appearance of an addressee, in relation to which we can say that he can *always* look, but the he doesn't always happen to *see*.

44 Even if we use the personal form 'the one who', we return -to repeat – to the traces of an activity or to the traces of the cause of this activity, and not to an individual.

45 Cf. Browne, op. cit.

46 It is better to say metadiscourse.

47 In the same way, in literature the author can 'slide into' one of his characters or even into the writing, which is then at the same time cause and theme of the text.

48 See the excellent schematisation in Segre's 'Contribution ...' op. cit.

49 Two different camera movements in the same shot (for example, a camera movement which includes a character who watches, and which isolates the scene observed by the character, maintaining in each a certain co-incidence between the axis of the look and the axis of the objects seen) constitute an improper 'subjective shot' given that, without a cut, there is coincidence but not identity between the point of view of the character and that of the camera.

50 A series where the order of the two shots or the two movements is free (and where, consequently, the construction will be either anaphoric or cataphoric).

51 For example, *Lady in the Lake* (Robert Montgomery, 1946).

52 Cf. G. Mannuccari, *La soggettivazione nel film*, Roma: Smeriglio, 1951.

53 On condition of not considering, as Greimas has, that the origin of semiotic structures are directly narratological; here we understand narrative as one of the regimes or genres particular to discourse.

54 In interpellation, the addressee can have a power equal to the character (as in the confusion created in *The Kid From Spain* [when the camera attempts to by-pass the translucent screens]), but this example shows that in any case the character knows what the addressee knows, whereas the addressee does not know what the character knows, constituting an advantage for the character (and behind him, the enunciator) over the addressee.

55 On these issues, see U. Melchiorre, *L'Immaginazione simbolica*, Bologna: Il Mulino, 1972.

56 Drawing inspiration from Greimas' 'semiotic square', we can give the following order to the four terms:

where A represents the *enunciator*, identifiable as 'the one who looks', and is represented by the *I*; B represents the *addressee*, identifiable as 'the one who is made to look', as is represented by the *you*; -B represents the *non-addressee character*, identifiable as 'the one – animate or inanimate – who is seen but who does not control the look' (in fact he looks but does not see), and is represented by the *he*; -A represents the *non-enunciative character*, identifiable as 'the one – animate or inanimate

– who is seen but does not look' (in fact he sees what he is made to see) and is represented by the *he*; the axis A – B represents the axis of characters, and is opposed to -B and -A, which constitutes the axis of non-characters; the axis A – -B represents the axis of *subjects*, in opposition to the axis B – -A, which represents the axis of *anti-subjects*.

THE IMPERSONAL ENUNCIATION,
OR THE SITE OF FILM
IN THE MARGIN OF RECENT WORKS ON ENUNCIATION IN CINEMA

Christian Metz

Not only are there different conceptions of enunciation, but the concept itself contains several distinct ideas (the latter probably contributing to the former). Two of those ideas have been accurately stated in Greimas and Courtés' *Dictionary:*[1] enunciation is a *production*; and it is also a transition, from a virtual instance (such as the code) to a real instance. There is also a third idea, which, in fact, is the first one in Benveniste and Jakobson and, in the narratological field, in Gérard Genette.[2]

What is meant by the word 'enunciation' is the presence, at both ends of the utterance,[3] of two human persons, or, rather, two *subjects* (it has to be kept in mind that for Benveniste the pair JE/TU [I/YOU] defines the 'correlation of subjectivity'). Of course narratology keeps telling us that enunciator and addressee are abstract and structural instances, 'places'; that it would be somehow silly to mistake them for the empirical enunciator and addressee (author, reader . . .); that enunciation is theoretically and practically different from *communication*, and so on. These ritual incantations do not have to be taken literally, at least not consistently. If narrator and author are doubtless usually differentiated (to take only this example), the locations of enunciation itself – enunciation being, supposedly, purely textual – are nevertheless usually perceived as persons of some kind. To think of these locations, clearly to figure them out, is only possible, one must admit, through *instances of incarnation*. On the other hand, these instances of incarnation are supposed to occupy the place of the locations of enunciation in the transmission process: thus, if someone tells me about the addressee, in order to understand what I am told, I have to think of the spectator, who is going to cast himself (in theory, or by miracle) in the role of the 'addressee'.

However, this does not mean that the features of its instances of incarnation have to be transferred onto the enunciative apparatus, as is done by those narratologists who, after defining some Ideal Reader (implied, immanent, and so on), describe the detail of his reactions in the vocabulary of human and fictional psychology. Moreover, terms such as *enunciator* and *addressee* bear hardly avoidable, and – in some cases as we will see – quite troublesome, anthropomorphic connotations, especially in film where everything depends on machines. If what is meant is the physical inscription of enunciation, using things' names would be more appropriate. I would suggest 'source (or origin) of the enunciation' and 'enunciative target (or destination)'. (The human subject reappears when someone comes to *occupy* the source or the target.) A long time ago, Albert Laffay accurately said that one could find in the heart of all films, with their 'ultraphotographic interventions' and many manipulations, a 'virtual linguistic source', an 'image exhibitor', a 'fictitious person' (note the word fictitious), a 'master of ceremonies', a 'grand picture-maker', and, therefore, eventually, an 'imageless structure' (this latter remark is exceptionally accurate).[4]

The instances of incarnation do not match the enunciative positions in a regular homological way. One would simply expect the spectator, comically called 'the real spectator' (that is, the spectator *tout court*) to be on the side of the target. In fact, he occupies both the source, in that he can be identified with the camera, and the target, in that the film watches him. This second, backwards, movement has been remarkably described by Marc Vernet: the third fictitious dimension of the screen creates a point of perspective that is directed toward us, 'an anonymous reflexive look, which breaks and launches again the dual relationship between the spectator and the image'.[5] The spectator would then be both an I and a YOU. This proposition, formulated in those terms, does not make much sense: this is a first indication of the inconveniences encountered in the use of personal pronouns. Personal pronouns can only lead toward *a deictic conception of enunciation in cinema*, which in my opinion is not suitable to the realities of film. This is, however, the most common theory in the terrain of cinema. It usually remains implicit, even more or less unconscious. It appears again, aware of itself for the first time, and vigorously articulated, in the work of Francesco Casetti, who is so far the best analyst of cinematographic enunciation.[6] Casetti summarizes the main enuciative configurations, which he identifies by their 'executive hyperphrases'. Taken together, these hyperphrases constitute some kind of *deictic formulary*. Thus, for the look at the camera: 'I (= enunciator) and HE or SHE (= character) look at YOU (= addressee)', and so on and so forth for all other significant 'forms' outlined by enunciation.

However, is an I that cannot become a YOU still an I? You may ask a psychoanalyst, whose answer is quite predictable, or a linguist, for whom the reversibility of the first two persons is an essential feature of their very definition.

The highest degree of this reversibility occurs in *oral exchange*. Oral exchange, as opposed to 'story', is Benveniste's prototypical form of 'discourse'. According to the same author, oral exchange is also the starting point of the whole theory of enunciation.[7] In a conversation, it seems that you can see or touch both the source and the target of enunciation (which in fact shy away from this contact, because they are nothing but grammatical pronouns). Source and target are, once again, mistaken for their instances of incarnation, for the two talking persons: what is seen as the source of enunciation is *another simultaneous utterance*, the mimico-gestual utterance produced by the same person, that is, by the speaker (hence the confusion). But still, the revesibility of the enunciative poles reaches its highest degree in oral exchange: the instances of incarnation are real human bodies that combine in a remarkable way two modes of presence: presence to each other, and presence right there at the very moment of their utterance (as opposed to written exchange, to the message on the answering machine, and so on, and above all to literature, cinema, painting). The reactions of the addressee might gradually modify and reprogram the words spoken by the enunciator because of the parallel and logically anterior exchange between the listener and the speaker. Enunciation theory was built largely upon situations that are exceptional because of their structural features (but very common in everyday life).

The reversibility of the persons is found at a lesser degree in *written dialogues*, transcriptions, and other 'reported speeches'. Benveniste,[8] as well as literary narratology,[9] paid attention to this phenomenon. Here, there is no more real feedback of the target upon the source, but (written) utterances that mimic other (oral) utterances and also mimic this retroaction. This imitation is made possible by the identity of the global code, that is the language, and especially the identity of deictic terms, which in general have similar written and oral forms, increasing the confusion.

Pragmatics, to whom nothing is alien, must have dealt with many more intermediate cases. For instance, the I in an official discourse, which nobody is supposed to answer, although the speaker is well known by everyone; or, again, the I in a pamphlet bearing a signature, and so on. Step by step, we reach the 'story', in which the reversibility of the persons disappears, since theoretically, only the third person is used. 'Enunciation in the story', to use another formula by Benveniste,[10] does not have markers. Casetti will argue that in certain cases, enunciation is 'assumed', implied by the mere presence of an utterance, or, in fiction, 'diegeticized'. (But at the other end of the variation spectrum, enunciation itself can be *uttered* [enunciated].)[11]

Before proceeding any further, a few basic reminders about the true deictics that are found in articulated language: I shall give the example of the French or English language. Since the exact list of deictics changes according to different linguists, I shall abide by the most common – namely, personal, possessive, and demonstrative pronouns,[12] time and location adverbs, verb tenses. We should not forget that the category of deictics overlaps to a great extent that of anaphorics; I shall provisionally use the term index to mean both deictics and anaphorics.

A first distinction can be made between 'dédoublés' and 'simple' indexes. The first ones have differentiated forms in the discourse and in the story: 'Yesterday/the previous day', and so on. ('Yesterday' is a deictic form, while 'the previous day' is anaphoric; the second does not refer anymore to a circumstance of the enunciation but to a piece of information already enclosed in the utterance.) Other indexes, however, keep the same form in story and discourse – personal and possessive pronouns of the third person and all demonstratives: 'this' is what you point at with your finger, as well as what points at the previous sentence. The distinction between 'unfolded' and other indexes is, of course, purposeless when applied to terms used only in discourse (personal and possessive pronouns of the first two persons), or only in 'story', such as the past perfect and the anterior past; the question of form doubling arises only for terms with two functions.

A second significant distinction can be made between deictics having *different signifiers for the same referent* according to the circumstances of enunciation, and deictics with only one signifier. In a conversation Mr Durand is called I when he speaks, but YOU when Dupont talks to him; 18 July is called 'tomorrow' if you speak on the seventeenth, but 'yesterday' if you speak on the nineteenth, and so on. This latter category matches approximately what language philosophers call the 'token reflexives':[13] the specific token of each enunciation is 'reflected', according to these philosophers' own terms, even in the literal meaning of the utterance. In order to know what the word *here* means, you have to know where the sentence has been uttered at that time. This is the group of the deictics *par excellence* (and maybe the only one),[14] both because this group has a very special mechanism of reference and because it contains the keywords *I* and *YOU* (which are also the words Casetti mentions). What is specific to this group is that it provides us with information on enunciation through enunciation itself; this group also is dependent on certain changes in reality, as opposed to the book or the film. Of course, personal and possessive pronouns of the first two persons belong to this group; so does the verbal triad present/past/future used to designate the same date according to the time of the speech; as well as the adverbs 'yesterday/today/tomorrow', 'here/there' – designating the same place according to whether you are close or distant – left/right,[15] and so on. These words which undergo changes differ from other words whose signifier does not change for a unique referent, even if the conditions of enunciation vary, that is if the sentence is uttered later, somewhere else, by someone else, and so on, and for the atemporal present ('The earth is round'), and for all demonstratives except those organised in pairs, Such as close/distant, *this one/that one*.

The only aim of this brief presentation was to emphasize the extreme precision of the deictic dispositive, even when it is transcribed in the simplest manner. The fact that all those structures are found in the dialogues of a talking movie is not surprising, since speeches have been recorded 'en bloc': the same comment can be made about the dialogues of a novel, since the mimicking transcription I have mentioned is always possible. However, is it a good idea – since we just took the (incomplete) measure of the structural constraints generated by this I, *constraints that also build its meaning* – to call this I the source of enunciation of a film or a novel taken as a whole, or the source of any other noninteractive discourse, which is completed before it is presented and does not give either to enunciation, nor to the reader-spectator any possibility for modifying it, other than – and this is a purely exterior exchange – to close the book or turn the television off? Gianfranco Bettetini gives those kinds of discourses – which include the majority of classical texts – the quite accurate name of 'monodirectional' which I shall keep.[16]

In addition, among the discourses prepared in advance which do not allow changes, a distinction should be made between linguistic discourses, such as literary narration, and audiovisual ones. In the latter, the speeches – which can be very close to actual everyday exchanges – must deal, however, with the Image. They do not carry the message alone; the body of the text partly escapes them. In a novel, nothing is speech, everything becomes writing but the language is sovereign and the idiom unchanged (the text's idiom is that *spoken* by the characters and the readers). The discourse is sprinkled with deictics (mimicked deictics, as we have seen) as well as with anaphorics, especially in passages of 'story'. Deictics and anaphorics are often expressed by the same word (such as *this*), so that the general impression remains. The spontaneous perception of the difference between story and discourse is often blurred by the anaphoro-deictic terms, for if the analysis did not go beyond these terms, discourse would become story without any change in the signifiers, by a one notch functional commutation, the role of the situation being mechanically replaced by the role of the context. (In pragmatic terms, one could say that the cotext has, as accurately as possible, taken the place of the context.) In addition, in writing the anaphor is less distant from the deixis, since the latter operates on 'situations' which are themselves pure products of the utterance. In discourse, in the novel's dialogues, the character will be able to talk of *this dog*, if we know from the book that there is a dog in the room right now; in 'story', the narrator of the same novel will be able to say 'this dog' if he refers to the preceding phrase where we learned that there was a dog in the room at this point: reconstituted deixis there, ordinary anaphor here.

In short, the story can assume the appearance of discourse, or remind us of some vaguely intermediate form. On the other hand – since things are connected but distinct – the written text always gives the impression of an enunciative presence to various degrees: this is because the text keeps in itself something from the deictic enunciation, the one whose use is most familiar to us. (The linguistic theory of enunciation – and this is not a coincidence – started as a theory of deictics.) Same remarks, *a fortiori*, for the 'oral text', fully oral, as sometimes on the radio.

'If it speaks [ça parle], it means someone is speaking': this is the general impression, even about a book. But the cinematic equivalent of this inner and immediate belief is far from certain. 'If they are images to be seen, this means someone arranged them': not everyone feels it clearly. The spectator spontaneously attributes the dialogues in the film to an enclosed, second-level instance; and he attributes the speeches of a potential off-screen narrator, or anonymous commentator, who pretends to be almighty, to an enunciative position, yet still unfocused and vague, or somehow blurred, or at least veiled by the image (on this subject, see André Gaudreault's remarks which seem to me very accurate[17]). The spectator is never able to pretend that the first, authentic enunciation does not come from the 'Grand Imager' mentioned by Albert Laffay, who orders images and even voices (*and the voices as images*), whose globally extralinguistic enterprise never gives the clear impression of a specialized, personalized, enunciative presence. But in most cases, this spectator does not think of the 'Imager'. On the other hand, he does not, of course, believe that things reveal themselves: he simply *sees images.* Although he supports (as I do) a theory of cinematic enunciation, André Gardies has a significant moment of doubt and declares that the notion of cinematic enunciation might only be an anthropomorphic metaphor.[18] André Gaudreault notes that a linguistic utterance is automatically ascribed to a precise person, whether or not this person can be identified.[19] He also notes that this certainty begins to fade as soon as nonverbal utterances are concerned. One has to keep in mind that the word *to utter* [énoncer], in common French, means only the act of speaking or writing (compare the expression 'I'énoncé du problème' [the utterance, the formulation of the problem]). This expresses the almost universal belief that the only true language is the linguistic language. Moreover, when David Bordwell condemns the very notion of enunciation in film studies, he uses a very similar argument, the nonlinguistic nature of the object.[20] One could say the same thing about Gérard Genette's statements that film could not, properly speaking, be a narration, because it is not a linguistic being.[21]

People who think that the expression 'cinematic enunciation' has any meaning should not ignore this point, which is indeed very strong. It compels us to make an important conversion: to conceive of an enunciative apparatus that would not necessarily be deictic (and therefore anthropomorphic), or *personal* (as are the pronouns that are called *personal*) and that would not too closely imitate this or that linguistic device, since linguistic inspiration works better from a distance. 'Often, indeed', as Pierre Sorlin puts it, 'the film indicates its relationship with the public by emphasizing that it is a film (an object fabricated from shot images and taped sounds), without involving the slightest trace of subjectivity'. He adds: 'In many films, the marks of enunciation do not refer to any delegated subject'.[22] In film, when enunciation is indicated in the utterance, it is not, or not essentially, by deictic imprints, but by *reflexive* constructions (François Jost had already expressed a very similar idea in an article[23]): the film talks to us about itself, about cinema, or about the position of the spectator.[24] It is at this moment that the kind of 'unfolding' of the utterance appears, which in all theories constitutes the condition without which one cannot speak of enunciation. The deictic unfolding – to be at the same time (and fictitiously if necessary) inside and outside – is not the only possible one. The metafilmic (metadiscursive) splitting, which is internal, may also support a complete instance of enunciation, all by itself if necessary. The reflexive return, as I shall attempt to demonstrate, might take many forms, which are frequently in films and numerous enough to cover the current inventory of enunciative positions: film in the film, *off*-address, *in*-address, subjective image, shot/reverse shot, flashback, and so on. The example of cinema (and many others, probably) invites us to broaden our idea of enunciation, and this time it is film theory that might, in turn, have some effect on general semiology and linguistics. It is not surprising that the various kinds of existing discourses, which are so diverse, offer diverse enunciation devices: and it could even be trivial to mention it if enunciation was not too automatically connected with deixis by some people. For what is enunciation basically? It is not necessarily, nor always, 'I-HERE-NOW': it is, more generally speaking, the ability some utterances have to fold up in some places, to appear here and there as in relief, to lose this thin layer of themselves that carries a few engraved indications *of another nature* (or another level), regarding the production and not the product, or rather, involved in the product by the other end. Enunciation is the semiological act by which some parts of a text talk to us about this text as an act. However, resorting to the complicated and quasi-inimitable mechanism of the deixis is not a necessity. The possible markers of enunciation are very diverse. In orchestral music, for instance, one marker is the characteristic sonority: when the oboe comes in, it does not only play its phrase, it makes itself recognisable as oboe, the musical message splits into two layers of information, each having a different status. In a film, if characters watch something from a window, they reproduce my own situation as a spectator and remind me both of the nature of what is going on – a film projection, a vision in a rectangle – and the part I am playing in it. But the textual construction which reminded me of it is meta-filmic, it is not deictic; or rather, in this example, the textual construction is meta-cinematographic since the rectangle of the screen is typical of the film as such. In a more general way, as François Jost and Jean-Paul Simon rightly put it,[25] cinema does not have a closed list of enunciative signs, but it uses any sign (as in my example of the window) in an enunciative manner, so that the sign can be removed from the diegesis and immediately come back to it. The *construction* will have, for an instant, assumed an enunciative value.

Gianfranco Bettetini correctly states that the film, despite its spoken words, is always on the side of the written, never on that of the oral (*CA* 106). It is true at least on one point, but a capital point: enunciator and addressee – at the global level of the work, not in inserted dialogues – do not exchange their marks along the way; and the addressee does not change by his reactions either the propositions or the proposal of the enunciation. This remains true, even where the canonical markers of enunciation unmistakably appear (for this happens), such as extra-diegetic commentaries saying 'You' to the public: this 'You' will never be able to respond. (Reciprocally, this example reminds us that deictics, even thus weakened, are not without any function in cinematographic enunciation.) Dominique Chateau notes that cinema instigates a 'discontinuous communication':[26] the two poles of enunciation, enunciator and addressee, cannot be exchanged, nor can they touch each other: transmission is split in two moments, recording (filming) and projection, separated by several technological and commercial intermediate steps. Marc Vernet, for his part, in a fine passage, describes the camera-gaze as the symbol of the encounter between reality and spectator:[27] this encounter is always desired, always missed, sometimes approached; it constitutes the fundamentals of film.

I come back to Bettetini. In the remarkable book he has devoted to these problems, *La Conversazione audiovisiva*, his position is both very rigorous and paradoxical. It describes film as 'conversation' – hence the book's title – a conversation between a simulacrum of the enunciator and a simulacrum of the addressee, both within the text, constituents of the enunciation apparatus; they mime an exchange and prepare for the possibility of later genuine interactions. The first paradox lies in Bettetini's choice of conversation as a metaphor for types of discourse which are radically different: the second paradox is that the book, which does not lack subtlety, insists on the difference: film is not interactive, it does not accept any response, the conversation of the books is imaginary, fantasmic so to speak. I shall not follow the way traced by the author, but it is not without appeal.

Film does not contain any deictic equivalents, with the exception, of course, of spoken words and written quotes. With the exception too, of one sort of global and permanent deictic – a very atypical one, to tell the truth – an actualizing and vaguely demonstrative '*Here is*' [Voici],[28] which is always tacit and always present and, in addition, proper to images rather than to film. (The image of an object *presents* this object, it contains some kind of designative elements that are little differentiated.) Otherwise, moving images with sound have nothing similar to verb tenses, personal or possessive pronouns, 'there' or 'the day after tomorrow.' It could be misleading, since the film is able to express space and time relationships of some kind, but only anaphorically, within the film itself, between its different parts, and not between the film and someone or something else. An appropriated construct of images might tell us 'The next day ...' (one evokes the night in between, makes clear that there was only one night, and so on), but this construct cannot tell us 'Tomorrow' – that is, one day after the day you watch this film. In a more general way, there always will be an important difference between textual arrangements that *evoke* the author's or spectator's figure, and words like I or YOU, that *designate* explicity the corresponding persons in a conversation.

As Francesco Casetti puts it without elaborating: despite the scepticism of most commentators, the film could really resort to a certain number of deictic configurations (*YY* 82). He mentions only two of them. The first ones are the technical traces, voluntary or not, which reveal the work on image and sound and remain in the final reel: that is, I'll grant, a mark of enunciation, but a typically metafilmic one; it is a fragment of secondary discourse, which tells us about discourse; it is in no way deictic, unless we call deictic all that shows or indicates something to us. The film credits, according to the author, also belong to the deixis. One could, of course, resort to my 'metadiscurive argument' as soon as one talks about film credits. Moreover, the film credits are entirely carried by the language, by the written and sometimes spoken language. However, it is true that the film credits inform us, if not about the reality of the production work, at least about the co-workers' and the author's name, sometimes about the shooting place, most of the time about the approximate date of the film. But this information is not given to us deictically. If in 1988 I watch a film that came out that same year, its credits do not tell me 'shot this year', but they bear (when they do) the date *1988*, which can be understood by everyone without specific information about the circumstances of enunciation. Deictic mechanisms are precisely what is to be avoided here, since deictics, taken in their purest form (variable signifier for a unique referent), would compel one to alter the reel again and again. (I hope I will be forgiven this caricatural hypothesis and these quite trivial reminders, aimed to react against the abusive use of the figurative or expanded sense.)

About film credits, Casetti recalls the still famous final sentence in *The Magnificent Ambersons*, 'My name is Orson Welles', spoken by Orson Welles himself (*DS* 42-43). The reflexivity appears clear. It is combined, this time, with an authentic deixis: had the same statement been said by the R.K.0. representative, we would have heard, 'His name is Orson Welles' (I indeed go on making absurd suppositions). The signifier would have changed, not the referent. The film admirably integrates the possessive to the general construct: it is the role of Orson Welles's voice, which 'takes up' the story's narrative voice and magistrally saturates the last minutes of the reel. By nature, this deictic construct is not cinematographic but purely linguistic; it contributes as such to the film and finds its effectiveness in the film itself.

The 'system' suggested by Francesco Casetti – since it is a system, and of great intellectual strength – rests entirely on cardinal points, which Casetti sees as the enunciative configurations in film, or as the *coordinates*, to use his own term, of cinematic enunciation. He is not unaware, of course, that film presents many other enunciative positions, such as the various forms of subjective framing studied in remarkable detail by Edward Branigan.[29] In Casetti, these various framings would probably be considered as relevant variants or derived cases. For his objective is different: it is deliberately synoptic and general, as in an aerial photograph. On more than one point, he takes up Bettetini's position, but he wants to be more 'technical'. He is the first to offer elements of formalisation for the whole enunciative apparatus of film in its main outlines. Therefore, it is not a coincidence that I am reacting to his text.

If you put aside two figures which are studied separately in the book (see *DS* 104 and *passim*), the flashback and the film in the film – other combinations of the same terms which I am getting to now – you are confronted with the following grid (see *YY* 89-91; *DS* 60-64): (1) *So-called objective shots* ('nobody's shots' in the Anglo-Saxon tradition); the formula is: I (enunciator) and YOU (addressee), we watch IT (the utterance, character, film). (2) *Interpellations* (= camera-looks and various addressees): I and HE, we watch YOU, who are then supposed to watch. (3) *So-called subjective shots*: YOU and HE see what I show you. (4) *'Unreal objective shots'* (= author's rare angles, which cannot be ascribed to a character, as well as similar constructions): 'As if YOU were I'.

The second case, interpellation, has a variant in which the enunciator does not assume a character's point of view, but the point of view of the whole scene, as when there are screens in the screen, mirrors, windows, folding screens, and so on (this connection seems a little loose to me); the formula is: 'THIS is for YOU, it is a film, that is ME'. The emergence of a reflexive idea, 'it is film', is to be noted in a general conception dominated by deictics. This phenomenon is much stronger than the author believes. He first states that personal pronouns will be for him 'simple equivalents of indicative nature' (*YY* 88); but later personal pronouns are the only elements to be part of his formula, until the reader discovers that they were barely metaphorical, and that their function was more than just indicative: Casetti indeed tells us toward the end: '[In enunciation] someone appropriates a language . . .; persons are being articulated (appropriation allows the distinction between an I, a YOU, a HE), etc.' (*DS* 142): we deal here with (nearly) true personal pronouns. I shall leave aside other aspects of the book; Casetti's concerns are noticeably broader.

Any conception of enunciation that is influenced too much by deixis contains, as soon as the analysis of spoken exchanges is left behind, three main risks:

anthropomorphism, artificial use of linguistic concepts, and transformation of enunciation into communication (= 'real', extra-textual relationships). Casetti himself does not often yield to those temptations; he warns us against them, but in the theoretical field the risk remains ('the risk' in the singular, because the three are one and cannot be dissociated).

First of all, when a film is being shown, there is in general one spectator (at least): the instance of incarnation of the target is present. But the instances of incarnation of the source – the filmmaker, or the production team are, most of the time, absent. Bettetini grants some importance to this dissymmetry (*CA* 99, 100). For this dissymmetry causes the true tête-à-tête to be distorted with regard to the so-called persons of the language: the tête-à-tête does not happen between an enunciator and an addressee, but between an enunciator and an utterance, between a spectator and a *film*, that is, between a YOU and a S/HE, distributed thus. The meaning of this YOU and this HE is blurred, since the only human subject that is right there and able to say I is precisely the YOU. It is also the common feeling, except in the specialized milieu of filmmakers, that the 'subject' is the spectator; books about psychoanalytic semiology, which deal at length with the 'spectator subject', certainly reflect this impression.

For Casetti, the enunciative poles are roles; same term in Branigan (see, for instance, *PV* 40). These roles will be invested by bodies later on (for instance *DS* 53; *YY* 78, 84), during the actual transmission; same term in Bettetini (*CA* 110).[30] The formula is beautiful and points at something essential. However, where the enunciator is concerned, there is no body. And since it is true that roles (or their equivalents in another theoretical frame) call for an incarnation – the nature of this call still remains enigmatic – the 'enunciator' is incarnated in the only available body, the body of the text, that is, a *thing*, which will never be an I, which is not in charge of any exchange with some YOU, but which is a source of images and sounds, and nothing else. *The film is the enunciator,* the film as a source, acting as such, *oriented* as such, the film as activity. This is how people think: what the spectator faces, what he has to deal with, is the film. Casetti's idea, that a body would be needed for the enunciator as well as for the addressee, is inspired by the first two persons of the verb in language.

Not being an I, the source of enunciation does not produce a YOU answering the I; neither does the source produce a HE on the screen. The utterance, the film itself, the character, and so on, do not have the features of a HE. HE is the 'non-person' of Benveniste, the absent person: the film is not absent. HE, especially, is the absent one, inasmuch as two present persons, 'I' and 'YOU', talk about him: the film, far from being an absent instance stuck between two present ones, would resemble rather a present instance stuck between two absent ones, the author, who disappears after the fabrication, and the spectator, who is present but does not manifest his presence in any respect.

Another difficulty is connected with 'watching' or 'seeing', which assumes great importance when cinema is at stake. Casetti sometimes uses these verbs with the enunciator as a subject, I; thus, 'I and You, we are watching it', as far as objective framing is concerned. 'I' can only designate the body or the role of the filmmaker. If it is the filmmaker himself (the body), he does not watch, he has watched (which is still not entirely accurate: he has filmed, and, therefore, watched; the 'utterer' [émetteur] does not watch his film; he makes it). If this is the role of the filmmaker, as is most likely the case, one does not understand either how this ideal figure, which is, so to speak, up-stream and exists before the film, can watch anything: from the source, nothing either watches or sees, the source produces, expands, *shows*. The parallelism between the enunciator (in the example of objective framing) and the addressee who sees is artifi-cially produced by deictic symmetries. The influence of the deictic model subtly dis-torts in various points this brand new system that has brought much to the terrain. For instance, the idea of the spectator as *interlocutor* (see *DS* 15) – an idea already familiar in textual semiotics – seems to me without any useful provocation as soon as the term is deprived of what constitutes its definition, the idea of immediate interaction. Moreover, if the film spectator is an *interlocutor*, what will users of truly interactive media that already exist be called? Scientific words are not exempted from keeping a minimal conformity with common language; they should at least not contradict it.

In order to designate what supports the target and the source, I prefer to use a vague and cautious formula, 'instances of incarnation'. For if it is true that source and target, which are basic and only text orientations of the text, call for *external* support, this support is not *real* because of that. Or at least it is real only, and there only, with the 'empirical' spectator or author as they say – in studies which are themselves empirical and which derive from inquiries, questionnaires, and organised experimental screen-ings, and so on. Research about enunciation does not make use of such methods; it is most of the time based on film analysis and remains 'internal'. However it constantly needs to *visualize a Figure of the Spectator*. Books on this subject all say that camera, for instance, is directed toward the spectator (or toward the addressee, since the ideality of the former sometimes makes the alleged distinction impossible), that the spectator looks toward the left of the picture, that he is connected with this character rather than that, and so on. In one word, the two 'real' poles, sender and receiver, are in themselves imaginary, and, however, necessary as mental support for the film analysis. Necessary and of a very legitimate use, if only we are clearly aware that this 'real' is nothing but the imagination of the analyst: the analyst, indeed, manages to construct his 'spectator' and 'author' on the basis of two information flows, the progression of the film, and the reactions of the individual (as well as the real . . .) spectator he himself is. In addition, this spectator will probably think that such brusque and unmotivated camera motion probably reflects an 'author's intention'. And this is the way things are in the film, or, at least, there is no other way to construct the film; but the true intention of Mr X, film-maker, is not known to anyone. As Edward Branigan has well expressed it, the work does not provide *any context* (see *PV* 40) – no 'frame'[31] in this perspective – as to where we put the figure of the author; in order to read a text, we are compelled gradually to make up an imaginary author, exactly as the author, in order to compose this text, could not help constructing an imaginary reader (see *PV* 39). Those remarks seem essential to me, as does Bettetini's insistence on the fantasmic nature of the protagonists in the 'audiovisual conversation' (see *CA* 110, 120).

In very beautiful pages on visual 'interpellation', Francesco Casetti declares that the place of the addressee, in the gaze at the camera, is the empty space in front of the screen, a space created by this blind look, the only off-screen space that will never become an on-screen space (see *YY* 79; *DS* 65, 73): acute analysis of a cinematic configuration which, however, cannot preclude (and refrains from doing so) the spectators' actual reaction, although the spectators are supposedly represented by this addressee, whose place is indicated to us. We can be sure that the major part of the audience has a far less subtle idea (or no idea at all) about the camera-gaze, and that its 'instinctive', affective, and visual responses vary considerably according to individuals and time. For one single film image there certainly is no point on the screen (or even around the screen) that cannot become the 'place' of one or more spectators. Hence the futility of some empirical investigations which choose between interchangeable or indifferent alternatives.

Textual analysis, even when enunciative, remains textual analysis. If you want information about audiences and filmmakers, you have to go and get them on the spot. You cannot dispense with experimenting or collecting facts. It is of no use to pretend with all the required discretion that knowledge of the enunciator and the addressee would give us at least probabilities or general frames to understand the author's intentions and the spectator's reactions. For these forecasts are so general that no empirical analysis would take them into account and they could prove to be wrong for any given spectator, even if they express a partial tendency common to everyone. The reason why is that you deal with two heterogeneous orders of reality, a text (that is, I repeat, a thing) and persons; many different persons and a unique text. Pragmatics, at least when it adheres to the text, has to accept this limitation, which it resents at times even though there is nothing there to be ashamed of. The spectator is exposed to multiple influences that were, of course, absent from cinematic prediction; it is therefore not contradictory to note that the film has 'positioned' the addressee on the right side of the screen and that this spectator has placed his gaze to the left (Bettetini's theory devotes much space to these disparities[32]). Enunciative analyses, for all these reasons, seem to keep all their usefulness and autonomy. Their 'realistic' pretensions are rather voluntary illusions of the moment and are explicitly contradicted soon afterwards. Francesco Casetti declares, for instance, that the YOU allows the interface between the world of the screen and the world of which the screen is only a part (*DS* 144) (thus, enunciation, as one can guess, would really be something in-between, it would have a foot in the world[33]); but two pages earlier, Casetti reminded us that the empirical YOU is definitively out of the reach of the film. It is true, but then what about the interfacial YOU? (The author has in fact an acute awareness of the uncomfortable and 'interstitial' aspect of the pragmatic undertaking as a whole [see *DS* 24].)

Another perhaps superfluous precision. I don't pretend here that enunciative configurations are deprived of any influence on the observable behaviour of the spectators (this hypothesis is as improbable as that of its unmistakable determination by the film). But in order to measure this influence, you must again go and see, that is, get out of the text.

Cinematic enunciation is always enunciation on the film. Reflexive rather than deictic, it does not give us any information about the outside of the text, but about a text that carries in itself its source and its destination. Edward Branigan considers that in fictional films, narration is a metalanguage with respect to what is being narrated (*PV* 3).

Two conversing friends exchange the I and the YOU, according to the physical reality of their speaking turns; the film 'speaks' alone all the time, it does not allow me to say anything and it cannot get out of itself (it was made before, once and for all). When the filmmaker appears on the screen, as Hitchcock does in his films – deictic and reflexive figure at the same time, as it seems – it is not, to take up another remark by Branigan (see *PV* 40), a filming Hitchcock that we can see, an author/filmmaker ('external' instance), but a filmed Hitchcock, a character, a little piece of film: metafilmic construction (since, on the one hand, we still recognise the filmmaker). The time always comes, the same book insists, when the film cannot reveal the conditions of its birth and touches upon an 'apersonal component' (*PV* 40; see also 172) (beautiful expression; it is the film as a thing, once again). Branigan also comments on the famous title lines of *Tout va bien* by Godard (see *PV* 172), where we see hands signing checks (thus, the filmmaker wanted to show the role of money in film production, and especially in his own): for the American analyst – he is pitiless but right, unlike those who fancy that it is *really* possible to 'show the apparatus' – these images that were supposed to be revolutionary are still an ordinary scene in the movie, since the act that shows them to us is not shown. To put it in more general (and simplistic) terms, we could say that without the help of a mirror the camera is unable to film itself – it is like our eyes, which we do not see – and that the so-called outside of the text can therefore be only text, reduplicated text, metatext.

The textual enclosure of cinematic enunciation is even clearer in common and, so to speak, anonymous figures. Thus, when someone tells us, as often happens, that in the 'first person on the sound track', in voice-over, the enunciator has provisionally borrowed the voice of one of the protagonists, this person only describes some strange ballet in which all the terms belong to the film: enunciated mark of the enunciator (see Casetti), 'voice' of a character, presence of an explicit narration, and so on – one example among many of the various metadiscursive twists which constitute cinematic enunciation by folding the different instances of the film over each other, in the exact same manner that there are several ways to fold a napkin.

The source and the target, considered in their literal inscription, in their discursive identity, are not roles, but *parts of text*, aspects of configurations of the text (that is how we notice the shot-reverse shot in the general organisation of a sequence of images). Source and target are rather *orientations*, vectors in a textual topography, more abstract instances than is usually said.

The source is the text as a whole, seen from its origin to its end, in the ideal downstream order in which it is woven; in Casetti's book, it is one of the film's directions, 'the film in the process of *being made*'. The designation is the same text concurrent from its ending point, being undone and freed in imagination: it is the moment of '*being given*' in Casetti.[34]

Casetti gives once or twice the example of a famous scene in *Gone with the Wind* (see for example, *DS* 69-71): a spectacular and emphasized crane shot 'abandons' Scarlett in the middle of the corpses and wounded bodies lying on the ground just after the battle of Atlanta. According to the author, the camera motion figurativizes both how the scene is constructed (enunciator) and how it wants to be read (addressee). We could say the same thing about any shot, but it is true. However, to switch from one of those figurativizations to the other, one has to turn the text over and watch it from the other side, even if it is to obtain two perfectly parallel constructions. (After all, the reader does not, in theory, decipher anything else than what the inscriber wrote, but their respective actions are oriented in opposite directions.)

Another case: subjective images. According to Casetti, the enunciator plays a slight role and the addressee, on the contrary, is very much highlighted, since he is 'syncretized' with a concrete character, through whose very eyes we see what we see, and who is therefore, like the addressee, a watcher (see *DS* 75). That is beyond doubt. But it is also true, if you turn over the text, that the enunciator regains his importance, in that the source is 'figurativized' in a character who is not only a watcher (as the spectator), but also someone who shows, like the filmmaker who stands behind him. This character has one eye in front and one eye in back, he receives rays from both sides, and the image can be perceived in two different ways, as in some drawings in which form and background can be inverted.

Casetti shows that he is very sensitive to the profound cause of these phenomena of reversion, although he does not comment separately on them. The 'point of view' in the film, he stresses (*YY* 81-82), can be the place of the camera or that of the spectator – both can coincide but cannot be confused – so that enunciation is, from the beginning on, divided between *showing* and *seeing*. I shall add, in a psychoanalytical perspective, that primary identification with the camera has the effect of transforming it into a retroactive delegate of the spectator to come (André Gaudreault has commented well on this notion[35]), and that the projective/introjective qualities of this machine, recorder as well as pointed weapon, make it as ambivalent as the view itself, about which it is impossible to say whether it is active or passive, since it both receives and enlightens. Hence a symmetry, a *reversibility* of source and target, of which I gave a few examples, and which is probably responsible for the theoretical recourse to deictics, which are also reversible in language. But these two forms of reversibility are quite different, even if the French language does not have two words to distinguish them in one case, signifiers physically exchange their location and actually start moving; in the other case, the spectator or the analyst reverses his perspective without touching anything.

Another striking example: the camera-gaze I have mentioned. It is of course a figure of the target; the destination provisionally coincides with the location of the camera (since the latter is being looked at), and it seldom happens that the reception instance of the film is solicited in such an explicit way, that is, that the spectator is directly addressed by a diegetic intervention. But this construction also highlights the source, which is, for now, clearly figured by the eyes of the observing character. The source follows and duplicates the vector of this look. Having noticed this, Casetti thinks the I has created an interlocutor for himself (hence the strong presence of the YOU), while taking advantage of this situation to assert itself (see *DS* 143). This is the outline for a novella, whose characters would play tricks on one another, look for psychic benefits, and so on. In fact, if the spectator, whether real or imaginary, and the analyst (always considered real), 'turn' the text 'over' the way the diegetic onlooker does, the latter serves as a source, but also as a target, for he is under the fire (!) of the camera.

And if you mentally orient the text the same way as the camera, this camera then becomes the target of the observer, and, nevertheless, being camera, that is, source, brings this look into existence.

This does not mean that figures of enunciation are all reversible. If I have insisted on those which are, it is to highlight both the abstract and textual (perceptive) character of those 'locations' I can source and target. They are not the enunciator and the addressee, who are fictitious people; they are not even exactly things; they are – as the chosen word would like to suggest – directions (belonging to the geography of the film), orientations discovered by the analyst. For it is true, in a way, that all the film's activity happens between two poles, or two plots: there are by necessity makers and watchers, whatever name they are given. But when they are marked at a precise point in the film, what is important is to describe the layout of this imprint that is yet depersonalized and transformed into a landscape. Even when the filmmaker addresses us with the voice-off of a person, of an anonymous and overhanging commentator, the result in the text is a vocal one-way crossing that has this profound organ as a source, and, since there are no target 'markers' (if one assumes the absence of any diegetic audience), that disseminates over the entire surface of the image, covering it as a coating.

Contrary to the previous figures, this one is not reversible, it marks the source and it alone: the 'movement' of the voice only makes sense (if I may say so) in one sense, and there is no way to turn over the text, since there is no coherent construction in which an off-voice could be the target. Nonreversible figures are numerous and common. Among them, of course, all cinematic addresses (in, off, semi-diegetized, on written text in silent movies, and so on). Likewise – without claiming to be exhaustive – the 'unreal objective' framings already mentioned, which are noticeably deforming but cannot be attributed to a character – and therefore correspond to a direct intervention by the author (these images were sometimes called 'author-subjectives' in film theory of the 1920s and 1930s). A classical and often-quoted example (with special astuteness by François Jost[36]): systematic low-angle shots by Orson Welles. Here, the notion of orientation can be understood in its almost literal sense, since the enunciation marker consists of the image's unusual coefficient of gradient. A work's 'manner' is a perpetual commentary on what the work says. This commentary is not developed. On the contrary, it is *wrapped* in the image. It is the incompressible coefficient of enunciative intervention, and the birth act of the metatextual gesture, yet still half stuck in what it will soon designate. To come back to source and target, I want only to say that they always consist of perceptible (audio-visual) movements and positions, or, rather, of reference points that allow the description of these movements and positions.

The kind of validity that is proper to textual studies of enunciation could, to a certain extent, be compared to that characterizing semiopsychoanalytic research. In both cases, if you assume that the analyst has the necessary training (knowledge, method), the whole value of his work depends on his personal qualities, since he is at the same time the scholar, and (together with the film), the very terrain of the research. He may declare that the specific pleasure that arises from the fictional film is due to a fetishistic splitting process, to a mixture of belief and disbelief. There is no need to quiz these people, who would be hard put to answer such questions. This is a general, or, rather, a *generic* truth; it concerns THE spectator. Anyone can find it within himself. It does not tell us – for instance – if, in this or that person, belief clearly prevails over disbelief, and if, in others, on the other hand, disbelief is dominant. There is no contradiction. The generic observation retains its interest, superior, I believe, to that of its variants or its local exceptions. However, in order to draw the curve of these fluctuations, which are inseparable from the 'real spectators' coming on stage, the only suitable methods are empirical ones, for the question that is then asked is empirical. At this point, the generic spectator – like the addressee in pragmatics: they are two analyst figures – has no longer much to say.

The content of these pages is a little cluttered. I shall now attempt, finally, to put things in order. I shall distinguish six points, which will hopefully clarify the matter.

(1) Taken globally, enunciation theory offers one weak point. Whatever the theory may say at times, it tends, more or less, in one phase or in one aspect of the analysis, to suppress the Author and the Spectator by using various and picturesque substitutes: implicit, ideal, and so on. These substitutes lend themselves to eviction and are always 'nonempirical' yet personalized. If it is true that you can always omit the 'real author' (but only because his real work is available), it is impossible to forget the spectator. An imaginary spectator, as I said, but imagined as real and not different from the real-real spectator, except that, in order to know his reaction, you only make plausible suppositions, not factual verifications. In order to suggest any interpretation of a cinematic sequence, someone has to have seen it, you have to have seen it yourself. The imaginary spectator deserves his name because it is unclear whether he reflects the general attitude of others, the entire public, or of any specific audience; but at the same time, he is real in the person of the analyst (and only the analyst, most of the time). It is unlikely that enunciation theory could do without the Spectator, that is the 'Receptor', whose figure is borrowed from a very different – and ritually repudiated – horizon, that of communication theory. Edward Branigan perceptively remarks that the thought of enunciation keeps in itself, despite its authentic autonomy, something of the scheme of communication (see *PV* 41). This 'something' can be reduced by hunting down

anthropomorphisms, but I don't think anyone is able to suppress it, for a 'real' analyst has to see the film.

(2) The obvious symmetry of enunciator and addressee hides a fundamental dissymmetry. If a given figure in film is attributed to the enunciator, it is because the analyst (on the side of the addressee) so decided. If it is attributed to the addressee, it is, again, because the analyst said so. The entire film is viewed from the perspective of the addressee, which leads us back to the great powers of the – or, rather, of *a* – real spectator. Which is only normal, for we talk about screening, not filming. In any field, the posture of analysis causes such an imbalance. You have to be aware of it and not be fooled by misleading symmetrical words, and to see instead the permanent risk of various torsions, which should, as much as possible be straightened out by an effort toward objectivization.

(3) I don't know if the words *enunciator* and *addressee* are really necessary ones, that is, if they designate something other than an imaginary author and spectator, or to be clearer, something else than the *image* of the author and the spectator. However, these words are convenient because of their visible kinship with 'enunciation'. In addition, they become necessary in the case of explicit enunciators about whom I shall talk soon. In practice, *enunciator* can of course be used to mean the author, without saying so, and *addressee* to anticipate gratuitously the reactions of the public. But no term is safe from such misuse.

The good thing about these lexical hesitations is that they emphasize that the often mentioned level of enunciation (in the singular) corresponds in fact to two different stages: a textual stage (the 'markers'; source and target), and a personal stage (imaginary author and spectator, enunciator and addressee; this is the level of attributions: the marker is ascribed to someone).

(4) In films and books, *explicit enunciators* are to be found, such as storytellers, when the work is narrative. But since the work is not always narrative, we need a more general term: enunciators, whom the text itself presents as holding a discourse. On the screen, they are never extradiegetic in Gérard Genette's sense,[37] for here are the images, the seeing and hearing apparatus which cannot be ascribed to this enunciator. As soon as the source of the entire film, the equivalent of its extradiegetic narration is at stake, enunciation loses its enunciator (and therefore its addressee), even if a voice-over covers the whole and speaks in the first person, even *a fortiori* if there is no voice-over. This is because the voice itself, as André Gaudreault points out,[38] is accountable only for what it says. I would add that the voice *does not explain why there are images.* In other words, the explicit enunciators in the film are always embedded, whether they pretend they are not, or are openly that way, like the narrators of a metadiegesis.

In regard to fictional films and their source, David Bordwell prefers to speak of narration rather than narrator,[39] and Edward Branigan speaks of 'activity without actor' (*PV* 48). In fact, if this body of images and sounds seems in a way *assembled* (= enunciation) it does not give the impression of this conscious, unitarian and continuous intervention, which imposes on everything the homogenous filter of a unique and familiar code, from which the ideal figure of an almost human character, such as, precisely, the enunciator, would emerge. Here again, I find myself close to certain of André Gaudreault's recent concerns.[40]

(5) One of the most permanent difficulties in this set of problems is that there are points (or lines) in the text which correspond in an obvious way, for a more or less long period of time, to the author or the spectator, and which are, however, part of the film like everything else: the so-called enunciation 'markers' (which are rather general organisational forms). These markers owe their names to the fact that theoretically they can be located within the text, but too often they are looked at less in relation to the text than to the entities they are the markers of, markers *of* the enunciator and *of* the addressee. I tried to introduce the apersonal words *source* and *target*, in order, so to speak, to reintegrate the markers in the cinematic flow, rejoining here in my own way Casetti's position on the same point.[41]

(6) All figures of enunciation consist in metadiscursive folds of cinematic instances piled on top of each other. In subjective framing, the gazing and at the same time showing character duplicates both the spectator and the camera. In 'interpellation', the character sends us back our own gaze, which usually does not allow any reply. And so on. It is as if the film could manifest the production instance that it carries in itself and that carries it only by talking to us about the camera, the spectator, or by pointing at its own filmitude, that is, in any case, by pointing at itself. Thus, in places, a slightly sliding-off layer of film is constituted. It detaches itself from the rest and settles at once through this very folding that puts it, as it were, on a double lane on the register of enunciation.

(*Translated by Beatrice Durand-Sendrail with Kristen Brookes*)

Notes

[1] Francesco Casetti makes this remark in his article 'Les yeux dans les yeux', about which I shall speak at length (see n. 6 for publication information). See Algirdas Julien Greimas and Joseph Courtés, *Semiotics and Language: An Analytical*

Dictionary, Bloomington: Indiana University Press, 1982, pp. 103-5.

2   See Gérard Genette, *Figures III* (Paris, 1972), p. 226. Genette grants the *narration* a status 'parallel' (to use his own term) to the status of linguistic enunciation. The latter, he says, has to do mostly with the feature of 'subjectivity in language', as Benveniste defined it.

3   I follow the terminology used by Catherine Parker in her translation of Tzvetan Todorov and Oswald Ducrot, *Dictionnaire des sciences encyclopédiques du langage* (Baltimore, 1979), except for *enonciateur*, which I translate by *enunciator*. Here is how the terminology of enunciation will be systematically translated in this paper:

	Enonciateur:	Enunciator
	Enonciataire:	Addressee
	Enoncé	Utterance

4   Albert Laffay, *Logique du cinéma (Création et spectacle)*, Paris, 1964, pp. 80-83.

5   Marc Vernet, 'Clignotements du noir-et-blanc', in Jacques Aumont and Jean-Louis Leutrat (eds.), *Théorie du film*, Paris, 1980, p. 232.

6   Especially in two texts, Casetti's article 'Les yeux dans les yeux', *Communications*, 38, 1983, special issue on 'Enonciation et cinéma', ed. Marc Vernet and Jean-Paul Simon, pp. 78-97; hereafter cited in the text as *YY* [published in the present volume]; and his book *Dentro lo sguardo (Il film e il suo spettatore)*, Milano, 1986; hereafter cited in the text as *DS*.

7   See Emile Benveniste, 'Les relations de temps dans le verbe français', *Bulletin de la Société de linguistique de Paris*, 54, 1959, pp. 69-82, republished in his *Problèmes de linguistique générale*, Paris, 1966, I, pp. 237-250. On p. 242 the author intro-duces 'discourse' after defining 'narration'; he mentions above all the spoken lan-guage, and immediately afterwards, the written text that reproduces or imitates the spoken text (novels' dialogue, letter exchange, and so on).

8   See n.7 concerning the written production that 'imitates' speech situations; in the same passage, Benveniste adds that a significant amount of written texts happen to be in the same case.

9   See Gérard Genette, 'Récit de paroles', in *Figures III*, pp. 189-203. Relating words is the only case where a literary text might operate by showing and no longer by telling, to quote the famous distinction by Anglo-Saxon critics. It only 'copies' (p. 190), writes down the words it wants to report. (That is why, in the logic of Genette's conceptions, one cannot talk seriously anymore about narration (*récit*) at this point of the text.)

10 Benveniste, *Problèmes de Linguistique générale*, I, p. 239.

11 See *DS*: 'enunciazione enunciata', p. 32; 'enunciazione diegetizzata', p. 38, 'pre-supposto', p. 40.

12   With of course the corresponding adjectives.

13   In English in the text. -tr.

14   Thus, for Benveniste, the definition of deictic words is that they organise the spatio-temporal in relationship to the I (those are therefore words whose signifier will change, the referent remaining the same). See Emile Benveniste, 'De la subjectivé dans le langage', in *Journal de Psychologie normale et pathologique*, 3, 1958, pp. 257-65; republished in *Problèmes de linguistique générale*, I, 258-66.

15   Not in all uses, for this example (see 'I am going to sit at the right of the driver').

16   See Gianfranco Bettetini, *La conversazione audiovisiva (Problemi dell'enunciazione filmica e televisa)* (Milan, 1984); hereafter cited in the text as *CA*.

17   See André Gaudreault, 'Système du récit filmique', lecture given a the University of Paris-III, 25 March 1987, pp. 17-18.

18   See André Gardies, 'Le vu et le su', *Hors Cadre*, 2, 1984, special issue on 'Ciné-narrables', ed. Michèle Langy, Marie-Claire Ropars, and Pierre Sorlin, pp. 45-64.

19   See André Gaudreault, p. 87 of 'Narration et monstration au cinéma', *Hors Cadre*, 2, pp. 87-98.

20   See David Bordwell, *Narration in the fiction film* (Madison, Wisconsin, 1985), ch. 2, pp. 16-26.

21   Quoted after Gaudreault, 'Système du récit filmique', pp. 3-4. On 26 Jan. 1983, in a letter to the review *Hors Cadre* and 22 Feb. of the same year, in a letter to Gaudreault himself, Genette asserted that film narration does not, properly speaking, exist, since film shows us stories that have been reconstituted (constituted) for this purpose; there is only narration when facts are signified in written or oral language.

22   Pierre Sorlin, 'A quel sujet?', in *Actes Semiotiques – Bulletin* 10, no. 41, 1987, a special issue on 'La subjectivité au cinéma, ed. Jacques Fontanille, pp. 40-51. The two quoted sentences are on pp. 43 and 49 respectively.

23   See François Jost, 'Discours cinématagraphique, Narration: deux façons d'envisager le problème de l'énonciation', in Aumont and Leutrat, pp. 121-31.

24   In a perspective broader than that of enunciative studies in the technical sense of the word, the notion of 'self-reflexivity in film' (where *self* seems to me redundant) has already been investigated in a very serious way by Reynold Humphries in Fritz Lang's American movies (*Fritz Lang, cinéaste américain* [Paris, 1980]) and also by a young Japanese scholar, Takeda Kiyoshi, in his analysis of theoretical writings of the 1920s and 1930s on film, in his thesis entitled *Archéologie du discours sur l'autoreflexivité au cinéma*, Paris, Ecole des Hautes Etudes en Sciences Sociales, 1986.

25 See François Jost, *L'Oeil-Caméra. Entre film et roman*, Lyon, 1987, p. 32, and 'Discours cinématographique, Narration'; and Jean-Paul Simon, *Le filmique et le comique*, Paris, 1979, p. 113. In this passage, Simon relies on some of my previous analyses (e.g. the tendency of grammatical markers to become part of the diegesis) in order to give them new developments.

26 See Dominique Chateau, 'Vers un modèle génératif du discours filmique', *Humanisme et entreprise*, 99, 1976, pp. 2-4. [Reprinted in this anthology]

27 See Marc Vernet, 'Regard à la caméra: figure de l'absence', *Iris*, 1, 2, 1983, ed. Jacques Aumont, Jean-Paul Simon, and Marc Vernet, pp. 39-40.

28 I made this point in 1964, in 'Cinéma: langue ou langage?', in my *Essais sur la signification au cinéma* (Paris, 1968), but without connecting it specifically to the problem of enunciation. François Jost rethinks the problem in a more precise way in 'Narration(s): en-deça et au delà', *Communications*, 38, 1983, p. 195.

29 See Edward Branigan, *Point of View in the Cinema. A Theory of Narration and Subjectivity in Classical Film*, Berlin: Mouton, 1984; hereafter cited in the text as *PV*.

30 Thus, the 'incorporeity' of the enunciator and addressee, in that they can both be reduced to textual positions; Bettetini expresses the idea from the other side, and with more caution.

31 In English in the text. -tr.

32 Esp. Ch. 4, 'La conversazione testuale', in *CA*, pp. 95 ff.

33 Francesco Casetti suggests several times in his book (pp. 20-21, 53-54, 57, 74, 145, 147, ff.), with both insistence and ambiguity, that the YOU would somehow be intermediary between the film and the world, that a constant come-and-go between the two would take place in the YOU. But in addition, the whole book correctly leaves the empirical spectator outside, so that one no longer sees who this mediator, that is called for and rejected, could be. Bettetini, by contrast, reminds us very simply (but this is useful) that the receptor's reactions cannot modify the text, contrary to what happens in spoken exchanges (see *CA*, p. 109).

34 In Italian 'farsi' and 'darsi'; see *DS*, p. 44, 79 ff.

35 See Gaudreault, 'Narration et monstration au cinéma', p. 93.

36 See pp. 198-99 of Jost, 'Narration(s): en deçà et au delà', *Communications*, 38, pp. 192-212.

37 That is fully accountable for the original narration, whether or not they are explicitly mentioned as characters; see Genette, *Figures III*, pp. 238-39.

38 See André Gaudreault, 'Système du récit filmique', working paper, beginning of

1987. In the meantime, this article appeared in revised form in an issue on 'Texte et médialité' in Jürgen Müller (ed.), *Mana*, Mannheim, 1987, pp. 267-78.

[39]   See Bordwell, *Narration in the Fiction Film*, pp. 61-62.

[40]   See Gaudreault, 'Système du récit filmique'. Between Gaudreault and myself, a quite rare phenomenon of crossed and almost simultaneous influence happened. He wrote the two 'Système du récit filmique' while taking part in a seminar where I was developing ideas close to the ones expressed here, but he put them in a different setting and gave them a new extension, so that I was myself led to borrow various theoretical elements from him.

[41]   With much talent and persuasive strength, Francesco Casetti shows his reader the paradox of enunciation: whatever its tricks are, enunciation always remains 'off-stage' (this is the author's expression), and it is only recognisable in the utterance. It is difficult to think of this situation and, even more difficult, to forget it. See esp. *YY*, p. 81.

THE AUTHORIZED NARRATIVE

François Jost

How often does one walk out of a cinema wondering whether such and such a detail in the shooting, the acting or the plot was *deliberate*? Whether, for instance, a piece of information provided by one sequence might be known to a character who was absent from it, or whether, on the contrary, it was an inconsistency in the narrative. Such questions, which regularly fuel conversations between friends, give rise to another, on the very nature of the narrative: how does the spectator distinguish between a paralepsis[1] and a mistake? What happens when an excess of information meets with no immediate and relevant interpretation? Theoretically, the answer is simple: for it to be called a paralepsis, the addressee must be able to attribute an intentional design to the excess of information; otherwise the latter is a mere mistake. It remains to be seen through what mechanism of attribution of intent one can tell the one from the other.

Authors on Credit

This is the well-known problem of the *unreliable* narrator, turned into a classic by Wayne Booth, and which is all too often reduced syncretically to phenomena of falsehood and irony, against the advice of the American theoretician, who also proposed examining the hypothesis of the mistake.[2] Where does one draw the line between truth and falsehood, mistakes and paralepses? These are the two distinct questions that must be solved, with the help of an analysis of *Une belle fille comme moi* (Truffaut, 1972).

In a bookshop, a young woman is looking for a thesis on women criminals. She is told that the book, which was to be published some years ago, never came out, and that no-one knows what became of its author. A flashback then follows: Stanislas Privine enters a jail in order to interview Camille Bliss, one of the prisoners. He prepares to make a tape recording of the interview of the young woman, but will soon become involved in her adventure.

After reading this summary, which has been deliberately reduced to the large narrative events, try to visualize it. Without being aware of it, you will reproduce some of the cognitive discrepancies that are present in the film.

The first of these is purely mechanical, for it originates in the faithful filmic transposition of the verbal narrative. *Le Chant de la sirène* (H. Farrell), which inspired

Une belle fille comme moi, is entirely narrated by the investigator. His intervention is minimal: apart from the narration of some elements necessary to the understanding of the story, he merely joins the transcripts of Camille's interviews end to end. The device of the tape recorder gives some plausibility to the phenomenal memory capacity implied by any *Manon Lescaut* type book within the book, in which one narrator repeats what another told him: two strictly focalized narrative levels are thus articulated in a perfectly natural way.

The filming of such an enunciative arrangement [*dispositif*] is bound to break its coherence straight away. For one of two things may happen: either the recording scene is shown without interruption, which runs the risk of boring the spectator; or it is replaced with a series of images and sounds. But then, as has already been said, a whole mass of audiovisual details add themselves to the indications given by the verbal narrative, which are inevitably more concise. This modal discrepancy is not a mistake, nor is it intentional: it is the only *constitutive paralepsis* in cinema: the image always shows infinitely more things than the words that it is meant to visualize.[3]

This gap gives rise to a second cognitive discrepancy between the knowledge of the intradiegetic addressee and that of the spectator. During the second interview, Camille describes her 'exploration' of her mother-in-law's (Isobel's) house: 'Chatting to the neighbours, I'd heard that Clovis's mother was literally rolling in it (...) The old bag always bunged her money into the old oven, the one in which she said she put her jams and her gherkins. I was pretty sure the money was lying in there, but I never discovered the trick. It would've meant pulling everything apart, and I didn't dare as long as she was alive'. While we hear her voice-over, we see her going down to the cellar, then the old 'bag' opening the oven, and at last Camille looking for something inside.

This, at first sight, is but an illustration of the young woman's words, which means, on a pragmatic level – once we have accepted the constitutive paralepsis – that the visual information offered to the spectator is, in theory, the same as that communicated to the intradiegetic addressee, which the spectator also hears, incidentally, from the voice-over. This illustration is so accurate that we are even shown images of Isobel, the mother-in-law, that no one has ever seen. However, this deliberate step-by-step visualization becomes less convincing in the rest of the flash-back: Camille tampers with the oven door, turning it into a potential guillotine. Not a word is said about it, and nothing suggests that the investigator knows about this shot. Nor does he allude to it when questioning the young woman at the end of her story.

The semantic interpretation of this gap between image and sound is not given in advance. The sudden withdrawal of the voice can be an explicit lie on the part of the narrator – the young woman – as well as a paralepsis designed to give us more information than is available to the intradiegetic addressee; a way, in other words, of endowing the narrative with a spectatorial focalization.

The third cognitive discrepancy arises as a result of the gap between what the character says and what we see. Thus, Camille gives Stanislas a pair of gloves, claiming that she has knitted them for him. He later learns, through one of the supervisors, that she has been punished for stealing gloves from her cellmate. Here, the matching of the context enables us to infer that she has told a *lie*.

The fourth discrepancy occurs when we mentally attempt to match the respective knowledge of different narrators and their perceptual experiences. As has been seen in the case of the novel, only a case of hyperamnesia can account for the literal rendering by one first degree narrator of the story told by a second narrator within his own narrative. Much more is needed in cinema: from the moment when the metanarrative is visualized, it must be assumed that the first degree narrator, who has received the product of a speech act, is capable of transforming it into a perceivable act. He not only renders the narrative, but also a visual and auditive field, which is a lot for information that was transmitted by hearsay! And yet, it is precisely this sort of acrobatics that is being offered to us in *Une belle fille comme moi*: Camille *tells* us that the rat-catcher *told* her how he had found her husband and her lawyer in the house where she had tried to murder him, and we view the scene through the eyes of the rat-catcher. This internally focalized narrative, supposedly filtered through the young woman's mind, is now embedded in another character's viewpoint, which, by definition, she cannot possibly share. This visualization also results in a generalized paralepsis, which is amplified even further when, at the end of the film, Stanislas suddenly remembers the episode of the bread oven, and the shots illustrating Camille's narrative (the old woman, the young woman's hand tampering with the door) which nothing permitted us to consider as being his own interpretation of Camille's words, since the scene had seemed to elude him at the time (this is, in fact, a superimposition of a paralepsis upon a paralipsis[4]).

The question is no longer to know how such filmic phenomena are understood, but how (and why) they are accepted. Once again, this is complicated considerably by the nature of the film as a double narrative: if a gap arises between images and verbal utterances, should one trust the latter rather than the former? This type of question can, of course, be eluded by the assumption that the image, by definition, cannot lie,[5] or by the *a priori* supposition of a trustworthy impersonal narrator as a support for fiction.[6] Such certainties are, however, easily shaken. *L'Année dernière à Marienbad* is a good enough proof of this. The character, *X*, occasionally struggles against the image, trying to bend it to suit his discourse. When, for instance, he tries to persuade *A* that he entered her room, he keeps repeating that the door was shut, in a desperate attempt to erase the image of the open door.

Does this mean that we side with the image? Probably not, for it is difficult to decide whether it represents another version of the event, that of *A* resisting *X*'s attempt to seduce her, or the 'real' version of facts. The same applies to *L'Homme qui ment* (Robbe-Grillet, 1968): in a film which shows a man standing up again after being killed, in which one hears a woodpecker over an image of glass crashing on the ground, in which German soldiers wear Lorraine crosses on their uniforms, in which the narrator says: 'The first time I came to the village, I went straight to the inn, which was also empty, as usual at this early hour...' while we are shown a room packed with people, it is difficult to determine whether this gap is an ironic distance introduced by the implicit narrator, as might be suggested by the many contradictions inherent in the diegetic world, or whether it is due instead to the personality of the character on screen, whom the title of the film advises us not to believe.

Audiovisual distortions are, of course, very different in the case of the lies in *Une belle fille comme moi*. Bernadette Lafont's style of acting, her retorts, the matching of her utterances with those of other characters, draw a portrait of Camille as a liar. The structure of the diegetic world is a stable one, and nothing urges us to question the stability of this psychological characterization. Her utterances are therefore interpreted by the spectator like those of anyone he might meet in real life. 'Hypotheses deducted from perceptive experience are generally very firm; the firmness of hypotheses founded on someone else's sayings is proportionate to the confidence one has in the speaker'.[7] Some sequences illustrate the typical behaviour of the character (as in the anecdote of the gloves) and play the part, for the spectator, of perceptual experiences enabling him to construct hypotheses on the truth of the speaker-narrator's utterances, and therefore on her psychology. It is such hypotheses that will allow us later to interpret certain audiovisual discrepancies as being proof that Camille is lying. This mechanism, of course, is only made possible by the deliberate coherence of this particular type of diegesis.

In order to attribute the responsibility for discrepancies between image and sound to a narrative authority, it is therefore necessary to use a criterion similar to the one defined by Lubomir Dolezel in the context of the *authentification* of fictional worlds in literature. In an extension of Booth's theory, according to which the degree of confidence on the part of the reader is in keeping with the norms of the text,[8] Dolezel distinguishes between two forms of narrative texture: in the first one, which is a narrative in the first person, or *er* form, all of the narrator's utterances are taken to be true, and the fictional world presented to us is entirely authentic. In the second form, or *skaz* form, the narrator does not take his function seriously: we are confronted with contra-dictory utterances, jumps from the first to the third person, from a limited to an omnis-cient perspective, in such a way that everything can be questioned at any moment, including the guarantee of authenticity constituted by the narrator himself: the fictional world is entirely inauthentic. A globally authentic fictional world such as the one in *Une belle fille comme moi* can, nevertheless, reveal discrepancies that cannot be attributed to the explicit narrator, and for which the implicit narrator is not accountable either. Apart from the 'constitutive paralepsis', which it is best to ignore inasmuch as it results from the very nature of the filmic material, we are left with these two well-known narratological infringements affecting the episode of the bread oven, with the following consequences for the narrative: during the visualization of a narrative reduced to the viewpoint of the character-narrator (Camille), an episode which has not been evoked verbally, and of which the intradiegetic addressee is probably unaware, is however, at a later stage, included in the latter's perceptions, due to a repetition of shots that he cannot possibly have seen as we see them. The rat-catcher's reminiscences embedded in Camille's story, as well as other passages that need not be mentioned here, result in similar contradictions.

As has just been said, such infringements are not attributable to the contra-dictory structure of the diegesis. Here, on the contrary, every sequence aims to partici-pate in the solving of an enigma (what has brought Camille to this?) and the film, by and large, is presented as authentic fiction. What, then, can explain such contradictions within the narrative? The relevant question now is not *how*, but *why* such phenomena occur. Are we confronted with a paralepsis or a mistake? The answer to this question will determine whether or not we accept a given phenomenon. Indeed, only two solu-tions seem open to the spectator: either he considers the phenomenon in question as unconscious and unplanned, carelessness, in other words, on Truffaut's part, or he at-tributes some communicative intention to the author (or does not ask himself any ques-tions, which is another way of accepting one of the two solutions *a priori*).

If one supports the second hypothesis, it is clear that no type of argumenta-tion on the coherence of the film can justify the contradictions, and that the latter can only be motivated by the intention to inform: the author intends to draw our attention to narrative hypotheses – Camille's character, her plans, Stanislas's gullibility – and this intention prevails over any concern with narratological coherence. Numerous examples illustrate the importance of this guiding principle in the overall structure of the film. To quote just one more: at the end of the film, Stanislas, who is in jail, is watching a live television programme in which Camille, now famous, is launching a programme of social rehabilitation of the area where she used to live, which will entail the destruction of the compromising bread oven. Stanislas discovers that she is accompanied by his own lawyer. He lowers his eyes, and the camera follows his glance, revealing the fact that the couple are holding hands. The movement of the camera, in a most unlikely fashion, has obeyed the movement of the character's eyes, powerless though Stanislas may be. The only intention here is to inform the spectator as quickly as possible that the story is at an end, and to make him laugh.

According to Dan Sperber and Deirdre Wilson, when communication is not reciprocated, the communicator may suppose that what he is trying to pass on automatically becomes obvious to both parties: such is the case of the journalist, the teacher, etc. If the communicator does not have such authority, he merely needs to subject his informative intention to a criterion of credibility. Understandably, the author's situation is always likely to oscillate between these two poles. Because of the precarious artistic status of film, the acceptance of narratological infringements is always subjected to a second factor: either the author gives priority to the intention to inform, and the film loses some artistic value, or he makes it artistically coherent, possibly at the expense of narrative communication. The structure of *Une belle fille comme moi* can, in fact, receive both types of interpretation: either narrative coherence predominates, and the infringements are paralepses committed in the name of some superior motive, communication of the story and satisfaction of the spectator; or artistic coherence is what guides the reception of the film, and the infringements are considered to be unworthy mistakes on the part of an author who should know his material. There is no need to choose between these two hypotheses, and as many supporters could undoubtedly be found for either. Only the following conclusions matter to us at this stage: first of all, the spectator's confidence in the narration is not limited to what enables him to construct the text, as Wayne Booth, and later Shlomith Rimmon-Kenan, would have it: if, as the latter wrote, 'the text makes it difficult to decide whether the narrator is trustworthy – and to what extent?',[9] it is because this decision depends on a construction by the implied author which, on the one hand, exceeds the text, and on the other hand, partly depends on the addressee's judgement.

Which exceeds the text, because the implied author, far from identifying with the narratological fact, like a disincarnate mega-narrator, a pure paper being, or to some obscure essence of the 'real' author, takes on numerous meanings constructed from the paratext as well as from the various epitexts (such as articles and televised interviews of the author). Before referring to authority, the term 'author' means 'someone who increases' (from *augere*, 'to increase') and more specifically, who increases confidence, credit, in other words, the salesman. The justification of this fact is, therefore, not to be sought in metaphysics, but in economics, as the times in which we are living ought to remind us. The interpretation of *L'Homme qui ment* and *Une belle fille comme moi* is also largely dependent on my feelings about the *authors* constructed by Robbe-Grillet or Truffaut through their interviews.

Which partly depends on the addressee's judgement, based on an in-built cultural capital (Bourdieu), including some knowledge of cinema, films and critiques, as well as a single act of reception, involving the addressee's observation and his attention.

We know that according to Booth, the implied author was to be defined as a 'second self' of the author, in whom the novel made us believe. In order to assess the usefulness of this concept, Genette postulates that this image of the author 'is only worth mentioning if it is unfaithful, because inaccurate' – faithfulness, in this case, meaning mathematical equality – finally concluding that there is no scope for a third authority other than the narrator or the real author.[10] In a recent book, Seymour Chatman rehabilitates the Implied Author.[11] I shall devote some time to his argument, in order to show how my 'constructed author' differs both from the 'real' author and from the *implied author*.

According to Chatman, the latter is neither an image, nor even a human representative of the real author, but the recording, the trace, of the textual invention that the reader constantly notices as he reads the text, if he can read between the lines. The *implied author* is immanent in the text, a textual object 'responsible for the textual project', inventing the discourse and the characters, and, at the same time, he is inferred by the reader, who has little freedom to find anything else in the text than what *awaits* him.

Why should this authority be necessary, according to the American theoretician? Three of these arguments are worth retaining. First of all, the example of the Hollywood film shows that a large number of real authors in a film does not prevent it from giving an overall impression of unity. This means that we postulate the existence of a single auctorial source, far removed from the reality of production.

Similarly, when trying to understand an advertisement, we are not interested in the decision-makers' and advertising agents' intentions, but only in the textual intention which dominates the world being represented, and for which the *implied author* is solely responsible.

As for the ideology of a text, is it not true that its potential difference with the author's own ideology shows the necessary existence of an intermediate agent? This argument is so commonplace that it needs no further development.

The idea that the writer's own self is partly present in his texts, that this self is not always that of the empirical individual, is one thing (Proust showed it better than anybody). The idea that the *implied author* is necessary every time that the reader or spectator, not knowing the genesis of the texts, has to rely on inferences in order to construct an author, is another. From a narratological point of view, what matters is not that the text might give an image of the author in contradiction with that of the real author (that is a problem for critics), but the fact that the reader's construction of the author affects his understanding of the narrative, as was seen in the case of the narratological mistake or infringement. But we see no reason why the view which I propose should compel us to consider the *implied author* as an intermediary authority between the author and the narrator, especially if we situate him within the text. How, indeed, can a purely textual authority be endowed with free will? When Seymour Chatman declares that 'the difference between *telling* and *showing* then comes down simply to the implied author's choice of signs',[12] does he refer to the real author, as one might imagine him through his writings, or to a textual authority suddenly endowed with an anthropomorphic form of autonomy?

The contradictions arising from Chatman's formulations are due to the fact that he sometimes situates the concept of *implied author* within the text, as tradition would have it, and sometimes within the spectator. This alternation rests on the rather optimistic assumption that this agent is 'reconstructed by the audience in each reading'.[13] However, although we may need a constructed author in order to explain some phenomena, there is no need to conceive him as an interface between the author and the receiver. The constructed author is the author as seen *by the spectator*: through the text, through his own capacity to perceive and understand, through the author's public manifestations, his critiques, etc. It is the diversity of this lateral knowledge that explains the possible variations in the narratological interpretation of a single narrative.

Trial of Intent

When discussing the function of the voice within the narrative, Genette is aware of the fact that he may be transgressing the boundaries of narratology by examining the relationship between the narrator and the author.[14] By showing that the border between a modal alteration and a mistake requires that the author should be taken into account, I have shown myself to be in favour of his full integration among the explanatory concepts of the narrative. I shall presently go further than this, in maintaining that the construction of the author can become, in the case of a factual narrative, the transcendental condition [in the Kantian sense] of the reception of the audiovisual document as a narrative, and even as an illocutionary act.

Since photography implies no actual history, the image frozen on film is generally considered as being outside the narrative. This is the theory of Metz's 'Notes

Toward a Phenomenology of Narrative',[15] but also that of André Gaudreault, according to whom the absence of any motion or tranformation in the frozen shot exclude it from the field of the narrative. Yet the mere comparison of a photograph with that slide-like effect created by the frozen shot shows us that the interpretation of this type of filmic image largely depends on the construction of the enunciator by the spectator.

The diegetization of photography involves my knowledge of the world or of the time when the shot was taken. In that sense, any narrative based on photography springs from some lateral knowledge, from 'narrative extrapolations' or from the imagination, and thus, from the verbal discourse that accompanies it.[16] If this way of creating narrative can indeed occur in a film using photography in a punctual manner, the freezing of the shot can also refer directly to the narrative, not through the content of what is being represented, but through the speech act inherent in this transformation of the filmic material: this is of course what happens with Godard, when the frozen shot constitutes a forceful statement on the representative status of the film by underlining the artifice of filmic movement. In that sense, it is not so much an assertive as a declarative act: 'I declare that I am making a film'.

This interpretation largely depends on what type of intention one attributes to the director. By not knowing Godard, or at least by not taking his concept of cinema into account, I run the risk of attributing this type of effect to any odd motive or, perhaps, to an attempt at a gratuitous act, devoid of any communicative intention, a self-contained pleasure (an argument which has been heard all too often!).

It must be stressed that the speech act is not detected at the level of the image itself, as may have been suggested by the hypothesis, put forward by classic semiology, according to which the animated image in itself, regardless of its organisation into a filmic document, is condemned to stating and asserting the presence of what was – or is, in the case of live pictures – in front of the camera. Viewed from that angle, different shots could only be distinguished from one another by their respective illocutionary *force*: whereas some could be seen as strong utterances, involving the speaker's commitment as to the existence of a situation which he has witnessed through the image (so much so that the absence of any pictures of war may make us doubt its reality), others would present reality through a sheer act of mediation, lessening the presence of a speaker and, in fact, their own illocutionary value. This variation in the perception of illocutionary force may explain, as I was already maintaining several years ago, why the filmic utterance, as a phenomenon, inspires such different reactions in the audience.[17]

The application to the image of the theory of speech acts raises two problems: the first of these arises from the fact that images, unlike language-systems [*langue*], contain no real 'markers' of illocutionary force, indicating the act accomplished by the author of the utterance (the visual devices enabling us to distinguish between dream and reality, fantasy and reality, etc., in works of fiction, are more like markers with a propositional content).[18] Thus, a series of pictures presented as a documentary can conceal a 'directive' act behind the assertive act. A novel, treated in its entirety – and not through the medium of a single utterance of the 'Once upon a time...' type – is, in fact, less remote than one may think from this essentially vague status of visual acts, as will be shown later.

Basically it is, of course, the assimilation of the image to a speech act which causes problems. We can just as easily argue that the film is trying to *tell* us something, as we can choose to perceive the referential dimension of the image, at the expense of its discursive aspect. In any case, it is only when the audiovisual document is treated as a whole that the notion of speech act is at all relevant. The same actually applies to novels, for the apparent Searlian paradox of 'the author conveys a serious speech act through the performance of the pretended speech acts which constitute the work of fiction'[19] is only a paradox if one admits that a text is a series of speech acts. Indeed, when Searle maintains that in telling a story, one pretends to 'make a series of assertions' about a situation, or that the narration pretends to be a reference, he limits his reasoning to the level of the sentence. This is also the angle from which he views the following extract from *Anna Karenina*: 'Happy families are all happy in the same way, unhappy families unhappy in their separate, different ways', concluding that this is a real, serious assertion, not a fictional assertion. This approach is in keeping with the refusal to consider the narrative as a specific speech act, though not so much with the idea, temporarily adopted by Searle, that the text is to be treated as a *whole*: 'to identify a text as a novel, a poem, or even as a text is already to make a claim about the author's intentions'.[20]

Such intentions, however, do not rest on isolated assertions, but on the text as a whole, which should not be assimilated to a 'series' of assertions that could simply be put end to end in order to determine the status of the text.

Genette supports this idea when he maintains that the 'whole is more fictitious than the parts'. It remains to be seen whether by 'pretending to make assertions (about fictitious people), the novelist actually achieves something else: the creation of a work of fiction'.[21] I am inclined to think that the auctorial act usually implies the following indirect aspect: in order to achieve a global speech act (be it assertive, directive or expressive), the author must achieve a multitude of (assertive or non-assertive) speech acts, to which the text cannot be reduced.

The novelist's first and foremost function may not be, however, to 'create a work of fiction'.[22] The 'fictional intention'[23] of the author might even be, in some cases, secondary to the speech act that he has in mind. When the 'message' precedes the very act of writing (as is the case in the *roman à thèse*), and is equally well expressed by various genres (essay, novel, play), can it not be argued that the text is primarily a directive act, necessitating an arrangement of feigned assertions? If this is true, a work of fiction should not be reduced to a fictional intention. Writing a work of fiction might – and ought to – result from the desire to write, as much as the desire to write fiction. These two intentions are not necessarily interchangeable (on this point, I agree with Jean-Marie Schaeffer, who remarks that texts can 'be composed of several different intentional acts'[24]). It should be up to the reader, or spectator in the case of film, to determine the communicative intention relevant to the reception of the document, with the help of the generic labelling. As was said earlier, this applies even more to the factual narrative, in which the identification of the communicative intention contributes to constructing the meaning. The case of Ceaucescu's trial is an obvious example: initially, the freeze-frames of the dictator and his wife were considered of no significance by the French television reporter, as if they had been due to transmission problems (which can result in similar effects) or to a lack of any pictures of the judges. The fact is that no one suspected the Rumanian people, in the throes of liberation, of any 'impure' intention, such as the intention to 'manipulate' images. At that stage, these shots, which were defined as 'fixed shots' rather than 'freeze-frames', could appear to be 'pauses', breaks in the visual narrative. But as soon as it became clear (within minutes, for the more alert viewer) that these freeze-frames were replacing moving images that had been censored, the absence of any motion was read as a proof that the document had been narrated, and was a global speech act, imputable to an organising authority, and in no way similar to the anonymous testimony of a surveillance camera.

The attribution of this freezing of the image to a programmed intention on the part of the communicator can of course have important narratological consequences, since it does, in fact, transform the broadcast into a narrative, manipulated by an anonymous author (reporter, television channel, political leader). Here, the term *paralipsis* becomes a euphemism for censorship. The recent events in Rumania have shown how quickly the same images could undergo a change of status in the addressee's mind, depending on the degree of confidence in the constructed author, the real difficulty being the problem of matching the latter with a real author.

The Constructed Author
If indeed, as was said earlier, the image contains no marker indicating its illocutionary force, the speech act implied by the audiovisual document remains to be determined (which is another way of saying that images do not speak for themselves).

The interpretation of this document is, therefore, organised into the three following phases.

1. The 'auctorialization' of the audiovisual document: I must assume that the image-sound complex being presented to me has been transmitted by 'beings more or less like myself', otherwise their communicative status is beyond me, and I am viewing the material in a state of pure aphasia[25] (I would have preferred to use the simpler term 'authorization' to describe this process, but none of its accepted meanings refer to what I am trying to convey, hence this neologism, which avoids any ambiguity). This is true, as has already been seen, on a factual level, but also in the case of non-figurative images: some effects obtained by scratching the surface of the film can be mistaken for defects, until their process of production has been identified. Similarly, *Arnulf Rainer* (Peter Kubelka, 1957-1960) is only a succession of white and black images unless one knows that the director is paying tribute to the paintings of his friend.[26]

Saying that the filmic utterance always belongs to the field of metalanguage – as I used to maintain, along with Metz, amongst others – is merely a way of saying that through reflexive audiovisual phenomena, a film refers to filmic language before referring to its transmitter. It does not, however, endow the filmic text with any discursive autonomy. By looking into the text itself for an explanation of this referential property of the film, we move towards an anthropomorphic type of analysis; if the text is not in itself responsible for any of its effects, the spectator will, of course, turn to its guarantor for an interpretation. Who is the author, and what does he want to tell us?

2. The identification of the author. Although this poses no problem with diaries or autobiographies (reference to the paratext is sufficient evidence), the author of an audiovisual document is disguised. In the case of journalistic material, repeated mentions of 'authorized sources' remind us – should we have forgotten it – that everyone, if not anyone, can become an *author*. The television viewer's 'task' often consists, of course, in identifying the author of the document being viewed. Is it the presenter? The press agency who transmitted the news? Or whoever wrote the news report sent to the agency? When viewing the pictures of an Iraqi mosque destroyed during the Gulf War, it was sometimes very difficult to choose between these three solutions; and yet this choice was crucial to the third phase.

This is a complex operation, not only because it depends on our lateral knowledge around the film or document, but also because it implies an act of nomination. Who is the author of *Une belle fille comme moi*? Is it Truffaut? The author of *Jules et Jim*, the New Wave film director, or a director who would have liked to be a novelist? The auctorial construction can vary depending on my choosing between a name and a specific description.

3. *The recognition of the intention.* As Roger Odin puts it, 'the institution determines the way in which the spectator produces *the image of the director*',[27] and the various paratexts also play a part in the auctorial construction. If, for instance, the 'topic' of a news bulletin is given the title of *narrative* rather than that of *report*, we immediately view the speaking authority as a narrator rather than a reporter, which implies a distance from reality and a transformation at a superior level, instructing the spectator to interiorize it.[28] In this respect, the reasons why *La Sortie des usines Lumière* cannot be considered as a narrative is the purely descriptive nature of the title, and the classification of the film as a *view*. Should the same film be retitled *Nous vaincrons*, the spectator would quickly find, in the profilmic material, the elements of a latent conflict, as can be found in the opening of *La Grève*. The same exercise could be tried with *Départ en vacances...* As for the process of identification of the author, it influences the hypothesis that the spectator formulates whenever a narrative contradiction arises, as in the case of the paralepsis. This hypothesis depends on the constructed author, on the spectator's confidence in him, and on the intention he attributes to him as a result of this degree of confidence. We expect different things from a 'literature lover', from the 'pope' of the New Wave who abuses the rules of credibility, or from an author who has become a part of the history of cinema.

On the other hand, by glorifying the role of Rumanian television, turning it into the main force behind the 'revolution', the French journalists were, in their own way, rewriting the script of the utterance and recasting the parts: the people invading the studios or fighting in the streets were presented as the only speakers, while the audio-visual document was stripped of its status as a speech act, based on live broadcasts and the *topos* of raw images, as on the reference to retransmissions from Rumanian television by French channels. The image of a transparent enunciator, humble mediator of the people, was thus constructed. It is easy to understand the disillusionment of the French journalists, when confronted with the irrefutable fact that this constructed enunciator had nothing in common with the textual reality of the manipulation of images. This example shows, once again, that if the analysis is to provide any explanation of the communicative facts, we must refrain from assuming any *a priori*, intangible order of narrative elements. The *a priori* determination of the narrative hierarchy of enunciative authorities offers no explanation for the reception of the product.

In this respect, the narrative authorities seem to be largely influenced by my image of them, which I have constructed from a multitude of clues, some of them outside the document: details on the transmitter's behaviour, viewing of other documents by the same transmitter, etc. Still on the example of Rumania, the existence of several versions of the Ceaucescu trial has reinforced the feeling that we were being 'taken for a ride', and that the speaking authority who emitted these documents was not only a narrator, but a lying narrator.

As I said before, we only understood progressively that what we had perceived to be the statement of a reality – the pictures of a trial – was in fact a plea expressed through the bias of the assertive value of the information. A plea for compassion, understanding, the perlocutionary effect was to become an arousal of pity, even support for the rebels' cause. This indirectness is what helps to turn information into propaganda. Similarly, the news report, broadcast during the Gulf War, on an Iraqi mosque reduced to ruins, could easily slide from a message of the type 'I am keeping you informed of American action' to 'I urge you to condemn the American aggressor', depending on whether the author of the document was a French journalist or the Iraqi army. The author, clearly suspicious of the illocutionary capacity of images, had removed any potential ambiguity by also showing a woman whose comments allowed no possible doubt on this matter.

Needless to say, the real initiator of such a document – whose identity is not always easy to determine – is not addressing a viewer analysing the images with the detached approach of a semiologist, but rather an addressee whose reaction is more influenced by affective than by cognitive factors. The addressee himself is also constructed, and only partly corresponds to a real audience.

There is no other way of discovering the author's purpose than the examination of any explicit traces of his intentions. This apparent truism should provide a basis for the abundant philology-inspired research on films presently being published. We should, indeed, refrain from mistaking the intention inferred by the spectator from the document for the real intention (journalistic criticism is in the habit of creating this confusion); also from believing that the study of iconography (such as the ressemblance between a certain scene from *Ivan the Terrible* and another filmic sequence) always reveals the author's intentions. Finally, we must remember that the intention may not actually be expressed anywhere: in this respect, there is an essential difference between the factual documents broadcast by the media and those accompanied by a paratext or rough version, the study of which can lead to a detection of the auctorial intention.

Apart from the rather embarrassing analogy with written material, another disadvantage of the persistent notion of filmic text is that it places on a single footing what I have referred to as audiovisual documents, for lack of a better expression: films, news reports, television programmes, as if they were all simple mechanical objects produced by the same enunciative mechanism. On the contrary, the narratological hypothesis on the author shows that an interpretation of these 'documents' implies their transformation into human objects, understood according to inferred human intentions, and therefore classified differently. If we do not watch images in the same way, depending on whether we expect information or entertainment, contemplation or emotion, is it not because we imagine a multiplicity of voices, and not a homogeneous enunciation, as the origin of the film?

(*Translated by Claudine Tourniaire*)

Notes

1   [Editor's note: for a definition of the term paralepsis, and its difference from paralipsis, see footnote 4.]
2   Wayne Booth, 'Distance et point de vue', *Poétique*, 4, 1970, p. 521.
3   To this constitutive paralepsis, Truffaut adds a strange handling of the tape-recorder convention: during the transition from the first verbal narration to its illustration, the camera zooms onto the recording equipment, which then seems to emit the sounds – and images – of the following scene (the accidental death of the father)... as if the machine was rendering a narration which has not yet been told!
4   [Editor's note: Here, Jost is referring to a distinction made by Gerard Genette in *Figures III*, Paris: Editions du Seuil, 1972, translated by Jane E. Lewin, *Narrative Discourse: An Essay in Method*, Ithaca, New York: Cornell University Press, 1980. In a discussion of what he terms *alterations* (momentary, or isolated infractions – those that do not bring the whole text into question), Genette notes that two basic types of alterations exist:

> The two conceivable types of alterations consist either of giving less information than is necessary in principle, or of giving more than is authorized in principle in the code of focalization governing the whole. The first type bears a name in rhetoric ...: we are dealing with a lateral omission or *paralipsis*. The second does not yet bear a name; we will christen it *paralepsis*, since here we are no longer dealing with leaving aside (-lipsis, from *leipo*) information that should be taken up (and given), but on the contrary with taking up (-lepsis, from *lambano*) and giving information that should be left aside. (*Narrative Discourse*, p. 195)]

5   This is also maintained by Sarah Kozloff, *Invisible Storytellers*, Berkeley: University of California Press, 1988, p. 114.
6   Robert Burgoyne, 'The Cinematic Narrator; The Logic and Pragmatics of Impersonal Narration', *Journal of Film and Video*, vol. 42, 1, 1990.

7   Dan Sperber and Deirdre Wilson, *La pertinence*, p. 122. [*Relevance: Communication and Cognition*, Oxford: Basil Blackwell, 1986].

8   'Pour une typologie des mondes fictionnels', in Herman Parret and H.-G. Ruprecht (eds.) *Exigences et perspectives de la sémiologie, Recueil d'hommage pour A.-J. Greimas*, Amsterdam-Philadelphia: Benjamins, 1985.

9   Shlomith Rimmon-Kenan, *Narrative Fiction*, London and New York: Methuen, 1983, p. 103.

10   *Nouveaux discours du récit*, p. 95 ff.

11   Seymour Chatman, *Coming to Terms*, Ithaca and London: Cornell University Press, 1990.

12   *Ibid*, p. 114.

13   *Ibid*, p. 75.

14   *Fiction et diction*, Paris: Le Seuil, 1991, p. 79.

15   In Christian Metz, *Film Language: A Semiotics of the Cinema*, trans. Michael Taylor, New York: Oxford University Press, 1974, pp. 16-28.

16   On this point, see *L'image précaire*, in particular p. 80 ff.

17   See 'Discours cinématographique, narration: deux façons d'envisager le problème de l'énonciation', in Jacques Aumont and Jean-Louis Leutrat (eds.), *Théorie du film*, Paris: Ed. Albatros, 1980.

18   On this point, see John R. Searle, *Speech Acts*, Cambridge: Cambridge University Press, 1969.

19   Searle, *Expression and Meaning* Cambridge: Cambridge University Press, 1979, p. 75.

20   *Ibid.*, p. 66.

21   *Fiction et diction*, p. 60.

22   *Ibid.*, p. 109.

23   *Ibid.*, p. 60.

24   *Qu'est-ce qu'un genre littéraire?*, Paris: Seuil, 1989, p. 161.

25   This is Searle's lesson: 'When I take a noise or a mark on a piece of paper to be an instance of linguistic communication, as a message, one of the things I must assume is that the noise or mark was produced by a being or beings *more or less like myself* and produced with certain kinds of intentions. If I regard the noise or mark as a natural phenomenon like the wind in the trees or a stain on the paper, I exclude it from the class of linguistic communication, even though the noise or mark may be indistinguishable from spoken or written words' *Speech Acts*, pp. 16-17; my emphasis. It is worth mentioning that Jaap Lintvelt is one of the few narratologists to include anthropomorphism among his criteria of analysis ('Une approche typologique', *Protée*, vol. 19, No 1, *Narratologies, Etats des lieux*, ed. François

Jost, Chicoutimi: Université du Québec, winter 1991, p. 11).

26 As Michel Contat puts it in the work quoted (p. 24), 'we may label as 'writing authority' the highly complex combination of affects, conscious or unconscious intentions, systematic bifurcations, psychosocial factors, seduction strategies, relationships with the literary institution, being activated by the writer; he remains, nevertheless, a being capable of making a decision, who committed a certain configuration of words to paper and then modified it'.

27 'Pour une sémio-pragmatique du cinéma', *Iris*, vol. 1, No 1, 1983. [Reprinted in this anthology]

28 On the subject of the 'instruction', see Roger Odin, ibid.

THE POLYPHONIC FILM AND
THE SPECTATOR

FRANÇOIS JOST

What we call 'literary narratology' was born in the 1970s, inspired by Gérard Genette, in a period dominated by what I would call the optimism of Roman Jakobson's model of communication. According to this model, a transmitter sends a message to a receiver who only needs to decode the message correctly in order to discover what the transmitter has encoded. In fact, within this framework the transmitter and the receiver have little importance, since in the communication process the message or the text as a whole passes, in Jakobson's words, 'from hand to hand without being altered in the process'.

The emerging film semiology of the 1960s proceeded in the same way. In spite of its declared desire to 'understand how we understand', every act of understanding is assimilated to a simple decoding process: to understand a film is to put into use codes that the semiologist has strived to find, classify and articulate. This emphasis on the code, even if it is the fashion of the period, also has another reason. In order to avoid being identified with a criticism which is too eager to speak about the world rather than about film, it is necessary to distance oneself from the world. If the reader constantly stumbles over the words, if he always pays attention to the text as a text, the spectator has an irrepressible tendency to pass through the images in order to reach reality. Even the most experienced semiologists sometimes watch a television programme or a documentary and only think of what is being shown, neglecting for the moment the way in which it is shown and forgetting even the presence of the camera.

The cinematic image, an analogy of the reality it records as well as a trace of this reality, or, in Peirce's terms, icon and index, seems sometimes to tell itself. Hence, in order to fight against the impressionism and the subjectivity of the critics, the only solution is to prove that the cinema is not the world. This is the concern of Metz in his *Film Language*, where he states: 'What distinguishes a discourse from the rest of the world, and by the same token contrasts it with the "real" world, is the fact that a discourse must necessarily be produced by someone ..., whereas one of the characteristics of the world is that it is uttered by no one'.[1]

Hence, in the late 1970s, some scholars, myself included, were concerned with determining whether the marks of subjectivity referring to a discourse may be recognised in a film. As we know, thanks to Benveniste, discourse is characterised less by being in opposition to the world than by the fact that it refers to a speaker identifiable through the deictic signs.

After having followed this first course of research, I personally reached the conclusion that filmic discourse is distinct from linguistic discourse for several reasons:

First thesis: filmic discourse has no equivalent to the deixis of natural language. There is only the enunciative use of signs, and not enunciative signs as such: the black screen, when it interrupts narrative continuity in Marguerite Duras' films, refers to discourse. If the black screen is part of a scene where someone has just turned off all the lights (as in *Manhattan Murder Mystery*, Woody Allen, 1993), it belongs to the story. (In passing, let me say that this feeling of filmic enunciation is for me a childhood memory: I could never tolerate those scenes where, after the hero had turned off the light and gone to bed, one could still see all the furniture around him as if it were still daylight.)

Second thesis, which follows from the first: cinematic discourse is much less a question of person, if I may put it that way, than the conviction on the part of the spectator that someone is 'speaking cinema' to him. Cinema invades the diegesis. Cinematic enunciation is first of all a metalanguage.

Third thesis: the feeling of enunciation varies. This invasion of cinema into the diegesis is, contrary to Descartes' *bon sens*, rather unevenly apportioned. For some, it starts with a light which is turned off, for others, with a black screen...

The second thesis leads us to a radical consequence: if enunciation is first of all a metalanguage, if discourse is characterized by the fact that 'the film talks to us about itself, about cinema, or about the position of the spectator',[2] it may be 'impersonal' and does not in any way imply a theory of narrative *instances*. This is the position of the later Metz, who in a sense is in opposition to the Metz of the 1960s, who deduced from cinematic discourse that someone relates it.

However, this thesis, which I myself defended, has revealed its limits: in fact, because for such a long time they have regarded film as a neutral object which the spectator must try to understand without ever involving himself in what he sees, film narratologists have come to neglect all human presence. Produced by machines, film itself would be no more than a mechanism understood by human machines. The fear of anthropomorphism has had consequences for the theory of cinematic enunciation: after the *auteur*, it is the narrator who has been suspected of carrying with him too many human connotations, and enunciation has been understood as an 'impersonal' process (Bordwell and Metz).

Of course I do not defend the return to impressionism, to emotional criticism, or to the abandonment of all semio-narratological research. But what bothers me in this reification of the film is that it leads inevitably to the anthropomorphism that it intended to combat: in considering that 'the enunciator is the text', one ends up by taking it for the Polynesian *mana* of Bergson, who 'attributes intentions to things and events'.[3] Animism is the inevitable tendency of any theory which posits the text as an autonomous entity.

Recording or Auteurization?

Contrary to what is often said, the image does not speak all alone, neither about itself nor about anything else, and it is useless to try to enumerate figures of enunciation to the extent that every moment of the film may refer to cinema if the spectator pays more attention to the expression than to what is expressed. For me, the question is therefore less one of knowing when and where the film speaks of itself than of determining whether one speaks to me through it and who speaks to me.

Thus, a document broadcast in June 1993 on French TV showed images of a man, or maybe an extra-terrestrial, held prisoner in an 'apartment equipped with a surveillance camera' (according to the commentary). The bad quality of the images, the jumps between the shots, the quasi-automatic changes in the axis of the shots, all gave the impression of a recording made by a surveillance camera. It was only at the end of the broadcast that we learnt that the document was false, a pastiche of automatic recording.

Isn't it evident that its meaning changes depending on whether it seems intentionally emitted or not? If I consider it the result of recording by surveillance cameras, it is purely a document: in that case I am more interested in what it shows me than in defects inherent to this type of technology. If, on the contrary, I *auteur*ize it, that is, I presume that it has been shown to me by a 'being more or less like myself' and who is trying to tell me something, or to make me believe something, the meaning completely changes: the issues of truth and untruth, of manipulation, of technical ability appear. The defects become marks of enunciation in which we look for a meaning that is not only in the film, but which is also in the pragmatic context of its emergence: while the mechanically produced document showed me something, the intentionally produced document is at the same time a discourse which tries to say something to me while *speaking* cinema, and a narrative which *tells* a story.

Enunciation and Narration

Unfortunately or fortunately, it is always up to the reader, or to the spectator in the case of film, to determine what the relevant communicative intention is, even when the name of the author or the credits may be a guide to knowing how the document should be received as a whole. 'Speaking cinema' and 'telling a story': by these two expressions which I just related to each other, I want to show that the same audiovisual signs may refer to the enunciation as well as to the narration, to a discursive intention as well as to a narrative intention, and that it is not legitimate to regard the film as being only a 'système du récit' (Gaudreault) or that narration and enunciation may be assimilated to one another and 'fuse' (Metz).[4]

If this easily reduces the question of the *récit* to that of cinematic language, it is because the theory of filmic enunciation is largely dependent on ideas inherited from Benveniste.

With reference to the linguist Oswald Ducrot, I would now like to propose a theory of polyphony of cinematic enunciation. It is not possible, within the limits of this paper, to go into these matters in detail. Here I will only present the general outline necessary for understanding my own theory.

A Theory of Polyphony
For Ducrot, the first person forms which one finds in an utterance do not refer only to the speaker in a Benvenistian sense. It is true that they may refer to the one who speaks, but they do not have to. In addition, the one who speaks is not necessarily responsible for the enunciation. In other words, the speaking subject is not identical to the speaker.[5]

Think of the television journalist who reads a telegram: even if he seems to be responsible for the text he is reading, he is not therefore the author. Ducrot thus distinguishes between the *speaking subject*, the one who really utters something, and the *speaker L*, the subject responsible for the enunciation as such.

But the one who speaks is not only the source of the utterance, he is also a social being, a 'complete person', who is not reduced to being responsible for his enunciation. When I say, in a sinister tone, 'I am happy', L is certainly responsible for the utterance, but the feeling is in fact attributed to the social being, who has, among other things, the ability to speak, but also to feel. This subject of enunciation, to which the utterance refers, Ducrot calls the *speaker λ*.

Cinematic Enunciation, Filmic Enunciation
Let us return to film. I reject the idea that a theory of enunciation should be conceived of as a nesting of levels where, at the top, we should find the one responsible for the narrative communication (the grand image maker, the *méga-narrateur*, etc.). I also refuse a theory which, prisoner of immanence, tries to reduce the enunciation to an easy to discover meta-textual game.[6]

Not only does the perception of the enunciation vary according to period, place, and individual, but also through the course of a film, for one particular spectator. Nevertheless, even if the spectator navigates by eyesight, we may uncover four levels or, to carry the metaphor further, four cardinal points which help him to orient himself.

Let us consider the second sequence from *Weekend* (Godard, 1967). The character played by Jean Yanne has crashed into a Dauphine while reversing his sports car. The owner of the Dauphine, alerted by her son, goes out to meet him. A dispute follows, in which the driver's passenger also joins in. The car's engine is present to such a degree that we hardly grasp what the characters are saying to one another. Why this confusion? Two answers come to mind.

The first is to blame this defect on the shooting technique, which has often been considered one of the characteristic traits of the *Nouvelle Vague*: this unintelligibility would come from the fact that the original sound recording is used in spite of the imperfection of the omni-directional microphone. All those who are familiar with Godard's films - and notably his later ones - draw another conclusion: this way of preventing the spectator from understanding too easily, of grasping the meaning, so to speak, is recurrent in his films, regardless of the shooting technique adopted (direct sound or postsynchronization). Far from being accidental, the mixing of noise and speech is the speciality of the *auteur*, his way of conceiving cinematic language, his style.

The question is not knowing which of these two 'readings', as they said in the 1970s, is the best (even if I, of course, as you, have my idea about that). The two exist, have existed, or will exist. What interests me is that they imply conceptions of enunciation which are quite different or, for a theory of polyphony, three distinct levels of enunciation.

If we think that the shooting circumstances are responsible for the inaudible dialogue, we consider this to be accidental, not volitional, but only something that the one responsible for the filming has been subjected to, in the same way as a sudden movement of the camera or a blur in a direct recording. At this level the mark, the defect refers to the film itself. This zero degree of subjectivity, where the machine is humanized to the point of making us feel the presence of a body through the camera or the tape recorder, refers to the *filmeur empirique* [cameraman, journalist, reporter, etc.] who shoots the film. This is the filmic enunciation. In a sense, any identifiable trace of the technical constraints of a given period may refer to the level of filmic enunciation.

If, knowing Godard, it seems to me rather that this mixing of noise and speech was done *on purpose*, that the shooting conditions were merely a result of a decision to go against the conventions of 'realism', which normally consists of letting speech have priority over noise in the mixing, in this case this special effect should be referred to as a discursive intention. The defect of intelligibility is not accidental, it is the way in which the supposed author speaks cinema. He is less concerned with giving us information on the story level (he even takes away such information) than with manifesting his own 'style'. This level, which is the level of cinematic enunciation, may have something to do with a communicative intention, which reduces the problem of language coherence, namely in the case in which the author uses all kinds of cinematic procedures to make us understand what he wants to say, or it may have something to do with an artistic intention, if this is more important than the communicative intention.

The Constructed Author and the Role of the Spectator

As I just suggested in my interpretation of the sequence from *Weekend*, there is nothing that *a priori* distinguishes filmic enunciation from cinematic enunciation: no formal element, no certain sign. It was my contextual knowledge that allowed me to differentiate the one from the other: my knowledge of Godard.

I do not mean to say that you have to be a cinephile to see a film or that you have to undertake extensive philological research (this would exclude almost the entire audience from my theory). Unlike certain scholars who aim, through their theorising, at an understanding of ideal essences, the being of the text, an ontology which the spectator should discover at the risk of erring, I am first of all interested in the diversity of the readings, even if they should be wrong. Even if the spectator is caught up by the illusion, the theory must be able to understand how the error is possible. And it has to answer these questions: why don't we always agree with our friends when we leave the theatre? What concepts do we need in order to explain this diversity of readings?

In such a perspective, what I just called 'knowledge' of the author designates the knowledge that the spectator has of the author of the film he is about to see, even if this knowledge may be limited by his ignorance. By the author I understand not only this person constructed with the help of interviews, publicity, posters, this social being who Ducrot named the *speaker* λ, but also a more abstract entity, which is the studio, the producer or the Hollywood institution. Every spectator has his author. Whoever that may be, he is considered to be responsible for the narrative or artistic communication, a person in whom the spectator either does or does not have confidence. (Let us not forget that author etymologically means 'the one who increases confidence', the seller.)

Narrative Enunciation

As I have now presented it, this system of enunciation is not yet complete. In particular, as the attentive reader will have noticed, it does not account for the opposition between narration and enunciation.

After the racket of the automobile engine, let us consider the silence of the trains. First of all, the silence of *Le petit soldat* (Godard, 1963): the deserter is reading in a train compartment. No noise is heard except for a very distant rumbling. Then, that of *Un soir, un train* (André Delvaux, 1968): from a train compartment, Mathias (Yves Montand) watches his wife, Anne (Anouk Aimée), who is in the corridor. We hear a knocking sound repeated at regular intervals. Flashback: Mathias is with Anne in the country. He takes her in his arms and observes in the distance a peasant cutting wood. The sound of the axe blends in with the rumbling of the train. Then, at the moment the train passes a small station, we hear the ringing bells of a level crossing, very loudly. There is a dissolve, and then a very rapid montage of images of a wall seen from the train, which speeds along, and a close-up of a flashing light, and the noise of an accident, of sirens and the cries of Mathias who calls out 'Anne! Anne!'. After a series of images showing Mathias walking along the sleeping compartment and a close-up where he is next to Anne, listening to her sleeping, the sequence ends on a fade. We rediscover Mathias in his compartment. It is silent. The train continues its journey without a sound in a snow-covered landscape. Mathias remarks that his watch has stopped.

Of course, trains are not silent. In opposition to the first Godard example, the quasi-silence in *Le petit soldat* cannot be due to accidental shooting conditions. What may the author's intention be? In the first case, I am not able to say exactly what it is, but when I see the film, it is evident that this intention has to do with a decision on the discursive level: in *Le petit soldat* as a whole, almost the only thing we hear of reality is speech. Any departure from this principle is significant (as when the French terrorists play on the car's horn, in the silence of the night, their 'Algérie Française', the signature of their crime).

In Delvaux's film, things are different. When the train leaves, you hear its movement quite distinctly. When it suddenly disappears, it is not because of a stylistic intention; it is rather meant to signify an event which has just occurred, perhaps without the knowledge of the spectator, and which is evoked by several images and sounds (a flashing light, the ringing bells). At the end we understand, if we had not already, that this sudden silence in the train means death. In this case, the sound is the bearer of another type of intentionality, a *narrative intentionality*. In other words, in order to understand this absence of noise, we have to refer it to an impersonal level constructed from the filmic system as such: the *implicit narrator*. Since its finality is determined by a narrative intention, by a desire to give us the information we need in order to understand the story, I shall call it *narrative enunciation*.

Polyphony as a Construction

How can the spectator refer these images and sounds to the intended level: the *filmeur*, the constructed author or the narrator? As I just suggested, it depends on his idea about the author, the place and the role that he attributes to him in the process.

To see this, we can look at a sequence from Woody Allen's film *Zelig* - a newscast about Hearst, consisting of the following shots:

1   Intertitle from 'Pathé News': 'Hearst hosts Zelig and Fletcher and shows how the rich and famous spend their leisure and honour their guests'.

2   General shot of Hearst's estate.

3   Shot of a small group outside the entrance to the estate.

4   Hearst comes out, Marie Dressler on his arm, followed by friends. We see the horizontal bar that separates the photograms. The camera wobbles and suddenly reframes the characters according to their movements. A person passes between them and the camera. Marion Davies and a friend move closer to the camera making faces, until they becomes blurred.

5   Charles Chaplin plays the banjo to Marion Davies.

6   Oblique shot: Jimmy Walker draws some dance steps and dances with himself.

7   Close-up: the shot misframes Jimmy Walker as he continues to dance.

8   Tom Mix holds a woman by the shoulder and poses for the cameraman. Suddenly a face is interposed between them and the cameraman: it is Zelig, played by Woody Allen. He then joins them, and bows.

9   Charles Chaplin with Adolph Menjou.

Several levels overlap. First it is a newsreel, which shows us images taken on the spur of the moment. This is the reason for imperfections which are not relevant as such: poor image stability, jagged camera movements and framing, poorly controlled movements of the people being filmed, passers-by temporarily filling the screen, etc. When two women being filmed speak to the camera and approach it, we recognise a characteristic trait of home movies, which is always subject to the filming conditions imposed by those who you are trying to film.

Evidently the obliqueness of the sixth shot also shows the improvised character of these images, as well as the third shot, which has the same characteristics as the preceding ones (blur, sudden movement of the camera, person speaking to the camera at close range ...). Only the fact that we recognise the actor Woody Allen allows us to infer its heterogeneity in the series: how can the 'real' Hearst, the 'real' Chaplin be at the same party as this character played by Woody Allen?

Hence, what we had taken for one piece of filmic enunciation falls apart and we begin to doubt. Several interpretations are possible, according to the spectator's knowledge: if he recognises neither Hearst nor Chaplin, he can think that it is an authentic newsreel. However, from the moment he recognises Woody Allen, he must form the hypothesis that some images have been reconstructed, they have been shot by the filmmaker and edited into the rest of the sequence. If he recognises Hearst and Chaplin, he forms this hypothesis immediately and he must admit that his sequence mixes an authentic filmic enunciation, confirmed by the final credits, and a false filmic enunciation.

Of course, these two hypotheses do not have the same status: whereas the first one fits all the criteria which we used in order to define it (the accidental, nonintentional, character of the images), the false filmic enunciation serves a higher intention: that of mixing reality and fiction completely by borrowing from the language of the 1930s newsreel and from the home movie. Nothing but its aim distinguishes the cinematic pastiche from the object it imitates. The cinematic enunciation overlaps the filmic enunciation entirely like a palimpsest which is perfect and absurd at the same time, since is borrows exactly the contours of the text upon which it is superimposed.

We understand better why I just said that the technical constraints of a period constitute an irreducible residue of the filmic enunciation, hard to perceive for the contemporary spectator: a sequence recording Zelig's voice allows us to hear a noise that in itself has no significance in a document of the 1930s; it is only to the extent that it is intended as a defect imitating an old film that it becomes meaningful: from being filmic enunciation it slides towards cinematic enunciation.

Enunciation: From the Question of Narrative Responsibility to the Identification of Enunciators

From all this we may conclude that it is not enough that a sequence lets us see or hear marked filmic phenomena, as Lotman said,[7] for us to immediately regard them as subjective. Or, at least, everything depends on what you mean by the term 'subjectivity'. The constructed author? The narrator? A character?

At this point it is evident that the question of cinematic enunciation is not one of actual responsibility in the narrative communication (that's a question of law). To put in that way, this question is not very interesting. For, if we admit that this responsibility is neither in the text nor the text itself, which would be to fall into anthropomorphism, whatever you might call the author, whatever form and power is conferred upon him, one thing is certain: he exists somewhere outside of the film.

Concluding in this way does not solve the problem of enunciation. In fact, as we have seen, for the spectator it is less a question of determining who speaks cinema than of deciding which point of view is adopted by this heterogeneous entity. Point of view is here used not in the perceptive or cognitive sense, but in the ideological sense, as one speaks of the point of view of the defence or the point of view of the prosecution.

The detour to Ducrot's theory teaches us that the speaker can very well express through what he says the point of view of another, without, however, reproducing exactly his terms. Thus, when I say 'Oh! I look like an idiot!', I am the source of the utterance, but I do not necessarily adhere to this judgment which represents the point of view of an enunciator who is not me. In a sense, something similar happens in the cinema. Behind every image and every sound, the spectator can discover the point of view of one of the masks that I have tried to identify (to which must be added those which depend on the characters and the explicit narrator, which I cannot treat here). A sound which is hardly audible can give us the idea that it is reality itself, unmanipulated, which is the enunciator, but it may also reveal the aesthetic intention of an artist. Of course, it all depends on the films. There are no figures of enunciation given *a priori*. Everything depends above all on the idea that the spectator has of this author who is responsible for the narrative communication.

Faced with his object of study, the theoretician can adopt two attitudes which were already pointed out by Descartes: 'Each thing should be considered differently according to whether we refer to the order of our acquaintance [*ratio cognoscendi*] or to the order of real existence [*ratio essendi*].'[8] Thus, in the order of existence, which is that of *Discours de la méthode*, God is the first reality, while, in the order of reasoning, which is that of *Les méditations*, he intervenes as a simple logical supposition: in order that clear and distinct ideas, among which the *cogito* itself, may be stable, we need someone to guarantee their eternity. And it is God who is asked to play this role. These two ways of using reason are not equivalent. While the one aims directly at reality, the other begins in the subject in order to establish gradually what is necessary for explaining the world.

To see a film is not to be presented with an enunciative system which is as rationally organised as the nesting of Russian dolls. It is not to discover some sort of *ratio essendi*. It is true that the number of enunciation 'masks' is not infinite, and it is up to the theory to describe it. In return, it is up to the spectator, at any moment of the film, to attribute the images and the sounds to the one or the other or to nobody (the total absence of sensibility exists on and off). Quite often, disputes and discussions with our friends are just the expression of this uncertainty or this enunciative openness. We have to accept that: the spectator is not the monolithic being described by semiology, he is rather a tissue of hesitations. It is up to the theoretician to retrace the sinuous meanderings of this spectatorial acquaintance.

Notes

1   Christian Metz, *Film Language: A Semiotics of the Cinema*, trans. Michael Taylor, New York: Oxford University Press, 1974, p. 20.

2   See Metz, 'The Impersonal Enunciation', in this anthology.

3   *Les deux sources de la morale et de la religion*, Paris: PUF, 1958 (1932), p. 185.

4   Metz, *L'Énonciation Impersonnelle ou le Site du Film*, Paris: Méridiens Klinck-sieck, 1991, p. 186.

5   Oswald Ducrot, 'Esquisse d'une théorie polyphonique de l'énonciation', *Le dire et le dit*, Paris: Minuit, 1984.

6   This is Metz's position in 'The Impersonal Enunciation': 'Enunciation is the semiological act by which some parts of a text talk to us about this text as an act'.

7   Jurij Lotman, *Semiotics of Cinema*, trans. Mark E. Suino, Michigan: Ann Arbor, 1976, chapter 3.

8   *Regulae*, regula 12.

'ENUNCIATION':
FROM CODE TO INTERPRETATION

JAN SIMONS

Cinema, Language and Cognition

Claiming, as one of the major goals of film studies, to understand how films are understood, as Metz wrote in his *Language and Cinema*, means conceiving a theory of film as a representation of the knowledge a person must have to be able to assign structures and meanings to filmic configurations. Since film theory is concerned with audio-visual representations and not with verbal expressions, there is no *a priori* justification for employing linguistics to represent this knowledge. Film theory is not necessarily a branch of linguistics, nor does a linguistic theory necessarily provide an appropriate framework for film studies. However, when considered as a cognitive theory, film studies shares with linguistics some psychological concern, which then suggests that it has as its aim the attempt to achieve psychologically interesting formal representations of spectators' knowledge of film.

In this paper I shall consider the representation of this knowledge through a discussion of the possible contributions generative and cognitive semantics can make to film theory. Emphasis will be placed on the work of Gilles Fauconnier, whose introduction into cognitive semantics of the concept of mental spaces offers one way of conceiving the meeting ground of language, cognitive science and cinema.[1] But first, I shall briefly consider the inherent limitations of Francesco Casetti's and Christian Metz's recent theories of enunciation, limitations that justify a move towards generative and cognitive semantics.

Deixis, Impersonal Enunciation and Levels of Narration

Because enunciation mediates between the abstract and virtual language system (*langue*) and the concrete and particular utterances of a language (*parole*), it can be and has been approached from both sides. Since film semiology never really came to terms with the 'system' of filmic language, it will come as no surprise that the problem of 'enunciation and film' has mostly been taken up from the side of actualized filmic discourse.[2] From this point of view, a film is seen as an 'utterance', the very existence of which is proof of a logically preceding act of 'enunciation', generally defined as the productive act by which 'the speaker appropriates the formal apparatus of a language'.[3]

Here the enunciation is seen as the place where the subject of language emerges as the mediating locus between the *langue* and the *parole*, the actual 'mise en discourse' of this formal apparatus.

According to Casetti the aim of a theory of cinematic enunciation is 'to give meaning to three current claims: to the idea that the film "designs" its spectator; to the idea that it assigns a "place" to its spectator; and to the idea that it makes its spectator follow a "trajectory". Thus, how the film construes its spectator, how it accounts for its spectator, fixes a place for him, and makes him follow a "trajectory"'.[4] The actual spectator is from this point of view a 'body' *outside the film* that is invited to occupy a 'role', designed *inside the filmic text*. The subject is thus conceived as a *signified*, which has to be systematically correlated with material filmic configurations as its *signifiers*. So Casetti proceeds to individuate four basic filmic configurations, correlated with four enunciative positions, that he paraphrases by 'deictic formula' (see the papers above).

Metz's argument, meant as a criticism of Casetti's 'deictic conception' of cinematic enunciation, can be reduced to the basic assumption that the relationship between language and film is one of *translation*[5]. Since the 'language of film' has no counterparts of the deictic expressions of natural languages, films cannot signify the meanings of, and thus may not be translated with such linguistic expressions. Again, the observation that film is not like a natural language is rather trivial.

A more fundamental point to be made, however, is that natural languages signify and refer to, but do not provide translations of non-linguistic realities. Rather, they provide tools for the description and interpretation of non-linguistic phenomena, including films, as well as for the expression of more abstract conceptualizations that have no perceptible counterparts in 'reality', such as the cognitive relationships spectators entertain with events on the screen.[6] For instance, spatial relationships expressed by prepositions like 'before' and 'behind' do not exist objectively and independently of their conceptualization by a speaker/hearer: these prepositions are not 'translations' of some objective, external relationship between a speaker and entities in his spatial environment. Rather, these relations are internal, subjective mental construals by means of which a speaker conceptualizes his relationships to other entities in its spatial surroundings.[7]

This is what Casetti's 'deictic' formulas aim to achieve: not to 'translate' pieces of film but to express judgments and interpretations a spectator associates with certain filmic configurations. However, the problem with his concept of enunciation is that it locates the spectator's judgments about his relation to the events represented on the screen in the film itself: it is the filmic enunciation that distributes roles ('I/you/he'), places ('here/there/elsewhere') and times ('now/before or after/then').[8] In the end, the spectator makes no judgments, no interpretations or has no intuitions about the relationship he is supposed to entertain with the events on the screen, but rather fits into a 'role', designed and prefigured in what is called the 'filmic enunciation'.

Ironically enough, it is Metz who points out this problem by showing that the formula Casetti proposes as descriptions for filmic configurations might just as well be reversed, depending from which side one wishes to approach a shot or a scene. For instance, for the subjective shot, Casetti proposes the formula 'you and he see what I show both of you'. On the other hand, Metz quite rightly argues that one might just as well substitute this formula for its opposite: 'You and I are looking at what he is seeing'. Metz explains this ambiguity with the double function a camera has in filmic representation since it 'sees' and 'shows' at the same time. Here one would rather wish to say that a camera as a technical apparatus only *records*, while seeing and showing are intentional perceptual, cognitive and communicative acts of a human consciousness. In the latter sense, the term 'camera' is not to be understood as a real, technical object, but as a 'reading label', a 'reading hypothesis which seeks to make intelligible the spaces of a film', sometimes by ascribing the origin from a 'vision' that brings a representation into being to a character.[9] The interpretation of a subjective shot is not fixed by some predetermined identification of the spectator/you with a character/he that is seen as a representative of the spectator on the screen, nor can a possibly ambiguous interpretation of a subjective shot be reduced to the technical properties of the recording instrument. Which interpretation is given depends on the way a spectator conceptualizes and rationalizes the access he or she is given to the data on the screen, that is, the epistemological context the spectator construes for the information about the represented events he obtains.[10]

In this perspective a 'text' is not its material or technical substratum, nor the string of images and sounds that are projected on the screen, but rather, as Branigan writes: 'a certain *collection of descriptions of an artifact* where the artifact must be one that materializes a symbol system, and the descriptions that are offered of it must be sanctioned by a society'.[11] The most general epistemological context Western societies provide as a description of texts is that the artifact or object that materializes the text must be understood as being produced or used by some human agency to communicate some meaning to other human agencies. Between this most general epistemological context (what Branigan calls the level of the 'historical author'[12]) and the lowest or most specific level, commonly described by the term 'internal focalization' several epistemological contexts at several levels of narration can be distinguished, labelled with several terms like *extrafictional, nondiegetic, diegetic narrator, character, focalization,* etc.

In this context the concept of enunciation indeed no longer has any use, since there are no 'roles' or 'posts' a text construes for the spectator to identify with, nor does it refer to processes by which the text refers to its coming into being. There are no roles, but 'levels' or 'epistemological contexts', which are not 'encoded' by structural patterns or stylistic devices within the text, but construed as descriptions and interpretations of the text by a spectator who tries to make sense not only of the data he or she is presented with, but also of the way he or she obtains knowledge of these events. Since these descriptions are interpretations and not 'translations', it is possible that different interpretations, employed for different purposes, might be entertained at the same time.

Generative and Cognitive Semantics

Spectators typically assign semantic interpretations to films which can normally be verbalized.[13] It would be a mistake to conclude from this that the properties natural languages share with a so-called film language are syntactic structures, or that film images should be analysed in terms of linguistic concepts like lexical categories, phrasal structures, etc. The possibility of verbalization of the semantic interpretation of film images, an instance of the more general ability of people to talk about what they see (and hear and smell) points to a level of mental representation where information, processed by visual, auditory and other perceptual systems, is translated into forms suitable for linguistic expression. Ray Jackendoff, who has developed a cognitive semantics within a framework of generative theory, identifies this level as the level of conceptual structure.[14]

The assumption of such a level is justified by the observation that linguistic, visual, motoric or other forms of input and output information do not 'suffice to explain the way we understand the world in terms of objects, their motions, our actions on them, and so forth. Rather, such aspects of our understanding must be encoded in an integrated modality-independent form that I will call a central format'.[15] As a lingua franca, a meeting ground for information from several sources, this central format or level of conceptual structure is also independent of specifically linguistic levels of representation like phonology and syntax.

In a different, non-generative approach to cognitive semantics, Mark Johnson and George Lakoff[16] also argue for a 'non-propositional' level of meaning, claiming that 'propositional content is possible only by virtue of a complex web of nonpropositional schematic structures that emerge from our bodily experience'.[17] At this non- or pre-propositional level meaning emerges in the forms of *image-schemata* (a recurrent pattern, shape and regularity in, or of, ongoing activities that order actions, perceptions and conceptions chiefly at the level of bodily movements, the manipulation of objects and perceptual interactions), *metaphoric mappings* ('a pervasive mode of understanding by which we project patterns from one domain of experience in order to structure another domain of a different kind'; *metonymic mappings* (by which one well-understood or easy-to-perceive aspect of something is used to stand either for the thing as a whole or for some other aspect or part of it).[18] Together with *propositional structures*, which identify elements, assign properties and establish relations among them, Gestalt-structures, etc. these form so-called *Idealized Cognitive Models* (ICM) that organise human knowledge.

In spite of differences of opinion about the status of syntax with respect to conceptual structure, the arbitrariness or symbolic nature of syntax, about whether syntax and syntactic categories as morphemes are semantically motivated or not, generative and cognitive semantics agree that:

- meanings and the concepts that instantiate them are not independent, objective, disembodied representations of objects, properties and relations as they are in the external world, but rather human *construals* of that world, which emerge from bodily and perceptual experience and interaction, organised by patterns of imaginative structuring, or, as Jackendoff puts it, dependent on the 'combinatorial space of distinctions available to the brain';[19]
- the meanings and concepts at this level of mental representation are not themselves linguistic or propositional, but rather consist of image-schemata, Gestalt-structures, metaphorical and metonymical mappings, visual '3D model structures', 'body representations' that 'encode internal states of muscles and joints, as well as the locus and character of body sensations such as pain, tension, heat, and so forth'.[20] Basic cognitive operations such as categorising take place also in nonlinguistic organisms, and involve for example an appreciation of the visual field when a categorisation is ostensively proposed. It is hard to imagine how the difference between the meanings of lexical items such as *duck* or *goose* could be captured by a decomposition of the concepts into distinctive features (what comes next after + animate, + animal, + birds, + waterfowl, +...?).[21] Another major implication of the non-compositionality of meanings is that the conditions that make up a word meaning (or concept) cannot be taken to be collectively necessary and sufficient to determine a categorisation. Rather, categories are to be seen as consisting of networks with prototypical members, clustered in the centre of the category with less prototypical members at various distances from the central members.[22] Network relations, preference rules, chaining principles and so forth seem to be more appropriate to characterize categorising relationships.

Although there seems to be no reason for a cognitive theory of filmic comprehension to make an arbitrary *a priori* distinction between cinematic and non-cinematic codes (as Metz does throughout *Language and Cinema*), nevertheless the principles that allow spectators to ascribe spatial-temporal relations to a series of images (and sounds) seem to constitute a focal domain of interest for any account of the way films are understood. This dimension of the comprehension of film involves procedures by which the spectator partitions the data on the screen into units, defined by spatio-temporal coordinates. Since visual scenes do not have spatial or temporal markers, the spatial and temporal relationships within a film are a matter of each spectator's judgments and interpretations of the data, for which for instance the data of a given shot have to be compared with the data of a preceding shot to see whether they can plausibly be located in a single time-space or are to be seen as separated by a 'filter' (see Colin's paper 'The Grande Syntagmatique Revisited', in this anthology), whether the events in succeeding shots are related by causal connections (in which cause and effect, spatial or temporal proximity, repetition, etc. all play a role[23]), whether there is coreference, or whether the singular events can be interpreted as distinct instantiations of a particular script, etc.

Giving due respect to the variety of factors involved, and also taking into account the principle of the 'separation of material and structure',[24] it should come as no surprise that the construction of spatio-temporal relations allows for some freedom in the matching of pieces of film with structural descriptions. The intuitive and sometimes quite ambiguous nature of the judgments about spatio-temporal relationships might be an indication that the principles of the segmentation of a film should be seen as 'preference rules' rather than a set of clear cut criteria.[25]

Mental Spaces and Subjectivity

For Gilles Fauconnier, mental spaces are mental representations which are 'distinct from linguistic structures, but construed in correspondence to cues provided by linguistic expressions'.[26] They are represented by structured and modifiable sets of elements and relationships that are satisfied by those elements. Linguistic expressions like prepositional phrases (*in John's mind, in 1929, from his point of view*, etc.), adverbial expressions (*probably, maybe, theoretically*), logical conjunctions (*if A, then.., either..or..*), propositional attitude verbs (*Max believes.., Mary wishes...*) and so forth may introduce new mental spaces, put elements into these spaces as well as the relationships satisfied by those elements, even though these mental spaces are not in themselves linguistic. Neither are they some 'imagined worlds': as the examples of possible introducers of mental spaces already show, they are abstract media for the conceptualizations of, for example, fictional situations as in novels or movies, future and past situations as under-stood by the speaker/hearer, hypothetical situations, abstract domains such as concep-tual domains (e.g. economics, politics, physics), mathematical domains, etc.[27]

For one thing, they may be construed on the basis of other than linguistic material, including pictures and films.[28] Another, maybe even more important reason to distinguish between mental spaces and the structures of linguistic (or other symbolic) expressions, is that the construction of mental spaces is underdetermined by grammati-cal structures. The construction of mental spaces is a matter of applying cognitive strat-egies, rather than structural interpretation: '(...) a sentence is always accompanied by the full scale of its semantic interpretations (as fixed by grammar), of which the inappriorate ones are eliminated by the speakers'.[29]

Mental spaces are not to be confused with 'possible worlds', since they have no ontological status: as mental constructions they have no existence outside of the mind. Rather, 'reality' is itself, as the speaker's mental representation of reality, neces-sarily a mental space or, as Jackendoff puts it: 'Whatever the nature of *real* reality, the way reality can look *to us* is determined and constrained by the nature of our internal representations'.[30]

Since mental spaces, among which must be counted a mental space that represents 'reality', are mental constructions, they normally presuppose some other mental space, from which they are construed. A linguistic or symbolic element that introduces a mental space *M*, will introduce this within another space *M'*, which Fauconnier calls the 'parent space' of *M*. Mental spaces can be explicitly introduced into other mental spaces by 'introducers' as in:

1 *Max believes that in Luc's painting the red flowers are yellow*

The mental space *M*, introduced by the expression *in Luc's painting*, is itself embedded in a mental space *M'*, introduced by *Max believes*. But the element, designated by the proper name *Max*, is itself an element of another mental space *R*, the 'reality' as con-strued by the speaker. This mental space *R* is itself not explicitly introduced by any linguistic expression, but rather pragmatically inferred. In response to an utterance like (1) another speaker might say for instance:

2 *In reality, Max believes that in Luc's painting the yellow flowers are red*

Another property of mental spaces is made clear by these examples: (1) and (2) only make sense if they are used to describe a mistaken belief of Max about the colour of the flowers in Luc's paintings. Still, those sentences are ambiguous about the mental space in which the flowers have to be located: in M or in M'? The elements of one mental space can thus be related to elements of another mental space by what Fauconnier calls 'pragmatic connectors', such that entities in one space can be introduced or designated by entities from another mental space, with which they are pragmatically connected, as for example in a well known example from linguistic and philosophical literature:

3   *Ralph believes that the blue-eyed girl has brown eyes*

The expression *the blue-eyed girl* designates an entity in an implictly inferred mental space R ('speaker's reality'), as well as an entity that is related to it by a pragmatic connector in mental space M, explicitly introduced by the expression *Ralph be-lieves*.

What could all this mean for the problem of subjectivity in cinema? First of all, of course, a mental space can be seen as the medium for conceptualizing situations and events, designated by a film.[31] Second, within this mental space, new mental spaces can be introduced, for instance by stories told by characters, represented by flashbacks, dream sequences, movies within the movie and so forth. Third, the mental space, intro-duced and designated by a film is itself embedded within a 'parent space' R, the reality as construed by the spectator. This 'parent space' R, which is the mental construal of the conditions and circumstances of the filmic communication and the participants in-volved in it, – the 'ground' as Langacker calls it – may be construed implicitly, or on the other hand be foregrounded explicitly.[32] In linguistic utterances, deictic expressions typically serve as cues for the more or less explicitly foregrounding of the ground of the speech event, but the absence of counterparts of such expressions in film certainly does not exclude the explicit foregrounding of the ground in the spectator's construal of the film.

For instance, Branigan proposes an account of how (classical) pictorial representations are comprehended, which consists of six elements.[33] Since pictorial rep-resentations do not exist by themselves, but are always brought into being, an *origin* will be conceived, from which the representation derives. The representation is brought into being from an origin by a force, that is, by a *vision*. Both these units of representa-tion are moreover linked in *time*, the third element of representation. There is a continu-ity when the units are a whole, or a discontinuity when they are disconnected, as in flashbacks, flashforwards, hallucinations or dream sequences. The next element of rep-resentation is a *frame*, which puts perceptual limits to what is represented (as in the opposition on screen/off screen for example). Then there is the *object* that is represented or 'framed', and finally what Branigan calls *mind*, 'that condition of consciousness – sentience – which is *represented* as (not *is*) the principle of coherence of the representation'.

As should be stressed, these six elements are not properties or parts of the material object that '*is*' the representation (the painting, the photograph, the film, etc.), but elements of the spectator's *mental construal* of this representation. This ICM of classical pictorial representation seems to fit rather well the cognitive model of mental spaces. The *object* can be considered as an entity within a mental space M, delimited by a *frame*, and brought into being, 'opened' or construed by a *vision* that originates from an *introducer*, the origin in parent space M', conceptualized as some kind of intentional consciousness that is capable of construing M. However, the model of mental spaces has some advantages over Branigan's account of 'subjectivity in the classical film' (the shortcomings and possible confusions of which are admittedly overcome in Branigan's later book *Narrative Comprehension and Film*).

Branigan has some major strong points with regard to other, structuralist or semiological accounts of subjectivity in film. First, he shows that it is possible to develop a 'logic of reading'[34] of pictorial representations, which does not rely on (counterparts of) linguistic elements such as deictic expressions for example. By simply assuming an *origin*, from which a *vision* brings a visual representation into being, Branigan's account avoids undecidable questions such as whether a character who represents past events by a flashback has to be identified with the 'I' of the enunciator/narrator who is 'showing' these past events, or rather with the '*you*' of the narratee, who is 'looking' at them (see Metz, 'The Impersonal Enunciation', above). Second, by presenting this 'logic of reading' as a procedure by which a spectator arrives at a *mental* representation of the film, Branigan also separates matters of point of view from material configurations of the film, such as 'the camera', properties of the camera as position, distance, angle, or 'the shot' that cease to be considered as decisive terms in our reading.[35]

However, there are some possible confusions and weaknesses in this account. The term 'frame' is used rather ambiguously, since it refers to the *perceptual* boundaries of pictorial representations (the frame that marks off on-screen space from off-screen space, for example), as well as to the *epistemological boundaries*, which mark more global and abstract mental representations, called 'levels of narration'. However, as the principle of separation of material and structure indicates, perceptual and epistemological boundaries become blurred in the spectator's mental construal of the 'origin' of a 'level of narration'. If 'levels of narration' or 'framed representations' are conceived as more abstract mental spaces, however, these ambiguities probably can be avoided, without losing all hope for a more or less formal representation of a cognitive model (as is the case in Branigan's *Narrative Comprehension and Film*).

Another problem is the notion of 'a frame which cannot disclose its own act of framing'.[36] According to Branigan, there ultimately is a frame 'beyond which it is impossible to go', the 'apersonal component' of the film. Of course, the buck has to stop somewhere, but the question is where to draw the line. For Branigan, this seems to be the point where a symbolic activity as the act of narration itself ('a particular relationship with respect to the symbolic process of the text') has to be construed as the 'origin' of the film as a whole. Metz makes use of this notion as an argument in favour of his conception of the 'impersonal enunciation', and of course, no real-life 'person' has to be posited as the ultimate source of a film. But this is something quite different from the claim that '*the enunciator is the film*, the film as source, acting as such, *oriented* as such, the film as activity' as Metz puts it ('The Impersonal Enunciation'). What could possibly be something like a 'film as an activity' or a 'film acting as such': a film is an inanimate object which, for its being active, orientated or whatever, presupposes some human agency, whether this agency is conceived as a person or not. Branigan introduces terms such as 'historical author' and 'extra-fictional narrator' as labels for this *origin* (see also Jost, 'The Authorized Narrative').

However, the major problem laid bare with the notion of 'the frame beyond which it is impossible to go' seems to be the conception of the way each spectator construes his or her own relationship to the events and situations designated by the film. This is doubtlessly due to the fact that most theories of point of view, enunciation or subjectivity in cinema, including Branigan's, are developed with reference to (classical) *fiction* films, and fictional worlds are typically construed as mental spaces structured by entities and relations that have no 'pragmatic connections' with 'reality' as understood by the spectator.[37] In other words, fictional worlds are typically introduced by (beginnings of) movies, novels, plays, etc. that leave the parent space from which they originate. In other words, the worlds they represent are construed with maximal objectivity, leaving the 'ground' outside their domain of conceptualization.[38]

In non-fictional genres on the other hand, the mental spaces construed out of the indications furnished by films such as advertisements, propaganda films, instruction films, news footage or documentary films, will be understood as populated with elements that are in some way pragmatically connected to each spectator's reality. Also the 'ground' of the filmic communicative event (which is, of course, the parent space as understood by the spectator) may be explicitly foregrounded by several forms of address, by referring to the 'historical' time and place of the event, by somehow relating to the real, everyday interests of the spectator, etc. Not only will the spectator construe in such cases a mental space R, in which he or she will conceive (a correspondent of) him or herself as the addressee of the filmic communication, but for the film, itself an element in R, some element will be assumed in R as its origin or as the agency that brings the film into being, be this agency some 'historical author', an institution, a commercial enterprise or whatever.[39]

But one might also wonder whether the intuitive notion of 'identification' could not be captured within the model of mental spaces. An indication of this is given by Branigan,[40] who proposes verbal (re)descriptions of the epistemological contexts, the 'levels of narrations', or, as is proposed here, the 'mental spaces' that can be discriminated within a film, amongst which conditionals like

3   *If a bystander* had been *present, he or she* would have *seen...* and *would have heard....* (implied diegetic narrator)
4   *Manny* looks at *x* (external focalization)
5   *I [Manny][now]* see *x [there][from where I stand]* (internal focalization), etc.

This suggests that the comprehension of film sequences involves the construction of mental spaces, in which the spectator conceptualizes an element as origin for the represented situation or events, which might be conceived as the 'mind' of a previously identified character (as in internal focalization) or of some unidentified, anonymous bypasser (who does not have to be actually present on the screen). But it also suggests the construction of hypothetical, counterfactual mental spaces, in which the spectator projects a correspondent of him or herself, which subsequently takes the origin of the represented situation as a pragmatically connected correspondent, somehow as:

6   *If a bystander had been present, and if I had been (in the position of) that* bystander, I would have seen...
7   *If I had been there, I would have seen Manny looking at x*
8   *If I were Manny, I would* see now x, etc.

This seems to be a promising way of formally capturing intuitions about spectators' comprehension of his or her relationship to film sequences, such as for instance Metz's notions of primary and secondary identification.[41]

Semantics, conceived in terms of mental spaces, opens up new, and more productive relationships between language and film. Language is not the only tool for comprehending and construing knowledge about the world, but it does provide a privileged entrance to conceptual structures, even if they are construed on the basis of non-linguistic cues and are themselves not necessarily linguistic in nature.

Coda

Once the 'meanings' of a text are no longer located within the text itself, but are identified as descriptions and interpretations in the cognitive activities of the spectator, there might again be room for terms like 'narrator'. Such terms no longer need to imply or suggest a reference to some identifiable 'person' responsible for the text, but rather label an epistemological context as conceptualized for the text. And once one sees verbalizations of filmic representations as possible linguistic descriptions of filmic images, a more relaxed attitude towards the relationship of language and cinema becomes possible, which might prove to be more productive than either an obstinate pursuit of the study of film with linguistic concepts or a firm rejection of any linguistically inspired approach, since the place where film and language meet is not some external space where autonomous semiotic systems correlate, but the mind of a human subject, where they interact at some conceptual level. However, to arrive at this mental meeting point, one has to transgress the border between 'sign' and 'mind', marked by the concept of enunciation which, on the one hand reaches out to the 'subject of semiology', but on the other hand firmly confines meaning and subjectivity within the boundaries of codes and texts.

Notes

[1]   Gilles Fauconnier, *Les Espaces Mentaux*, Paris, Minuet, 1984.

[2]   Again, the theoretical justifications for this approach are rather weak. By comparing a filmic 'unit' like the shot with a linguistic unit like the word, Metz notes 'five radical distinctions' (*Film Language: A Semiotics of the Cinema*, trans. Michael Taylor, New York: Oxford University Press, 1974, pp. 115-16): 1) the number of shots is infinite, like the number of utterances, but unlike the number of 'words' of a language; 2) shots are the 'creations' of the filmmaker, as the utterances are the 'creations' of a speaker, but unlike the 'words' that pre-exist in a lexicon; 3) the amount of information a shot delivers is indefinite; 4) the shot is an 'actualized unit', like an utterance but again unlike the word that as part of the lexicon is a purely virtual unit; and 5) a shot has only very weak paradigmatic relationships with other shots, while words are always part of a more or less articulated semantic field. The weakness of the argument, which locates film completely on the side of the

actualized discourse, becomes clear if one realises that first of all natural languages also manifest themselves only in actualized, concrete utterances (how else could one observe a phenomenon like language?); and second, all modern linguistics was actually inaugurated by the gesture, which separated the 'language system' as a theoretical object from the actual manifestations of language. But a theoretical description of a language system is a quite futile enterprise if it does not aim at describing the infinite set of sentences of a language, as Metz seems to suggest.

3   Emile Benveniste, *Problèmes de Linguistique Générale*, tome II, Paris: Gallimard, 1974, p. 82.

4   Francesco Casetti, *Dentro lo Sguardo. Il Film e Il Suo Spettatore*, Milano: Bompiani, 1986, p. 23.

5   This is coherent with the structuralist conception of a) semiological systems as independently existing systems b) the 'natural world', since it is endowed with meaning as a semiological system in its own right; c) the relationships between different semiological systems as one of 'correlation' of units of one semiological system as 'signifieds' with units of another semiological system as their 'signifiers'. This correlation accounts for the 'translatability' of non-linguistic semiological systems into 'natural languages' that 'semanticaly code the figures of the natural world' and 'lexicalize and manifest abstract semantic categories that generally remain implicit in other semiotics'. A.J. Greimas and J. Courtés, *Sémiotique. Dictionnaire Raisonné de la Théorie du Langage*, Paris: Hachette, 1979, pp. 340-41.

6   Or, for that matter, in reality. What would something like a *desire* or a memory look like? What is a thing like 'before' or 'after'? Those prepositions express the way speakers conceptualize their relations with other entities in his or her spatial (or, by metaphor), temporal environment, but they do not 'denote' some perceptible entities. Neither do they 'translate' some objective relationship, which exists independently of its cognitive conceptualization.

7   See George Lakoff, *Women, Fire and Dangerous Things. What Categories Reveal about the Mind*, Chicago and London: The University of Chicago Press, 1987, pp. 416 ff.

8   Casetti, *Dentro lo sguardo*, pp. 27-28.

9   See Edward Branigan, *Point of View in the Cinema. A Theory of Narration and Subjectivity in Classical Film*, Berlin, New York, Amsterdam: Mouton Publishers, 1984, p. 53 and p. 57.

10 See Branigan, *Narrative Comprehension and Film*, London and New York: Routledge, 1992, p. 113.

11 ibid., p. 87.

12 ibid.

13 See, for example, Michel Colin, *Langue, Film, Discours*, Paris: Meridiens Klincksieck, 1985, pp. 112-113.

14 See Ray Jackendoff, *Consciousness and the Computational Mind*, Cambridge, Mass.: The MIT Press, 1987, p. 125.

15 Jackendoff, *Languages of the Mind. Essays on Mental Representation*, Cambridge Mass: The MIT Press, 1992, p. 3.

16 Mark Johnson, *The Body in the Mind. The Bodily Basis of Meaning, Imagination, and Reason*, Chicago and London: The University of Chicago Press, 1987; George Lakoff, *Women, Fire and Dangerous Things*.

17 Johnson, *The Body in the Mind*, p. 5.

18 See Johnson and Lakoff, ibid., passim.

19 Jackendoff, *Languages of the Mind*, 1992, p. 2. See also Jackendoff, *Consciousness and the Computational Mind*, 1987, p. 126.

20 Jackendoff, *Languages of the Mind*, p. 14 and p. 15.

21 ibid., p. 44.

22 See Johnson, *The Body in the Mind*, p. 192; Lakoff, *Women, Fire and Dangerous Things*, pp. 91 ff; Ronald Langacker, *Concept, Image, and Symbol. The Cognitive Basis of Grammar*, Berlin, New York: Mouton de Gruyter, 1991, pp. 2-3.

23 See Branigan, *Narrative Comprehension and Film*, pp. 39-40.

24 ibid., p. 141.

25 See Fred Lerdal and Jackendoff, *A Generative Theory of Tonal Music*, Cambridge, Mass.: The MIT Press, 1985, pp. 39-40; Jackendoff, *Consciousness and the Computational Mind*, p. 143.

26 Fauconnier, *Les Espace Mentaux*, p. 32.

27 See Lakoff, *Women, Fire and Dangerous Things*, p. 181; Fauconnier, *Les Espaces Mentaux*, pp. 47 ff.

28 David Bordwell describes the film viewers' activity as follows: 'In the course of constructing the story the perceiver uses schemata and incoming cues to make assumptions, draw inferences about current story events, and frame and test hypotheses about prior and upcoming events', *Narration in the Fiction Film*, London: Methuen, 1985, p. 39. The construction of a story, or rather a *fabula*, can obviously be regarded as construing a mental representation (see Bordwell, ibid., p. 49). Jackendoff draws attention to the 'parallels in grammatical, lexical, and inferential patterns [which] suggest that the underlying logic of pictures and beliefs is pretty much the same – in particular that the ordinary language concept of belief is cognitively modeled on that of pictures', *Semantics and Cognition*, Cambridge,

Mass.: The MIT Press, 1983, p. 212.

Fauconnier asks: 'What about images? Paintings, photographs, aren't they real objects? Well, obviously the objects are real, but their interpretation as images is mental', *Les Espaces Mentaux*, p. 31.

[29] Fauconnier, *Les Espaces Mentaux*, p. 71.

[30] Jackendoff, *Languages of the Mind*, p. 159.

[31] See Lakoff, *Women, Fire and Dangerous Things*, p. 281.

[32] Langacker, *Concept, Image, and Symbol*, p. 318.

[33] Branigan, *Point of View in the Cinema*, p. 57.

[34] ibid., p. 16.

[35] ibid., p. 19.

[36] ibid., p. 40.

[37] Although this does not preclude the application of a strategic principle, according to which background assumptions across adjacent spaces must be maximized: 'As far as their *implicit* presuppositions and in general other contextual assumptions are concerned, space M and its parent space R must be structured as similar as possible', Fauconnier, *Les Espaces Mentaux*, p. 113.

[38] See Langacker, *Concept, Image, and Symbol*, p. 318.

[39] See also Roger Odin, 'Du Spectateur Fictionnalisant au Nouveau Spectateur: Approche Sémiopragmatique', *Iris*, no. 8, 1988, p. 129.

[40] *Narrative Comprehension and Film*, pp. 111-12.

[41] Christian Metz, *Psychoanalysis and Cinema: The Imaginary Signifier*, trans. Ben Brewster et al, London: Macmillan, 1982.

SECTION 3

THE PRAGMATIC TENDENCY IN THE NEW FILM SEMIOLOGY

INTRODUCTION

Jan Simons

I. Pragmatics

The actual interest in pragmatic approaches to film can be considered a logical outcome of the so-called 'second semiology', marked by a shift in focus from the film as a 'textual system' to the 'role of the spectator'. Pragmatics was originally defined by Charles Morris as 'the relations of signs to interpreters', in opposition to semantics (the study of 'the relations of signs to the objects to which the signs are applicable') and syntactics (the study of 'the formal relations of signs to one another'). Later Morris defined pragmatics in a more general way, as 'that portion of semiotic which deals with the origin, uses, and effects of signs within the behaviour in which they occur'.[1] In an even more general way one might say that a pragmatic approach relates a text to its *context*, that is, to 'the "environment" in which it appears, or at least intends, to operate'.[2]

This last definition might be too general, since it does not exclude branches of film studies such as film history or film sociology, which obviously also relate films to their 'environments'. The distinctive hallmark of the pragmatics of film is its linguistic origin and inspiration: pragmatic approaches are primarily interested in the way the 'environment' of a film affects the way a film as a 'signifying object' is comprehended or is intended to be comprehended by its spectators.

II. Pragmatics and Film

Since, in Metz's famous phrase, film semiology sees as its primary aim 'to understand how films are understood', and since classic film semiology came to the conclusion that film lacks a strongly codified syntax, as well as a paradigmatically organised semantics, pragmatics seemed to offer the only possible way to account for the comprehension of film. If it is indeed impossible to construe something like a film grammar or a film semantics (that is, if for film no abstract, Platonic language system can be assumed), then film can only be located in 'the messy universe of language', as Metz indeed does: 'the image is therefore always *speech*'.[3] There is, of course, no 'speech', no 'language use' without language users and without communicative contexts within which language is used.

One branch of film pragmatics focused on the way the spectator is 'addressed' by the film. The main question of this branch of research was whether and how the spectator's position is 'inscribed' in the filmic text, just as they are codified by first and second personal pronouns and other deictic expressions in linguistic utterances. This question has been the core of the so-called enunciation theories, of which Francesco Casetti might be considered the most outstanding representative (see Section 2 of this anthology).

Other ways in which the spectator is affected by the film were studied by scholars who turned to speech act theory rather than the studies of deictic expressions. Daniel Dayan tries to 'make Austin speak film' by studying how stylistic devices can be 'exploited' within a film to 'programme' responses and attitutes of the spectator towards characters and events represented in the film, and thus perform functions that are analogous to those of the different types of speech acts that were distinguished by Austin.[4]

Elena Dagrada's study of 'the diegetic look', presented in this section, also belongs to this strand of pragmatics, along with for instance Nick Browne's study of 'views' and 'glances' as elements of a film's rhetorical structure. Yet, what is notable in these studies by Dagrada and Browne is an emphasis on moments in films where a disjunction is effected between what the film text 'programmes' and what the spectator comprehends (see Browne's study of the Dry Fork sequence from *Stagecoach*).[5]

Nonetheless, these studies by Browne and Dagrada are based on the premises of the deictic and speech act theories, since they assume that, by themselves, films traditionally 'programme', 'perform', 'assign', or 'position' spectators. Odin calls this form of pragmatism 'immanent' and 'timid'.[6] In opposition to this immanent pragmatics, Roger Odin's semio-pragmatics of film is extrinsic. It returns to Metz's famous formula of film as a 'language sans langue' and draws radical and far reaching consequences out of it. In 'For a Semio-Pragmatics of Film', Odin claims that 'an image never indicates what procedures are to be followed for its reading'. Rather, the reading of a filmic image 'does not result from an internal constraint, but from a cultural constraint'. Furthermore, Odin argues that Metz's *Langage et Cinéma* should be read not as a description of the immanent codes of the film language, but rather as 'the *framework* of the cognitive labour of the spectator'.[7]

In rejecting the view that the spectator is not a derivative of the immanent structures of the text, Odin instead defines the spectator as 'the *point of passage of a bundle of determinations*'. The cognitive labour of the spectator itself is determined by a 'framework' of 'cultural constraints', which have an external existence from this spectator in what Odin calls 'the cultural space'. The film spectator is subjected to social institutions, which regulate the operations a spectator has to perform in order to come to an appropriate understanding of the film. In a number of essays, Odin discusses the institution of the fiction film, and how it differs from the institutions of the documentary, home movies, and so on. In 'A Semio-Pragmatic Approach to the Documentary Film', he argues that, when watching a fiction film, the spectator must perform a total of five operations: the construction of a diegesis, narrativization, 'mise en phase' ('alignment of the filmic relations to the diegetic relations in such a way that the spectator is made to "resonate" to the rhythm of the events told'), the construction of an absent enunciator, and finally fictivization.[8] For Odin, there is just one essential difference between documentary and fiction films – when watching a documentary, the spectator must posit the enunciator as real, rather than absent, in order to guarantee the truth of the images.

It seems logical to consider the framework of the cognitive operations performed by the spectator as part of the knowledge the spectator has of film.[9] This suggests that film pragmatics should (again) follow the example set by linguistics, and put cognition at the forefront of research. Film theory would then indeed have made the transition from sign to mind.

Notes

[1]   See John Lyons, *Semantics*, volume 1, Cambridge: Cambridge University Press, 1977, p. 115; François Rastier, 'La Triade Sémiotique, le Trivium et la Sémantique Linguistique', *Nouveaux Actes Sémiotiques*, no. 9, 1990, pp. 12-13; and Francesco Casetti, 'Pragmatique et Théorie du Cinéma Aujourd'hui', *Hors Cadre*, 7, 1989, p. 102.

[2]   Francesco Casetti, *Teorie del Cinema 1945-1990*, Milano: Bompiani, 1993, p. 278.

[3]   Christian Metz, *Film Language: A Semiotics of the Cinema*, trans. Michael Taylor, New York: Oxford University Press, 1974, p. 67.

[4]   Daniel Dayan, 'Le Spectateur Performé', *Hors Cadre*, 2, 1984, pp. 137-49.

[5]   Nick Browne, 'The Spectator-in-the-Text: The Rhetoric of *Stagecoach*', in: Philip Rosen (ed.), *Narrative Apparatus, Ideology*, New York: Columbia University Press, 1986. For other examples, see Nick Browne, *The Rhetoric of Film Narration*, Ann Arbor: UMI Research Press, 1982.

[6]   Roger Odin, 'La Sémiopragmatique du Cinéma sans Crise, ni Désillusion', *Hors Cadre*, 7, 1989, p. 83.

[7]   Roger Odin, ibid, p. 84.

[8]   For a more detailed list of the operations that a spectator must perform when watching a fiction film, see Roger Odin, 'Du Spectateur Fictionnalisant au Nouveau

Spectateur: Approche Sémiopragmatique', *Iris*, 8, 1988, pp. 121-39, and Odin's forthcoming book *Cinéma et effet fiction*.

9   This view is presented, for example by Ib Bondebjerg, in 'Narratives of Reality. Documentary Film and Television in a Cognitive and Pragmatic Perspective', Copenhagen: unpublished paper, 1993.

FOR A SEMIO-PRAGMATICS OF FILM

Roger Odin

A necessary starting point is the definition of our aim. Semiology means two things to us:

a   an attempt to 'understand how a film is understood' (to use Christian Metz's expression[1]),

b   an attempt to understand the mechanisms of the film-spectator relationship.

We are convinced that this programme can only be carried out if we see *pragmatics* as playing the *leading part* in the production of *meaning* and *affects*.

It is probably possible, albeit slightly over-simplistic, to distinguish three main current trends in the attitudes of linguists towards pragmatics.

Some prefer a complete separation between the fields of linguistics and pragmatics, and see any aspect of the latter as being part of a theory of action (pragmatics being then considered as the study of the application of linguistic formulas to a given context);[2] others try and implement some sort of 'integrated pragmatics'.

The latter current seems to embrace two distinct trends: for some linguists, linguistic analysis consists in identifying the informational content characterizing the utterance, then in determining its value and its illocutionary force[3] – this is what Alain Berrendonner calls the 'theory "in Y"'[4]; others prefer to renounce the notion of 'literal meaning',[5] and largely reduce the utterance to 'instructions' given to its potential interpreters, 'expecting them to search the discourse for relevant information, and use it in such a way as to reconstruct the meaning intended by the speaker'.[6]

Although the latter position seems the most acceptable within the field of linguistics, it does not seem possible to apply it unaltered to film as a subject for analysis.

The language of images is, indeed, characteristically devoid of any such instructions on the level of the utterance: an image never indicates what procedures are to be followed for its reading. In order to understand an image, therefore, it is necessary to follow procedures with no indication, within the image itself, 'of their nature, or of the order in which they are to be carried out'. In other words, any reading of an image consists of 'applying' to it processes that are essentially external to it. This reading does not result from an internal constraint, but from a cultural constraint.[7]

The sequential nature of film, which enables it to record 'the chronicle of a series of events', does not contradict the above remarks: a filmic chronicle follows a 'series of states, but without extracting or stressing the tranformation processes: it is indeed a dynamic product, and therefore completely different from the static views offered by photography or by drawing, but it is nothing more than a series of states'.[8]

Consequently, the only internal constraints involved in filmic communication are the obligation of *compatibility* between the procedures through which meaning is produced, and the form, disposition and consecution of the permanent marks imprinted[9] on the film, which are accurately reproduced every time the film is projected.[10]

We must, therefore, confront the shocking fact that not only does a film produce no meaning by itself,[11] but all it can do is to *block* a number of possible investments of meaning.[12] The only effect of internal constraints is to prevent the application of certain reading rules.

Seen from this angle, the elementary mechanism of the production of meaning could be described as follows:
a. the spectator proposes a meaning, and puts it to the test in the structure of the image.
b. if this proposition seems compatible with the constraints of the structure of the image, meaning is then produced.

It must, however, be stressed that where film is concerned, these constraints are extremely flexible, and always easy to evade. Filmic images, which disappear as soon as they appear, are fundamentally changeable, transitory, evanescent; they have to be seized as they rush past, on the spur on the moment, and with no hope of ever retrieving them; they follow one another unrelentlessly, allowing us no rest, no chance to take control, making it impossible for us to check and verify them (at least under normal projection conditions[13]). Predictably, the spectator is prone to deviant constructions, which do not even respect the disposition and the order of the marks imprinted on the film.[14] He has every reason to infringe the rules.

Although internal constraints are never imperative, some films, because of their structure, impose greater constraints than others (blocking the application of certain rules on the production of meaning more or less stringently).

In some experimental films, for instance, the configuration of the marks changes randomly between two frames. Under such conditions, the application of rules in the production of meaning is practically impossible, except on a very punctual level (such films are not in fact intended to function as forms of communication, even though they still carry some meaning: no film can totally block the production of meaning).

In classic narrative film, on the contrary, any alterations occurring between two frames, between two shots, between two sequences, obeys certain rules of coherence. The marks are imprinted on the film in keeping with the operation of these rules. This does not mean, of course, that the spectator is forced to apply the rules – since they are not incorporated into the film itself – but that nothing in the film itself will oppose an application of the rules by the spectator.

What is meant by *spectator* needs some explanation, since all propositions on the production of meaning seem to emanate from him.

The definition given by Christian Metz in his interview with Marc Vernet and Daniel Percheron is, to a certain degree, relevant to us: 'For me, the spectator is not the individual who goes to the cinema as a whole, concrete person, but only a part of him which goes there. It is the psychological mechanism necessary to the functioning of the institution, but only for the duration of the show'.[15]

For us, the *spectator* is a constructed entity, an actant; more precisely, he can be defined as the *point of passage of a bundle of determinations*.

Seen from this angle, the production of meaning is entirely based on *external* determinations. It is, indeed, exclusively through these determinations that the process of filmic communication can become operational: the closer the link between the determinations affecting the spectator and those affecting the direction, the more likely it is that the spectator-actant's constructions will match those of the director-actant.

All things considered, it is precisely because the Subjects producing the meaning (director and spectator) are not free to produce any odd discourse (because they can only express themselves by obeying the constraints of the 'discursive prac-tice'[16] characterizing their time and background) that communication can take place.

All determinations do not, however, have the same field of temporal and spatial application.

Some of them operate in a fairly stable way, and cover a vast geographical area (this is the case of determinations affecting the analogical reading of images, and narrative reading). Others, on the contrary, are particularly short-lived and/or limited in space (for instance, determinations affecting the interpretation of historical clues: recognition of certain characters or events). These determinations (and the processes of production of meaning that they trigger off) seem to be what M. Tardy describes as 'semiogeneses': the 'emergence of original modes of signification, furtive codes which only last for a moment'.[17]

Yet others are directly linked to language learning: the recognition of objects involves semes and semantemes[18] and there is, as Michel Colin points out, a 'discourse' in film.[19]

Others, finally, arise from the institutions constituting the filmic field: fiction film, documentary film, pedagogic film, home movies, industrial film, experimental film, etc.

By *institution*, we mean a structure activating a whole bundle of determinations. What we call a 'spectator' is simply the *point of passage* [20] of the determinations characterizing a given institution.

It is, of course, these institutional determinations that primarily interest the specialist in film semio-pragmatics, for they are the ones most specific to the filmic field (other determinations relate to the general cultural space).

Let us give some examples of what these institutions can directly affect.

1   The institution affects the hierarchical ordering of relevant features in the material of expression, but also of codes. This order provides the basis for the evaluation of the *degree of cinematic specificity* of the productions presented to the spectator.

The dominant filmic institution is thus characterized, from the point of view of the definition of film according to relevant features in the material of expression, by the predominance of the following features:
- iconicity (figurative images)
- mechanical duplication of reality
- reproduction of motion.[21]

Any occurrence of a feature of sub-categorization other than one of these three features, in the context of dominant film, is perceived by the spectator as a lowering of the degree of cinematic specificity of the passage in question.

The experimental filmic institution, on the other hand, applies a reversal of this hierarchical system. In this context, film productions of the highest degree of cinematic specificity are those that would be deemed to have the lowest specificity according to the dominant filmic institution. Here, priority is given to:
- non figurative images
- fixed images, or images manipulating the deconstruction or construction of motion
- and images produced by other means than the mechanical duplication of reality (for instance: images drawn by hand onto the film itself, as in some films by MacLaren).

The same observations apply to codes: whereas the dominant film institution considers productions that obey the rules of narrative coding as being of the highest degree of cinematic specificity,[22] the experimental film institution reserves this recognition to films that block the process of production of a narrative.[23]

Each institution is thus characterized by a certain definition of the filmic object in terms of material and codes.

2   The institution determines certain aspects of the *production of meaning*. For instance, the same phenomenon, such as an absence of sound, will be interpreted as

devoid of significance in the institution of silent film, and as a mistake (a mechanical failure) or a special effect, in the context of the institution of sound film. However, it must be said at this point that linguistic determinations, which are not exclusive to a film institution, are predominant. Institutions nevertheless have the power to block or facilitate the application of these linguistic determinations (thus, the experimental institution tries to block certain discursive determinations).

3   The institution determines the way in which the spectator produces *the image of the director*. In the institution of experimental film, for instance, which is a subdivision of the 'artistic' institution, the spectator acts in the Author's name (as Benjamin said, 'art is a question of surnames'). The institution of fiction film, on the contrary, demands the obliteration of any such marks of enunciation (the film is meant to function by itself, as if it had never been produced by a director). In the institution of pedagogic film,[24] the director is constructed by the spectator as the one possessing Knowledge, whereas in the institution of newsreel film, he is constructed as the one possessing Sight, the one who has seen. In this sense, the instruction given by the institution of newsreel film can be described as follows:

a. the director and the camera were there when the events happened; they saw them;

b. these events would have happened in the same way if the director and the camera had not been there.[25]

This last point is one of the differences between fiction film and newsreel film: the spectator watching a fiction film knows that the events that he sees happening on screen have been specially produced by the director, in front of the camera, even if he agrees, as long as the projection lasts, to pretend that the events existed by themselves (this reminds us of the familiar question on the suspension of disbelief: 'I know very well ... but all the same').

4   The institution also determines the spectator's *affective positioning*. As Metz has shown, the dominant film institution produces a spectator-actant at once isolated, motionless and dumb, whose psychological positioning lies somewhere between the waking state, day-dreaming and dreaming, and who is willing to produce this comprehensive imaginary construction: the diegesis.[26] As for us, we have tried to show how the institution of home movies produces a spectator who is more a 'participant' than a real spectator: he takes part in the direction of the film (having held the camera), in the action taking place on screen (having been filmed), in the installation of the projection equipment (having set up the screen and projector), and, finally, in this type of event that consists of the collective creation of a memorial diegesis by the members of the family.[27]

Thus, each institution has its own specific way of positioning its spectator. Hence the necessity, when analysing a film, of specifying which institutional framework one takes as a viewpoint; also the necessity, for the theoretician of film, of analysing the different ways in which institutions produce their spectator: which largely remains to be done.

Remarks on Terminology

We propose calling *'reader-actant'* the arch-lexeme subsuming the different ways in which institutions produce their spectator, and reserving the term *'spectator'* for the *'reader-actant'* produced by the institution of dominant film. We will, of course, have to find appropriate denominations for the *'reader-actants'* of other film institutions.

The choice of the arch-lexeme 'reader-actant' is explained by our wish to avoid, as much as possible, denominations implying that the production of meaning rests exclusively with the director-actant (such as the transmitter-recipient and sender-addressee pairs). In this respect, the notion of 'reader' seems less loaded, implying more of a really active process of production.

Alongside these denominations (reader-actant vs director-actant), we shall refer to the *directing space* and to the *reading space*. We shall also call *'direction-film'* the film endowed with meaning produced within the directing space by the director-actant, and *'reading-film'*, the film endowed with meaning produced within the reading space by the reader-actant. This terminology seems more adequate to us than the traditional notion of 'filmic text' (which gives the misleading impression that the film is in itself endowed with meaning), in that it clearly states that meaning is produced in both spaces, that these two productions are quite independent from each other, and are directly linked to the work of the actants concerned: the 'direction-film' and the 'reading-film' are thus opposed (as productions endowed with meaning) to the *'reel-film'* (the film as a series of marks imprinted on the film base) and to the *'projection-film'* (the film as a series of light or sound resonances, as it appears on screen awaiting an investment of meaning on the part of the 'reader-actant').

5   Finally, the institution determines *the production of affects by the film itself*. Indeed, at every stage of the projection, the 'reading-film', as it is constructed by the reader-actant under the influence of determinations, retroacts on this reader-actant, triggering positive or negative emotional reactions, which are themselves conditioned by the influence of institutional determinations. The film analyst, having determined the institutional context which constitutes his viewpoint (having, therefore, specified the rules influencing the construction of the reader-actant by the relevant institution), will be expected to examine the way in which the 'reading-film' plays with the reader-actant's affects. It could be argued that this implies a return to Charles Bally's 'stylistics of effects', but, of course, with a different set of presuppositions, for the analysis does not aim to reveal the feelings of the 'speaker' (in our terminology, the director-actant),

but only to show how the 'reading-film' shapes the affective reactions of the reader-actant in a certain institutional context.

For the purpose of our work on fiction film, we choose to designate, by the notion of 'mise en phase', the specific affective relationship produced by this type of film, in the framework of the dominant filmic institution.[28]

By *'mise en phase'*, we mean the following: at every major stage in the story being told, the film produces a relationship between itself and the spectator (an affective positioning of the latter) which is *homologous* with the relationships occurring in the diegesis.

In Lacanian terms, the 'mise en phase' could be said to activate the inscription of the spectator on the imaginary axis.[29] Indeed, the power of the 'mise en phase' is such that it enables the imaginary axis to benefit from figures which would otherwise be perceived as more or less strong marks of enunciation counteracting the spectator's fictional positioning. In other words, no figure is in itself inappropriate on the level of the imaginary axis: even a direct look into the camera (probably the most loaded figure from the point of view of the utterance, and the biggest taboo in fiction film[30]) can be put to use on the imaginary axis, as long as it corresponds to a homologous relationship within the diegesis (this applies to the glance directed at the camera during Henri's defloration of Henriette in Jean Renoir's *Partie de campagne*[31]). In *La Jetée* by Chris Marker, everything points in this direction: this film, at first sight, shows all the hallmarks of an experimental film, relying almost entirely on the freeze frame[32] – a highly loaded figure from the point of view of the utterance, in the context of the dominant filmic institution – and yet it succeeds, thanks to the 'mise en phase', in producing a highly intense fictional effect.[33]

Conversely, certain films that should, *a priori*, operate on the fictional level (since they tell a story) block the process of 'mise en phase', and so fail to produce a satisfactory film-spectator relationship in the context of the dominant filmic institution; such films are then perceived by the spectator as 'bad' films. This is the case of *Le Tempestaire* by Jean Epstein, which both triggers off and blocks the process of 'mise en phase'.[34] We propose to call 'phase displacement' [*déphasage*] the series of processes counteracting the 'mise en phase'.

Finally, it must be said that a film that has been rejected by the dominant filmic institution due to such 'phase displacement' can operate in the context of some other institution, for which no 'mise en phase' is compulsory. For this reason, *Le Tempestaire* comes into its own with institutions that allow a second reading (such as film clubs or courses on film study); it then operates on a 'performative' level. Let us remember that the term 'performative' applies to 'texts that are characterized by a relative change of focus, from the content being told to the process of telling'.[35] Viewed from this angle, *Le Tempestaire* can be seen as a remarkable parable on how fictional film operates (but not as a fiction film).

These observations on the functioning or malfunctioning of a film in a given institutional context lead to the introduction of the notion of *sanction* into the notion of institution.

The notion of sanction is, indeed, central to the notion of institution: 'The institution is a symbolic network, liable to social sanctions', as Castoriadis wrote in *L'institution imaginaire de la société*.[36] Similarly, Berrendonner defines the institution as a 'normative power, subjecting the individuals to certain mutual practices on pain of sanctions'.[37]

The displeasure felt by the spectator viewing *Le Tempestaire* from within the institution of the fiction film is the sanction pronounced by this institution against a film that blocks the process of 'mise en phase'. In the same way, boredom will be the sanction pronounced by someone going to see a documentary in the frame of mind of someone going to see a fiction film. Inversely, someone going to see a fiction film in the frame of mind of the reader-actant of a documentary would probably be considered 'insane', for he would be accused of confusing different levels of reality.

It can be seen that the sanction may apply to the film itself, if its treatment of the material is unacceptable to the institution within which it is meant to operate, or the reader-actant, if he infringes the institutional determinations that are imposed on him (this reminds us of the necessity of the distinction between the spectator in the flesh, and the reader-actant as constructed by the institution: for conflicts may arise between these two entities).

We have just demonstrated the existence of different filmic institutions, and (too briefly, no doubt) outlined a framework for possible further reflection. The next question is: should we distinguish between *several* 'film' objects necessitating very distinct semiological approaches (corresponding to the diversity of filmic institutions), or should we, on the contrary, construct *one* film semiology, integrating variations of instructions and treatment within a single approach?

The answer is far from obvious. For instance, Eric de Kuyper's comment on experimental film (which he renames the 'bad form') is that 'this deconstruction of film may be done with film, but should probably be excluded from the filmic field proper. The deconstruction (...) is so successful that, let's face it, it no longer belongs to the cinema'.[38] Dominique Noguez (though not hostile to experimental film) supports a similar solution, wondering whether it might not be sensible to question the very idea of a 'single corpus', 'the very idea that there is one cinema'.[39]

This position seems to encounter a number of problems, of which we only recently became aware. One of them is that everything does not change as one moves from one institution to another.

One finds, for instance, the same filmic treatment (basically strong and discontinous) in home movies, experimental films and documentary films. It is the reading instructions that change: production of a family fiction,[40] with the institution of home movies; production of the experimental effect, with the institution of experimental film;[41] and production of an authentic effect, with the institution of the documentary film.[42]

Inversely, the same instruction (at least on a certain level) can be compatible with different, not to say opposite treatments. This is what happens, in our opinion, between the institution of home movies and the dominant filmic institution: both institutions instruct their reader-actant to produce a fiction (a family fiction, a really 'fictional' fiction) and this fiction is actually constructed in both institutions, although the figures through which this fiction is constructed in the institution of home movies are precisely those that would prevent it in the dominant filmic institution (broken up narrative, jumps, blurred images, address to the camera...); and, inversely, movies constructed in the style of the fiction film (continuity, coherence, no address to the camera...) provokes a reaction of rejection in the reader-actant as a member of the family.[43]

Finally, even when two institutions are differentiated by instructions and by the filmic treatment which is being applied, this does not mean that they operate independently of each other. There exists, paradoxically, a strong link between the dominant filmic institution and the institution of experimental film. Eric de Kuyper stresses this particular point, and proposes, consequently, the term 'marginal' film as a substitute for 'experimental' film: 'This cinema will be called *marginal*. Simply in order to remind us that what is written in the margin of a text bears a relation (any relation, but some relation) to this text, to the large corpus to which it is linked, on which it depends, on which it is commenting or which it is refuting by means of notes and arguments. But it is in the margin, whether it likes it or not'.[44]

Experimental film could be considered, to a certain extent, as the negative of classic fictional film,[45] justifying the formulation of appropriate transformation rules.

It is in fact probable that the institution of classic fiction film enjoys a privileged position in the filmic field, for everyone has assimilated the norms of fiction film. There is therefore a risk, whenever we watch a documentary or an experimental film, of a conflict between the fictional determinations that we all carry within ourselves, and the determinations characterizing these institutions. No theoretician can afford to ignore this phenomenon.

We shall therefore state the existence of a law of *co-determination* between institutions, and consider that the institutional *heterogeneity* of the filmic field is a *structured* one.

This idea of heterogeneity is not self-evident. We know that Ferdinand de Saussure, for instance, saw heterogeneity and systematicity as being in contradiction. Since then, a number of linguists (Labov, Weinreich, Herzog...) have attempted to reconcile the two;[46] it does seem that if one wants to avoid being out of touch with what is really happening in linguistic communication, if one refuses, in other words, to abandon the level of performance, the notion of free variable should be replaced by that of *variable structures* contained in the language and *determined by different social functions*. In this respect, a language is a *diasystem* composed of several *dialects*, and every speaker has a number of different codes at his disposal; competence then appears to be the command of a *regularly* differentiated system.[47]

In the same way, the heterogeneity of the filmic field can be described as a structure within which each institution uses a specific filmic 'dialect' and fulfils a specific *social function*. This notion of function actually needs some clarification, for we may well have to distinguish, along with Michel Pêcheux,[48] between the *apparent* function and the *implicit* function. The institution of home movies, for instance, fulfils the apparent function of storing memories, and the implicit function of strengthening family bonds (and therefore a certain social order).

Our semio-pragmatic bias therefore leads us to contemplate the construction of a sort of *polylectal* grammar of film. By way of conclusion, we shall point to one major problem which has so far been ignored: the problem of the origin of institutions, and of their very existence.

(*Translated by Claudine Tourniaire*)

Notes

[1] Christian Metz, *Language and Cinema*, trans. Donna Jean-Umiker Sebeok, The Hague: Mouton, 1974, p. 74.

[2] This is the neopositivist attitude (Morris, Carnap) recently revived by Alain Berrendonner: *Eléments de pragmatique linguistique*, Editions de Minuit, 1981.

[3] The main representatives of this trend are Austin, Searle, Ducrot, Recanati, Orecchioni.

[4] Berrendonner, *ibid.*, p. 11.

5 For an examination of this concept, see John R. Searle: *Expression and Meaning*, Cambridge: Cambridge University Press, 1979.

6 Oswald Ducrot, *Les mots du discours*, Editions de Minuit, 1980, p. 12.

7 F. Bresson, 'Compétence iconique et compétence linguistique', in *Communications* No 33, 1981, p. 187-89.

8 *Ibid.*, p. 188.

9 Approaching this question during Metz's seminar, one of the participants (the experimental film director Giovanni Martedi) remarked that this statement was questionable: the quality of the film is affected by time, and the marks may change quite considerably after a long period.

10 This also needs qualifying: the marks vary depending on the power generated by the projector, the dimensions of the projector gate, etc.

11 Sol Worth was already expressing the same idea: 'There is no meaning in a film itself', in 'The Development of a Semiotic of Film', *Semiotica*, 1969, 1-3, p. 289.

12 Paul Willemen also remarks: 'Texts can restrict readings (offer resistance), they can't determine them', in 'Notes on Subjectivity. On Reading Edward Branigan's 'Subjectivity Under Siege'', *Screen*, 19, 1, 1978.

13 Obviously, things happen quite differently if the reading takes place at the editing table.

14 Raymond Bellour quotes some significant examples of deviant reading in the introduction to his study *L'analyse du film*, Paris: Albatros, 1979, 'D'une histoire', in particular p. 13.

15 'Entretien avec Ch. Metz', in *Ça Cinéma*, special Christian Metz issue, 7/8, 1975, p. 37.

16 Discursive practice: 'a set of anonymous, historical rules, always determined in time and space, which have defined, at a certain time and for a given social, economic, geographical or linguistic field, the working procedures of the utterance process'. Michel Foucault, *The Archaeology of Knowledge*, trans. A.M. Sheridan-Smith, New York: Pantheon Books, 1972.

17 M. Tardy, 'Sémiogénèse d'encodage, sémiogénèse de décodage', in *The Canadian Journal of Research Semiotics*, Spring 1979, Vol. VI, No 3, VII, No 1, p. 111.

18 On this point, see Metz, 'Le perçu et le nommé', in *Vers une esthétique sans entrave*, Mélanges Mikel Dufrenne, 10/18, 1975, pp. 345-78; and my own article: 'Quelques réflexions sur le fonctionnement des isotopies minimales et des isotopies élémentaires dans l'image', in *Versus*, 14/3, p. 69-91.

19 Michel Colin, *Prolégomènes à une 'sémiologie générative' du film*, Thèse de Doctorat ès Lettres, 1979. [Published as *Langue, film, discours: Prolégomènes à une sémiologie générative du film* , Paris: Klincksieck, 1985.]

[20] E. Veron: 'The subject is therefore, in our opinion, the *point of passage* of the rules on production and recognition processes...', in 'Semiosis de l'idéologie et du pouvoir', *Communications* 28, 1978, p. 19.

[21] On this definition of film in terms of relevant features of the material of expression, see Metz, *Language and Cinema*, pp. 227-235; and the chapter 'Préliminaire' in my thesis: 'L'Objet cinéma', in *L'analyse sémiologique des films*, to be published.

[22] 'The basic formula, which has never changed, is the one that consists in making a large continuous unit that tells a story, a "movie"... '. Metz, *Film Language: A Semiotics of the Cinema*, trans. Michael Taylor, New York: Oxford University Press, 1974, p. 45.

[23] On this point, see Dominique Noguez, *Eloge du cinéma expérimental*, Publication du Centre Georges Pompidou, 1979.

[24] On the functioning of the pedagogic film, see Geneviève Jacquinot, *Images et Pédagogie*, Paris: PUF, 1977.

[25] On the functioning of the news report, or documentary film, see Bill Nichols, *Ideology and the Image*, Bloomington: Indiana University Press, 1981, chapters 6, 7 and 8.

[26] Metz, 'The Fiction Film and its Spectator', trans. Alfred Guzzetti, in Metz, *Psychoanalysis and Cinema: The Imaginary Signifier*, London: Macmillan, 1982, pp. 99-147.

[27] See my own article, 'Rhétorique du film de famille' in *Rhétoriques sémiotiques, Revue d'Esthétique*, 1979, 1/2, 10/18, pp. 340-373.

[28] On this point, see my own study, soon to be published: *Partie de campagne: un exemple de 'mise en phase'*.

[29] This notion of 'mise en phase' seem to correspond quite accurately to what Michel Colin calls 'secondary identification'; indeed, the 'mise en phase' attempts to get the spectator to enter into the relational system, in other words the discourse, of the film (see *Langue, film, discours*, Paris: Klincksieck, 1985).

We also discovered at a later date that the expression 'mise en phase' was also used by Ph. Hamon to explain what happens in a realistic text, and especially descriptions; Hamon mentions an 'aesthetics of the process of mise en phase (set/character/ spectator)', and points out that 'the description is a kind of tonal operator (producing a positive or negative effect, euphoria or dysphoria) orientating the consumption of the text by the reader in the light of a global aesthetics of homogeneity' (Ph. Hamon, *Introduction à l'analyse du descriptif*, Hachette Université, 1981, p. 20). This coincidence is all the more interesting as the realistic text is the equivalent, within the literary space, of the classic fiction film within the filmic space.

[30] On this taboo, see, for example, Alain Bergala, *Initiation à la sémiologie du récit en images*, Les Cahiers de l'audio-visuel, p. 31-32, and Francesco Casetti 'Les yeux

dans les yeux', *Communications*, 38, 1983, pp. 78-97 [published in the present volume].

[31] The look directed at the camera, which is a kind of rape of our spectatorial self, is actually simultaneous with the 'rape' of Henriette by Henri.

[32] The only exception to the systematic use of the freeze-frame is shot No 282, which actually shows the woman opening her eyes (reproducing the movement).

[33] On this point, see my own article: 'Le film de fiction menacé par la photographie et sauvé par la bande-son. A propos de *la Jetée* de Chris Marker', in Dominique Chateau, André Gardies, and François Jost (eds.), *Cinémas de la modernité, films, théories*, Colloque de Cerisy, Paris: Klinsieck, 1981, pp. 147-172.

[34] On this point, see my own article 'Mise en phase, déphasage et performativité dans *Le Tempestaire* de Jean Epstein', *Communications* 38, 1983, pp. 213-38.

[35] C. Kerbrat Orecchioni, 'Note sur les concepts d'Illocutoire et de Performatif', in *Linguistique et sémiologie*, 4, 1977, p.82.

[36] C. Castoriadis, *L'institution imaginaire de la société*, Paris: le Seuil, 1975, p. 184.

[37] Berrendonner, ibid., p. 95.

[38] Eric de Kuyper, 'Le mauvais genre. II', in *Ça Cinéma*, 19, p. 33.

[39] Dominique Noguez, 'Théorie(s) du (ou des) cinéma(s)?', in *Cinémas de la modernité*, p. 43.

[40] According to this instruction, the breaks play the part of a 'stimulant' of memorial activity; at the same time, they enable each participant to reconstruct *his* own diegesis fairly free of constraints. On the concept of 'family fiction', see my own article 'Rhétorique du film de famille', pp. 364-67.

[41] It seems as if the instructions given by experimental film could be summarized as follows: read the breaks as a deliberate attempt, on the part of this type of film, to distinguish itself from classic fiction film, as manifestations of the desire to produce 'another' type of film; and enjoy these breaks. The 'experimental' effect certainly deserves a more detailed analysis; some relevant comments can be found in Noguez, *Eloge du cinéma expérimental*, especially in chapter 1: 'Qu'est-ce que le cinéma expérimental?'.

[42] Here, unlike what happens in experimental and home movies, the instruction orders the reader to consider the breaks as signs of the cameraman's presence on site, and of the difficulty of shooting live events. Once again, a detailed analysis of the 'filmic document' effect is needed; a few comments can be found in Nichols, *Ideology and the Image*.

[43] Many an amateur film director, 'corrupted' by the fetishism characterizing fiction films and prevailing in amateur film clubs, has learnt this the hard way, after a few family quarrels...

44   Eric de Kuyper; 'Le mauvais genre. I. (Une affaire de famille)', in *Ça Cinéma*, 18, p. 45.

45   This emerges very clearly from the first chapter of Noguez's study: *Eloge du cinéma expérimental*.

46   See 'Empirical Foundation for a Theory of Language Change', by U. Weinreich, W. Labov, M.I. Herzog, in W.P. Lehmann & Y. Malkiel (eds.), *Directions for Historical Linguistics, A Symposium*, Austin and London: University of Texas Press, 1968.

47   Similar comments can be found in: A. Delveau, H. Huot, F. Kerleroux, 'Questions sur le changement linguistique', *Langue française* No 15, 1972, and S. Lecointre and J. Le Galliot, 'Le changement linguistique: problématiques nouvelles', *Langages*, 32, 1973.

48   Michel Pêcheux, *Analyse automatique du discours*, Paris, Dunod, 1969, pp. 13-14.

A SEMIO-PRAGMATIC APPROACH TO THE DOCUMENTARY FILM

Roger Odin

The objective of a semio-pragmatics of film and the audio-visual is to attempt to understand how audio-visual productions function in a given social space. According to this approach, the act of making or seeing a film is not immediately a fact of discourse, but a social fact obtained by adopting a *role* that regulates the production of the *film text* (which means film as a construction endowed with meaning and generating affects). A role can be described as a specific psychic positioning (cognitive and affective) that leads to the implementation of a certain number of *operations* that produce meaning and affects. *A priori*, there is absolutely no reason for the actant director and actant reader to adopt the same role (the same way of producing meaning and affects). However, it is only when the same role is adopted by these two actants that what can be called a *space of communication* is created. A space of communication is a space in which the production of meaning and affects are harmoniously formed during the filmmaking and the reading. From this space of communication derives the feeling of mutual comprehension between the actants, which gives the impression that communication resides in the transmission of a message from a Sender to a Receiver.

The choice of a role by the actants is to a great extent linked to the intervention of *bundles of determination*, which derive from the social space. These bundles of determination, which constitute the actants as social Subjects, function like instructions to produce meaning and affects. In a given social space and field of communication, all the bundles of determination do not have the same power. It is for this reason that we cannot understand anything about what is going on in the field of audio-visual communication, in our social space, if we do not posit as our point of departure, and in all further considerations, the fact that the dominant bundle of determination – perhaps one should say *still* dominant, because it does appear, as we shall have the opportunity to point out at the end of this article, that things are slowly beginning to change – is the bundle of determination that constitutes the space of *fictional* communication.

This bundle, whose existence predates the cinema (it is what made the novel so popular), and whose intervention made itself felt at different degrees in the ensemble of cultural productions has, in fact, the characteristic of manifesting itself *within* each of us, to the point of appearing like 'a desire inherent in our psychical structure'.[1] More precisely, some see in it a manifestation of the Oedipal and of the 'configuration based on the narcissistic redoubling between man and woman that has ruled, since the end of the 18th century and throughout the 19th century (which we have just left behind us), the relation of desire between the two sexes'.[2] Indeed, it is advisable to be prudent when confronted with the temptation to universalize and even more to naturalize this desire, but one thing is certain: in our Western societies and in the field of the audio-visual, the space of fictional communication is the dominant space of communication. It is so dominant that, in the social imaginary, we often have the tendency to simply assimilate cinema and fiction film. Furthermore, the productions that do not conform with the constraints of this space find it very difficult to function correctly.

This is precisely the case with the documentary film. This manifests itself both on the film-making level and on the reading level: not only does making a documentary always appear less prestigious than making a fiction film – there are only a few documentary film-makers who have been able to gain recognition as an 'auteur', and when this happens it is very often retrospectively, because they have succeeded in the fiction film. Moreover, the documentary in a general sense is considered to be a temporary locus while waiting to be able to make fiction films. But also, for the spectators themselves, the documentary appears like something that we hardly have the desire to look at spontaneously, since it is often regarded as something that is fundamentally boring: 'The docukoo really annoys the kids, and how ...'. This terse formula by Raymond Queneau may be generalized without risk to the ensemble of spectators.[3]

But before continuing along this line of inquiry about the documentary, it is necessary to briefly describe the dominant regime of communication – the fictionalizing regime. Though it is not a question here of developing a theory of fiction,[4] it seems indispensable to us to comprehend the functioning of the documentary in our social space and to briefly explain the different operations that constitute the process of fictionalization.

There are a total of five operations:

1 *Construction of a diegesis*: production of a world (we must note that this operation presupposes the anterior operation of 'figurativization': the construction of figurative images);
2 *Narrativization*: production of a story, of a narrative;
3 *'Mise en phase'*: alignment of the filmic relations to the diegetic relations in such a way that the spectator is made to 'resonate' to the rhythm of the events told;
4 *Construction of an absent Enunciator*: the presence of the Enunciator is both indicated and effaced in such a way that the spectator, although knowing very well that

an Enunciator does exist may, however, believe that the world and events that are shown to him exist in themselves (we recognise here the mechanism of belief described by Octave Mannoni: 'I know very well ... but all the same';[5]

5   *Fictivization*: the (absent) Enunciator functions as a fictive origin. He accomplishes the act of enunciation 'without undertaking the commitments that are normally required by that act' (the obligation to guarantee the truth of what is articulated, to provide proof if requested, to commit himself personally to this truth: the sincerity rule ...).[6]

How does all of this concern the documentary? It is necessary to realise that the documentary is compatible with the majority of the operations that intervene in the process of fictionalization. Most documentaries construct a world (a diegesis) and comply with the rules of narrative structuration, even if it is to tell the story about how a barrel is made or the different stages of metamorphosis of the dragon-fly. More rare are without doubt the documentaries that bring into operation the 'mise en phase'. However, a certain number of these do exist, like those by Walt Disney and F. Rossif that are devoted to animals: everything is done 'to set the spectator on the right track', to involve him affectively in the dramas that take place in nature. The process that constructs an absent Enunciator is itself very frequent in the documentary. All the productions that function in accordance with the ideology of transparency (direct cinema, 'candid eye'-cinema, cinéma-vérité...) strive to give us a view of the things of the world as if there were no intermediaries, as if the world were there in front of us instead of on the screen.

Indeed, only the operation of fictivization is radically incompatible with the documentary. To make or read a film in a documentary perspective is always to construct an Enunciator who functions as a *real* origin. It is this operation, and nothing else, that founds the process of *documentarization*.[7] The operations involved in the construction of a diegesis, in narrativization, in 'mise en phase', and in the construction of an absent Enunciator can intervene concurrently with the implementation of this process, but they are not part of it, as opposed to what takes place in fictionalization where they are an integral part of the process. We can even say that a documentary will have a higher degree of 'documentarity' the more it blocks a greater number of these operations.[8] On the other hand, a documentary will have more chance to be accepted by the public if it mobilizes more operations belonging to the process of fictionalization, i.e. the more it resembles the fiction film. Television-makers know this very well: 'The reportages that are most appreciated and about which the critics make the most complements, are those that tell a story. The more they conform to narrative, the greater their success'.[9] If, in addition, they function in accordance with the 'mise en phase' it is even better. The only documentaries to have real success with the public (leaving aside the cinephiles) are precisely those that put into practice the first three or four operations of fictionalization (which is the key to the success of the series devoted to animals mentioned above).

However, this strategy to win-over the public to the documentary has a disadvantage: the more the documentary employs operations deriving from fictionalization, the more there is the risk that if the affirmation of documentarization (the construction of a real Enunciator) is not extremely strong, it may very well turn out that fictionalization will triumph over it. Nothing is more difficult to get included in a film than this documentarizing communication pact. Its acceptance has the effect of dislodging the Addressee of the film from his comfort as a spectator by placing him in the position of a *real* Addressee, i.e. an Addressee having to take seriously, in reality, what he is offered to watch. Faced with the perspective of such a positioning, the Addressee of the documentary film mobilizes all of his defences, and the simplest solution usually open to him (since it is the most readily available solution within our social space) is not to take into account the documentarizing injunction and to take up again as quickly as possible the position of a fictionalizing spectator.

We could, it seems to us, account for the very curious positioning that results from this alternating as a process of belief of double relief:

- first time: I know very well that what I am offered to watch emanates from a real enunciator, but I react as if it were a fictitious Enunciator (a refusal of the documentarizing injunction);
- second time: I want to believe that it concerns the production of a fictitious Enunciator; consequently, I can from now on allow myself without any problem to believe in the reality of what I am offered to watch (re-engagement to a fictionalizing positioning).

Be that as it may, the dilemma that all documentarizing production is embroiled in can now be formulated very precisely:

- either it attracts only a small audience, because it clashes too directly with the fundamental desires of spectators,
- or it reverts to the dominant space of fictional communication.

Now we would like to attempt to show quickly what happens in a certain number of Institutions that are attempting, despite all these difficulties, to promote documentary productions or, more simply, to make them function. Our hypothesis is that their degree of success in this attempt essentially depends on the way in which they negotiate the setting up of the documentarizing pact.

However, before coming to this investigation, it is necessary to return briefly to the conditions governing the setting up of the fictionalizing pact. What really characterises the fictionalizing pact, what explains why it functions so well is, on the one hand, that its Sender (the person responsible for the *mandate*[10]) seems to merge with the spectator Subject himself – the spectator Subject has the feeling of being himself his own Sender, even though the real Sender is in fact the social space. On the other hand, the manifestation of this mandate is so strongly interiorized that it takes place unconsciously. As soon as we are in the field of the cinema, the Desire for fiction is present, without which the Subject needs to decree it. This is a sort of 'natural' pulsation (quite evidently cultural) that animates the Subject without passing through the intermediary of a certain 'wanting' (even less of a 'having to do'). It is advisable to keep this in mind if we want to understand the problems that exist for the Institutions which promote documentaries.

Within the framework of this article, whose aim is to explain a method rather than carry out a systematic analysis of the documentarizing communication space, we shall be content to briefly examine the case of three Institutions that appear interesting because of the very different ways in which they offer to the addressee the documentarizing pact: School, the BPI at the Georges Pompidou Centre, and Television.

School. School is one of the great users of documentary productions while being itself an important producer of them. However, it seems that things are not working out as well as we would wish, because these productions rarely attain their pedagogical objectives. Indeed, there are many reasons for this, some of which (linked to the structure of the films themselves) have already been given prominence by Genevière Jacquinot.[11] We would only like to insist here on the difficulties arising from the institutional modalities setting up the communication pact. Within the framework of School, the documentarizing pact appears, in fact, as something imposed from the outside by an authority (the Teacher, himself representing the School Institution) endowed with the power to sanction and operate in the manner of 'Having to do'. Such an injunction can only conflict violently with the fictionalizing desire that animates the student-Subject from within. The conflict will be even stronger as long as the student-Subject considers the offer to watch a film to be equal to the instruction to fictionalize. In this perspective, we can say that the Teacher gives two contradictory instructions: to fictionalize and to documentarize. Faced with these two instructions issued by the same Sender the student-Subject can neither choose nor escape. We recognise here the characteristic schema of the 'double-bind'.[12] The ways to answer this type of paradoxical injunction are relatively limited: the first consists of strictly adhering to the injunction despite its illogicality – namely, in the case that concerns us here, to watch the film (this is what is common to the two injunctions) without fictionalizing or documentalizing, i.e. without taking any interest in it whatsoever. The second consists in 'withdrawing' from the game, in breaking off the communication (for example by taking refuge in day-dreaming or by talking to one's neighbours). And finally, the third consists in contesting more or less aggressively the source of the paradoxical injunction (uproar, dissension with the teacher, etc.). It is of course clear that none of these responses can have a positive effect on pedagogical communication.

The B.P.I. Apart from its role as library, the B.P.I. (Public Library of Information at the Georges Pompidou centre) produces a certain number of documentaries and makes freely available to its users documentaries on video. In addition, the B.P.I. organises a festival that specializes in this type of film: the Festival of the 'Cinéma du réel'. Within this institutional framework, and in opposition to what takes place in School, the documentarizing pact is not in any way forced upon the Addressees: it establishes itself prior to the arrival of the users at the B.P.I. by an internal negotiation (between the user and himself) or, to be more exact, between the fictionalizing *Desire* that the user has in him and his decision to see a documentary film: his *Wanting* to see a documentary film. This means that when the user enters the B.P.I., he has already decided to put himself in the position of a documentarizing spectator. Even if that does not regulate everything (namely, it can happen that the Desire for fiction returns during the showing of the film and causes annoyance towards the documentary film) it is, however, certain that the documentarizing communication has a much greater chance of functioning correctly within this context than within the context of the School.

Television. Television offers through a variety of programmes transmissions that correspond to different communication pacts: the spectacular pact of the variety shows, the ludic pact of the television games, the fictionalizing pact of the films and serials, the advertisement pact, the documentarizing pact of the 'magazine' programmes and news-broadcasts, etc.[13] All these pacts have in common the fact that they are offered as a choice to the television viewer without any apparent external constraints (acceptance of the contract seems to depend only on his *Wanting*) and prior to the transmission itself (by the television guides that publicize the programmes or by the announcements that appear on television during the day). Here we find ourselves in a situation quite similar to what we described in relation to the B.P.I.: the television viewer *positions himself* in the role of a documentarizing tele-viewer before seeing the transmission. Moreover, it appears that these transmissions are very well received by television viewers, so much so that Television still remains one of the few transmitters of this type of production.[14]

Nevertheless, we can wonder if this analysis of the functioning of television in terms of communication pacts is quite correct. In fact, there are good reasons to support the argument that television functions less in the way of a *contract* and more in the way of a *contact*. Let us note first of all that very frequently the television viewer switches on the television without prior contract and allows himself to be guided by the flux of images and sounds without any other positioning than to enjoy this flux. More generally, we can say that television establishes with its viewer a relationship that is based more on the, almost physical, power of a whole set of variations of rhythm and intensity, rather than on the production regulated by meaning and affects. The present evolution of television is moving clearly in the direction of a strengthening of this tendency already inherent in the medium itself: fragmentation of the transmissions by commercials, shortening of the length of transmissions, internal cutting up of the transmissions themselves in short sequences having their own rhythm and 'treatment'.[15] All concur in such a way as to make television a medium that we watch just for itself independent of the content of the transmissions (the famous formula of Marshall McLuhan: 'The medium is the message' applies perfectly here), a medium of fascination (we are not far from hypnotism), rather than one of communication. Under these conditions, we can say that all the transmissions are watched with the same *indifference* and the opposition between fictionalization and documentarization (to remain within the two types of contract which we are concerned with in this article) is thus suspended, emptied of its signification and its pragmatic relevance to make room for a positioning which consists of allowing ourselves to be carried along by the *energetics of the flux*.

This energetic positioning does not only exist in relation to television: an ever increasing number of films function according to this principle (the *Mad Max*, *Rambo* and *Rocky* series, etc.).[16] All video clips also pertain to this positioning (and we know the success of the music stations that diffuse these products). Finally, it is evident that the popularity of discos and huge spectacular concerts goes in the same direction. It is therefore not absurd to formulate the hypothesis of a modification in the demand of the social space itself. Perhaps we are witnessing the end of the domination of the fictionalizing Desire, and simultaneously the disappearance of the distinction between fictions and documentaries. If this mutation proves to be true, the whole functioning of the field of the audio-visual would find itself in confusion, and furthermore, in all probability, that of the unity of social space. Because when the conscious awareness of the distinction between the real Enunciator and the fictitious Enunciator disappears, it is the social body itself that is in danger. The 'uncivil'[17] man who functions only by way of emotional contact replaces the 'public' man who functions by way of contract. The demise of the documentary and of fiction would therefore announce the 'end of the social'[18], but luckily the 'cassandras' are not always right.

Notes

[1] Jean-Louis Baudry, 'The Apparatus: Metapsychological Approaches to the Impression of Reality in the Cinema', in Philip Rosen (ed.), *Narrative, Apparatus, Ideology*, New York: Columbia University Press, 1986, p. 307.

[2] Raymond Bellour, *L'analyse du film*, Paris: Albatros, 1979, p. 22.

[3] We could quote quite a few documentary film-makers who attest to this difficulty of the functioning of the documentary. Jean Rouch recognises that the Cinémathèque Française itself has made very little effort in this direction: 'What is certain is that the documentary has not often been programmed, neither by the Cinémathèque, nor elsewhere, because it has always been considered as a complement to a programme. And as a programme complement, the documentary has never been the subject of criticism, or only very rarely. The first film that I made, *Au pays des mages noirs*, produced in 1946, was shown as a complement to Rossellini's *Stromboli*, and was not mentioned anywhere at the time', interview with Jean Rouch in *Documentaires* (*Bulletin de liaisons et d'information des documentaristes associés*), 4, December 1987, p. 1.

[4] For a theoretical discussion of this point, cf. my forthcoming book *Cinéma et effet fiction*.

[5] Octave Mannoni, *Clefs pour l'imaginaire ou l'Autre scène*, Paris: Le Seuil, 1969.

[6] On this point, cf. John Searle's 'The Logical Status of Fictional Discourse', in *Expression and Meaning. Studies in the Theory of Speech Acts*, Cambridge: Cambridge University Press, 1979.

[7] For a detailed analysis of this process, see my article 'Film documentaire, lecture documentarisante', in J. Lyant and Roger Odin (eds.), *Cinémas et réalités*, Saint-Etienne: Ceirec, 1984, pp. 263-280.

[8] For another approach to the degree of documentarity in terms of levels of documentarizing enunciation mobilized by film, cf my article cited in footnote 7.

[9] Here we quote Thierry Mesny, documentary film-maker and theoretician of the documentary. Cf. Mesny, *Analyse du documentaire cinématographique et télévisuel dans sa construction interne et ses aspects structuraux*, Doctoral thesis (3rd cycle), 1987, under the direction of Christian Metz, Ecole des Hautes Etudes en Sciences Sociales.

[10] It is a known fact that each contract can be designated two functions: F(mandate) and F(acceptance). Cf. the entry 'Contract' in A. J. Greimas and J. Courtés, *Semiotics and Language: An Analytical Dictionary*, Bloomington: Indiana University Press, 1982, pp. 59-60.

11 Genevière Jacquinot, *Image et Pédagogie*, Paris: PUF, 1977.

12 On this notion, cf Paul Watzlawick, Janet Beavin, and Don D. Jackson, *The Prag-matics of Human Communication*, New York: Norton, 1967.

13 Such an approach is being developed by Francesco Casetti.

14 To cite an example, TFI announced 230 hours of documentary programmes in 1986.

15 The documentary film-makers complain about this reduction of time allowed to them and especially about the disappearance of the 52 minute slots. Cf. Christophe de Ponfilly, *Cahiers du Cinéma* 402, December 1987, p. IV.

16 On this point, see my article 'Du spectateur fictionnalisant au nouveau spectateur: approche sémio-pragmatique', *Iris*, 8, 1988, pp. 121-139.

17 Richard Sennett, *The Fall of Public Man* (New York, Norton, W.W. and Company, 1977)

18 Jean Baudrillard, *In the Shadow of the Silent Majorities*, trans. Paul Foss, Paul Patton, and John Johnston, New York: Semiotext(e), 1983.

THE DIEGETIC LOOK. PRAGMATICS
OF THE POINT-OF-VIEW SHOT

ELENA DAGRADA

1. Point-of-View Shot[1] and Subjectivity

The confusion that often surrounds theorisations of the Point-of-View shot can be said to have resulted from the lack of a clear definition of this filmic practice. The reasons for this lack can be found above all in the ambiguous usage of the expression 'point-of-view', often employed to describe the POV shot. Although at first, within a cinematic context, this term takes a perceptive meaning,[2] other layers of signification (psychological, ideological, emotional, valuational, and so on) usually overlap the visual one. Consequently, it is never quite clear whether the POV shot is supposed to express something (psychology, ideology, or the evaluation of a character), or whether it is a unit of language which can be distinguished from all other instances of filmic language.

Three main phases characterize the studies of the POV shot. The first one emerged during the 1920s, with the birth of Cinematic Expressionism, i.e., with the discovery that it was possible to charge a shot with meaning (subjectively *vs* objectively) by means of perspectival distortions, optical illusions or certain angles. At that time however, this particular kind of shot could represent indifferently a character's look or the author's worldview (*Weltanschauung*). Thus, it was impossible to define the POV shot as a linguistic structure, because its diegetic specificity had not been recognised yet. The use of the term therefore, remained linked to a generical idea of subjectivity, ascribed either to the screen character or to the film's author.[3]

A second phase developed in France between the 1940s and the 1950s, with the debate on the New Psychology and its major theoretician, Merleau-Ponty[4]. This school posited the connection between the POV shot and the spectator's psychological identification with the screen character. In this way, the author's subjectivity was henceforth eliminated from theorisations about the POV shot. But nevertheless, the issue of psychological identification with the character was introduced as a qualifying aspect so that every other cinematic practice which could provide it was considered as a kind of POV shot. Once again, it became difficult to define such a variable object in terms of cinematic language, precisely because the POV shot was almost everything that could express the psychological 'point of view' of the character, and because the approach to the POV shot would be psychological rather than linguistic.

The third and last phase of the sudies on the POV shot has developed from recent investigations on cinematic language.[5] Within this context, the POV shot is now considered as a linguistic structure, but the terminology which describes it still makes use of concepts such as 'point of view', 'focalization', 'distribution of knowledge', 'narrative voice', etc.

In most cases, therefore, the POV shot is considered as a narrative concept which is still supposed to express some sort of subjectivity, rather than as a linguistic unit of the cinematic language.

We can infer that all this is caused by the tendency to mistake the POV shot for subjectivity. On the contrary, the POV shot is uniquely a unit of language which can function in a text in many different ways, whereas subjectivity is a sylistic pattern which can be suggested through many other structures of cinematic language.

This mistake, as we have seen, on the one hand prevented a clear definition of the POV shot on the basis of cinematic language; and on the other hand, it also prevented the investigation of the possible applications which the POV shot may have in a filmic text. The range of possibilities of the POV shot extends beyond the subjectivity of the looking character. Often, instead, quite the opposite occurs, as we shall see later.

Thus, in order to understand that the POV shot is something more precise than the screen character's 'point of view', and also that it operates in the text through more complex processes than just a generical 'psychological identification', it is necessary to recognise its linguistic status and to abandon the conviction that it has to 'express' something, specifically, the character's subjectivity.

2. The Spectator's Role

Even more than the POV shot, the figure of the spectator has occupied an important place in recent studies of the cinematic language. The interest in this topic has developed within a radical reorientation in the discipline of semiotics, where a shift from structuralism to pragmatics has taken place.[6] Pragmatics, as we know, deals with the relationship between the text and its addressee. In pragmatics, the notion of reader as passive recipient of a meaning that is independent from him, is transformed into the notion of reader as active agent who attributes meaning to a text. Consequently the reader, or the spectator, can be defined in terms of *competencies* which will enable the actualization of the text.[7]

These competencies cover two distinct areas of textual operations. The first area refers to the basic grammar skills necessary to the actualization of the initial discursive level of the text. The second one instead refers to more complex reading operations, such as being able to predict and to interpret, to make forecasts and infer, to establish connections among various parts of a text, to construct its general meaning and to compare it to the meaning of other texts, and so on.

In other words, the spectator can be defined as an ensemble of textual and intertextual competencies, directly responsible for making the signification of a text possible. The ensemble of these competencies constitutes *in the text* the figure of an ideal spectator, or Model Spectator,[8] whose reading activity is crucial to the making of a text. Because the text depends on the spectator's contribution to the production of meaning, it strategically predicts and posits moments of signification – or textual nodes[9] – where the spectator's inferential activity is most stimulated and weighted.

We will therefore consider the spectator as a *role*, inscribed in the text, where his ablility to engage basic grammar competencies will enable him to recognise filmic structures such as the POV shot,[10] and also where his ability to undertake more complex reading tasks constitutes a sort of interpretive itinerary through the whole text, disseminated with those textual nodes which most stimulate his interpretive activity.

One of these nodes is, potentially, the POV shot.

3. The POV Shot as a Textual Node

As I pointed out, it is important to recognise that the POV shot belongs to the realm of cinematic language and that its perceptive structure is crucial to the spectator's filmic vision.

The composition of the POV shot varies according to the number of shots, generally divided into three units, as in the pattern ABA1. In this pattern, A (antecedent) and A1 (consequent) provide a context for the character's look within time and space, B represents, instead, the direction of that look, the distance and the angle of incidence from which it originates.

This structure can also follow a different pattern. The units may be more than three, or the antecedent/consequent shots may be missing. In this case, the presence of a character looking at what appears on the screen[11] will be indicated through codified elements, e.g. out of focus image, frame of glasses or telescopes which surround the vision, and so on. In either case, however, the POV shot is bound up with the representation of the trajectory of the look and of its diegetic nature.

The POV shot is a *unit of cinematic language which represents on the screen a diegetic look*: this is the reason why it differs from all other instances of the cinematic language. In fact, in a film, every shot illustrates objects and things filmed from a particular 'point of view' which is never casual, but which is thus expressive and meaningful. During a POV shot however, this 'point of view' belongs to a fictional character whose look mediates the images unfolding on the screen. And it is with that diegetic look that the spectator's reading activity will have to come to terms.

In fact, the filmic text regulates the viewer's interpretation also according to the point from which the vision is organised. The filmic vision is selected, structured and organised *for* the spectator. And during a POV shot, the look of the spectator and the character's diegetic look coincide and overlap.

In this way, the POV shot delimits both the realm of the look and of signification, thus forcing the perception and the inferential activity of the spectator within the coercive coordinates of a diegetic look. One can say then that the POV shot is a potential textual node which regulates the spectator's interpretive activity.

4. Inferential Paths

The POV shot informs the spectator's inferential activity according to the mode of the diegetic look.

The character, who in the POV shot becomes the subject of the look, will function as a *cluster of contents* textually established through the narration. These contents also exist beyond the character's subjectivity and are often linked to other contents led by the object of his look, according to a series of textual relations which are also established through the narration. Consequently, due to the mediation of the diegetic look, during a POV shot the spectator will be stimulated to actualize part of these contents and to render the textual relations significant through a process which assigns a new meaning to the object of the look (or event to the subject, as we shall see later). The spectator can also modify or confirm all the hypotheses which had so far informed his reading, and he can make forecasts, i.e. he can negotiate the textual node *through* a character – all this following two possible *inferential paths*.

In the first one, the spectator's inferential activity proceeds from the looking character to the object of his look. In the second one, it goes the opposite direction, from the object of his look to the looking character. In both cases, however, it is the looking character who carries, inscribed in his role, the contents that the spectator will actualize. What varies in this process is the direction and the very object upon which the spectator exercises his inferential activity.

4.1. First Path

This first case is the one evoked whenever the POV shot is said to 'express the point of view' of the character. But actually, we can affirm more precisely that the spectator assigns a new meaning to the object seen through the POV shot, redoubling the cognitive activity or the passional investment of the looking character.

A good example of this process occurs in *The Wrong Man* (Alfred Hitchcock, USA., 1957). This film tells the story of Christopher Emanuel Ballister, a quiet double-bass player at the Stork Club of New York, who is wrongly accused of being the thief responsible for several robberies in the neighbourhood. Ballister's misfortune starts when he goes to the Associated Life Insurance Company to ask for a loan and the secretary mistakes him for the thief who had previously robbed the company.

The sequence where the secretary, Miss Dennerly, believes to have recognised the thief when Ballister goes to her window is filmed with a long POV shot illustrating Miss Dennerly's look. Here, common gestures such as keeping one's hand inside the coat (photo 1a), approaching a window (photo 1b), or putting one hand in the inside pocket of the jacket (photo 1c) to take some paper out and give it to the secretary, are expanded in time and in the several units of the POV shot in order to become charged with the tension felt by Miss Dennerly, who fears finding out what the man might be hiding in the inside pocket of his jacket.

Although the spectator knows very well that the pocket contains just paper, when he sees it through Miss Dennerly's look the bulging pocket acquires the negative connotation of a menacing object, such as a gun, or something similar. Thus, the viewer's textual competence, his previous knowledge about Ballister, the inference made about the title (the *wrong* man) and about the opening credits, including the words of Hitchcock who appears on the screen prior to the beginning of the film, all are momentarily suspended. Miss Dennerly's look, in fact, leads the spectator even for the short period of time of that sequence to actualize those contents in a manner congruent with her textual role and with her cognitive activity: first surprise, then diffidence, suspicion, belief in Ballister's guilt, and accusation.

The Wrong Man uses this progression of contents to trap the spectator within the unfolding of a plot which he cannot escape, although he is aware of its falsity and distortion. He cannot escape precisely because of the look of the character who leads his inferential activity along a path that goes from the looking subject to the object of his look.

4.2. Second Path
This second case is more complex and posits a spectator's inferential activity which is opposite from the previous one. Here, in fact, the spectator assigns a new meaning to the looking subject by interpreting him through the object (usually another character) seen during the POV shot. In this case, it is clear that the spectator cannot actualize contents tied to the looking subject's 'subjectivity' – i.e. the POV shot does not 'express the character's point of view' – although he will actualize in any case contents which are inscribed in the textual role of the looking character.

1 a.

1 b.

1 c.

241   **THE DIEGETIC LOOK.**

I will examine for this purpose a POV shot from the film *The Nutty Professor*, (Jerry Lewis, USA, 1962), which not only illustrates very clearly this second path, but moreover, which could not be explained or understood otherwise.

The film concerns Dr Kelp (Jerry Lewis), a professor of chemistry at an American University, who like his literary predecessor, Dr Jekyll, is obsessed by a problem which he is unable to solve. Only here the nature of the problem is different: Dr Kelp is obsessed by his ugly physical appearance, which according to him is the reason for his failure with women. Therefore, after an unsuccessful attempt at gymnastics, he decides to turn to chemistry, prepares the most traditional potion, and drinks it. The transformation begins, and in the midst of it Kelp starts having convulsions while his body slowly becomes deformed and covered with animal fur. He then rushes to a wardrobe and, after throwing it on the floor, takes something out of a box and swallows it. The camera then cuts to the next shot, a POV shot, which follows the pattern BA, that is without antecedent. In this way, the spectator is denied seeing the definite result of the looking character's (Kelp) physical transformation.

The viewer's intertextual competence[12] tells him that in a situation such as this one the transformation usually proceeds from beautiful to ugly. Thus he interprets the fur on Kelp's body as the sign of a metamorphosis that proceeds in the same direction, and abductively[13] infers that a transformation from ugly to very ugly has taken place. Furthermore he feels he is allowed to read the following POV shot as a deductive confirmation of his inferential activity.

In fact, the POV shot begins with a close-up of a tailor (photo 2a) who, looking at Dr Kelp (looking at the camera)[14] is visibly upset while talking about his client's new clothes. Then the camera moves, simulating Kelp's walking among people (the sound of his footsteps is amplified) until he arrives at the students' ballroom. As he walks, he runs into people who are astounded at his presence (they too look into the camera representing Kelp's look). Some grow pale and some are startled (photo 2b). A man draws a woman close to him (photo 2c) as if to protect her. When Kelp enters the ballroom, everybody reacts very strongly: the band stops playing, people stop dancing (photo 2d), and two waitresses drop their trays. This long POV shot thus leads the spectator to convince himself that his previous inferences were indeed correct: Kelp has turned into a monster. Here, the viewer's reading follows a winding inferential path which goes from the object of the look to the looking character, and in so doing he falls into the trap which the text has set for him in order to achieve a comical effect. As the looking character appears on the screen, the spectator now sees Buddy Love/Hyde, a handsome young man who acts as a playboy: and the spectator laughs at his inferential mistake and at the naivety of making it.

2 a.

2 b.

2 c.

2 d.

THE DIEGETIC LOOK.

It is important to notice that the text itself has not lied. Rather, now the spectator can read the POV shot retrospectively and realise that Kelp's need for a tailor was motivated by his new strength, and not his deformity. In the same way he can realise that the people in the street were so confused because of Kelp's attractive appearance that they could not hide their emotions. The man's gesture of protection with that woman now indicates that he felt his love relationship threatened by the presence of such a handsome boy. And even the growing of the fur now acquires a new meaning: it represents only a temporary phase of a transformation which, once completed (and once having swallowed the content of that box), will automatically eliminate the fur. The text has indeed not lied. It has simply *foreseen* the spectator's interventions as a result of complex textual inferences, based on intertextual competence, made possible by the existence of this second inferential path: from the object of the look to the looking subject.

Despite its extreme peculiarity, this case occurs more frequently than one would think.[15] It occurs regularly whenever the POV shot portrays the look of an evil character (a monster, a murderer), and the spectator is led in his inferential activity by the object of that look, the character's victim. This kind of situation, of course, stimulates the spectator to actualize contents which cannot express the looking chracter's 'subjectivity', and moreover which do not allow a 'psychological identification' with him. Actually, this second case contradicts the belief that the POV shot must produce the psychological identification between the spectator and the looking character.

5. Conclusions

To speak of inferential paths in order to designate the modalities of production of meaning activated in the spectator by the POV shot allows us to address three important questions.

First of all, inferential paths allow us to *explain* the way that the POV shot semiotically operates in a text (as interaction between the spectator's interpretive activity and the looking character's role), rather than merely registering the results of that process.

Inferential paths also posit the possiblility of discovering the potential variety of these results, rather than imposing a single and unquestionable one according to the specific cultural and methodological approach which is in effect.[16] In particular, it denies the common belief which assigns to the POV shot the task of representing always and only the characters' 'point of view', and of creating a 'psychological identification' between character and spectator. On the contrary, as I pointed out in the discussion of the second path, this is not always the case.

Lastly, inferential paths permit us to distinguish the POV shot from the expression of the character's subjectivity. The subjectivity, as I said before, is a stylistic pattern that does not always come as a consequence of the use of the POV shot. In the same way, the POV shot as a unit of cinematic language does not encompass all the instances of subjective syle.[17]

The POV shot is *primarly* a unit of cinematic language. The code which regulates it stipulates that a certain structure (on the plane of the signifier) corresponds to the representation of the character's look (on the plane of the signified). This code is a filmic convention[18] accepted by the spectator even though he knows very well that it is the camera (or an optical illusion, or some other device) which stands for the screen character's look. And by virtue of the same convention, the POV shot is not supposed to 'signify' anything else[19] (a not inconsequential point), even though it acquires different connotations according to the various genres through which it is more frequently employed (horror film, thriller, film noir, etc.).

Nevertheless, it is possible to investigate the numerous ways in which the POV shot operates in a text. Its linguistic characteristics, in fact, make the POV shot a potential textual node that stimulates and regulates the spectator's inferential activity.

Thus, during a POV shot the spectator is supposed to activate a part of his audiovisual competencies, which from the very beginning of the history of cinema the first POV shots have contributed in instituting.[20] To locate them means to try to explain in terms of semiotic operations the experience of viewing and interpreting a film.

(Translated by James Hay)

Notes

[1] [In accordance with recent English and American studies about the cinematic language, I have decided to translate the Italian term *soggettiva* (corresponding to the French one *caméra subjective*) with the term *Point-of-View shot* (POV shot). This term designates the unit of cinematic language which represents on the screen the look of a character.

Moreover, the term *language*, translates here the Italian *linguaggio*, in opposition to *lingua* as a closed system of abstract rules. *Linguaggio*, instead, is an open system of rules *in action*. The term *linguistic* refers in the same way, to the status of film as *linguaggio*. – trans.]

[2] Jacques Aumont, in 'Le point de vue', *Communications* 38, 1983, distinguishes

with great precision four definitions that the term 'point of view' has had through the years in cinema studies. The first one (POV 1) designates the material, topological *point* where the vision represented on the screen originates. The second (POV 2) indicates the screen *representation* of POV 1 in terms of perspectival coordinates. The third (POV 3) defines the narrative subject (author or screen character) which is supposed to embody the look represented by POV 2. The fourth (POV 4) describes the mental attitude (psychological, ideological, moral, intellectual, evaluative...) attributed to POV 3. Aumont rightly points out that cinema studies have always privileged the narratological aspects (POV 3) over material and representational ones (POV 1 and POV 2).

Moreover, studies concerning the POV shot have not only privileged definitions 3 and 4, but they have also distorted, or even ignored, defintions 1 and 2 whenever they did not serve the needs of expressiveness. As far as I am concerned, I will only investigate definitions 1 and 2, which for convenience I will both name 'perspective point of view'. The term designates representation (POV 2), in its perceptival coordinates, from the point (POV 1) where the vision appearing on the screen originates. Although the POV shot represents the screen character's look, I will not attribute to him here any narrative role (POV 3). Rather, I am interested in freeing the POV shot from all notions of narratology (POV 3) and expressiveness (POV 4), in order to come to the notion of the POV shot as a *unit of filmic language*.

[3] It is interesting to notice that this issue of double subjectivity ascribed both to screen character and author is present in the notion of *soggettiva libera indiretta* (free indirect POV shot) elaborated by Pasolini (cf. 'Il cinema di poesia', in *Empirismo eretico*, Milano: Carzanti, 1972). Pasolini's notion in fact, shares with the POV shot only the terminology, because of its metaphorical suggestions. Cf. Elena Dagrada, 'Sulla soggetiva libera indiretta', *Cinema & Cinema* 43, 1985.

[4] Cf. especially Maurice Merleau-Ponty, 'Le cinéma et la nouvelle psychologie', a paper given at IDHEC on March 13, 1945, printed in *Sens et non-sens* Paris: Nagel, 1948. Cf. also Jean Mitry, *Esthétique et psychologie du cinéma*, II, Paris: Éditions Universitaires, 1965.

[5] Among others, I will cite Edward R. Branigan, and particularly his recent work *Point of View in the Cinema. A Theory of Narration and Subjectivity in Classical Film*, Berlin-New York-Amsterdam: Mouton, 1984.

[6] Psychoanalytically oriented studies have also focused upon the figure of the spectator, but they have disregarded his cognitive and interpretive function. These studies have therefore assigned the spectator a *place*, rather than a *role* within the text.

[7] In 1969, Sol Worth was already writing 'There is no meaning in a film itself. By

common signification, or meaning, as used in film, I mean the relationship between the implication of the maker and the inference of viewer'. Sol Worth, 'The Development of a Semiotic of Film', *Semiotica* 1, 3 (1969), rpt. in *Studying Visual Communication*, ed. Larry Gross, Philadelphia: Pennsylvania University Press, 1981, p. 43. These ideas have been developed by Roger Odin in 'Pour une sémio-pragmatique du cinéma', *Iris* 1, 1, 1983 [translated and reproduced in this volume].

[8] There are a number of authors who have constructed a model of textual theory around the idea of an implied author and reader, or spectator: Wayne C. Booth, *The Rhetoric of Fiction*, Chicago: University of Chicago Press; Wolgang Iser, *The Implied Reader*, Baltimore and London: Johns Hopkins University Press, 1974; Seymour Chatman, *Story and Discourse*, Ithaca-London: Cornell University Press, 1978; or Model Reader (Umberto Eco, *The Role of the Reader*, Bloomington: Indiana University Press, 1979). These theorisations only disagree over the importance that one should attribute to the felt need to combine such an abstract figure with the empirical syncratic one, of the relationship between text and receiver. Regarding this argument see in particular Francesco Casetti, *Dentro lo sguardo: Il film e il suo spettatore*, Milano: Bompiani, 1986; Cesare Segre, 'Semiotica e filologia', in *Semiotica filologica*, Torino: Einaudi, 1979.

[9] I borrowed the expression 'textual node' from Umberto Eco, *The Role of the Reader*, op. cit.

[10] The consciousness of the empirical spectator is relatively unimportant within this process. And it is even less important to decide whether the viewer knows that what he sees is called a POV shot. What is crucial, instead, is that in some way he recognises the *convention* which assigns to a particular shot – or series of shots – the representation of the character's look. In the same way a speaker makes use of a series of grammatical and syntactic structures without necessarily being aware of the rules which govern them.

[11] Much has been written about the cinematic devices which indicate that the screen image represents a diegetic look. These devices vary from the more traditional ones (glasses, binoculars, locks framing the vision, a blurred image connoting drunkeness, fatigue, blindness, etc.), to the more sophisticated ones, such as the hand held camera simulating the character's movement, the noise of his footsteps, breathing, heartbeat (usually amplified), and so on. This list is potentially endless. It is important here to emphasize that all these various devices are the result of a cinematic convention. In order to be recognised as such, the POV shot must, in fact, respect these conventions; while the viewer, in order to recognise and interpret what he sees as a POV shot, must be aware of the conventions which generates it. Al-

though these conventions do not directly pertain to pragmatics, they nevertheless are preliminary for a proper pragmatic practice of a POV shot in a text. In the same way, the 'felicity conditions' in Austin (*How to Do Things With Words*, Oxford University Press, 1962), establish the terms of accomplishment of a speech act.

[12] Unlike the titles of the Italian and French version of this film, the American one does not assign the task of activating the spectator's intertextual competence either to the title, or to the character's name, Kelp. This competence is, however, activated through the parodic reference to Stevenson's work, *Dr Jekyll and M. Hyde*, and also through various quotations from previous film adaptations of the novel, especially the sequence illustrating Jekyll/Kelp's physical transformation, announced by the amplified sound of his heartbeat and the growing of the fur. The Italian and the French titles, on the contrary, explicitly invite the spectator to exercise his intertextual competence. The French one (*Docteur Jerry et Mister Love*) does so by redoubling the title of Stevenson's novel. The Italian one (*Le folli notti del dottor Jerryll*) does so by emphasizing the assonance Jerryll/Jekyll, although the character's name in the film remains Kelp.

[13] Charles Sanders Peirce classified three kinds of logical inferences derived from classic syllogistics (*Collected Papers*, Cambridge, Mass.: Harvard University Press, 1931-35). The first one is deduction, a process which, given a rule and a case illustrating it, the result can be inferred with complete certitude. The second one is induction, and it occurs when, given a case and its result, the rule which governs it can be inferred with a certain amount of risk. The third one is abduction, which instead takes place when, given a result, the rule which governs it and originates a case is hypothesized with a very high amount of risk. Inductive and abductive reasoning are often employed in the interpretation of texts. Regarding this argument see in particular Umberto Eco, 'Il cane e il cavallo: un testo visivo e alcuni equivoci verbali', *Versus* 25, 1980.

[14] It is interesting to note that the POV shot neutralizes the potential transgressive act of looking into the camera by rerouting that act within the diegesis. That look thus addresses an element of the fiction (the looking character), and not something outside the space of the fiction (the camera). Cf. Alberto Farassino, 'Gli occhi abarrati', *Il piccolo Hans* 15, 1977.

[15] In *The Birds* (Alfred Hitchcock, USA, 1963) we find another example where the second inferential path occurs. I am referring to the POV shot of Melanie Daniels (Tippi Hedren) looking at the mother of the two little children, frightened after the bird's attack at the gas station. During this POV shot – and through the object of Melanie's look – the spectator is stimulated to interpret Miss Daniels as a possible

cause for the bird's attack. And this inference is the first of many others through which the spectator will be invited to discover a cause for the mysterious events. Besides, the text itself creates an atmosphere of ambiguity by suggesting many possible explanations without privileging anyone of them in particular. Ambiguity will thus be maintained throughout the unfolding of the story, and even beyond its final solution.

[16] According to film critics of the 1950s, for example, *Lady in the Lake* (Robert Montgomery, USA, 1946), almost entirely shot in POV shot, betrayed a sort of ontological limit of the POV shot just because it did not produce the psychological identification between spectator and screen character.

[17] Even Branigan (*Point of View in the Cinema...*, op.cit.) makes this confusion. He distinguishes between POV shot and subjectivity, but he still asserts that the POV shot necessarily implies a process of subjectiveness.

[18] The importance of a semiotically-oriented reading of this issue has been explored in Umberto Eco, 'On the Contribution of Film to Semiotics', *Quarterly Review of Film Studies* 2, 1, 1977.

[19] There are other instances, besides the most evident one cited in our second inferential path, where the POV shot does not 'express' the character's subjectivity. For example, this occurs every time the POV shot serves only the purpose of hiding the face of the looking character from the spectator or when the POV shot simply illustrates the space of a visual field. In *Knife in the Water* (*Noz W. Wodzie*, Roman Polanski, Poland, 1962) the screen character is looking at the coast from a boat, first with one eye and then with the other. The camera portrays this vision by showing the image of the coast from the perspective of the left eye and then from the right one in order to simulate a human perception of the world. This POV shot does not mean anything beyond itself. Or it may signify precisely the fact that the POV shot may not want to signify anything else.

[20] Cf. for example, *Grandma's Reading Glass* and *As Seen through a Telescope* (Georges Albert Smith, GB, 1900). As the titles indicate, the POV shots in these brief films had to provide a recognizable context (both in the screen image and as a sequence of shots) in order to enable the spectator to recognise the character's look.

SELECTED BIBLIOGRAPHY

1. Special Journal Issues

Actes Sémiotiques, 41, 1987, 'La subjectivité au cinéma', ed. Jacques Fontanille.

CinémAction, 47, 1988, 'Les théories du cinéma aujourd'hui', ed. Jacques Kermabon.

CinémAction, 58, 1991, '25 ans de sémiologie', ed. André Gardies.

Communications, 38, 1983, 'Énonciation et cinéma', ed. Jean-Paul Simon and Marc Vernet.

Communications, 51, 1990, 'Télévisions Mutations', ed. Francesco Casetti and Roger Odin.

Degrés, 64, 1990, 'Approches du cinéma (I)', ed. André Helbo.

Degrés, 65, 1991, 'Approches du cinéma (II)', ed. André Helbo.

Hors Cadre, 7, 1989, 'Théorie du cinema et crise dans la théorie'.

Hors Cadre, 10, 1992, 'Arrêt sur recherches'.

Iris, 1 and 2, 1983, 'Etat de la théorie: nouvelles méthodes, nouveaux objets', I and II.

Iris, 9, 1989, 'Cinema and Cognitive Psychology', (contains a dossier on Michel Colin).

Iris, 10, 1990, 'Christian Metz et la théorie du cinéma', ed. Michel Marie and Marc Vernet.

2. Books

Aumont, Jacques, and Jean-Louis Leutrat, *Théorie du film*, Paris: Albatros, 1980.

Bettetini, Gianfranco, *La conversazione audiovisiva: problemi dell'enunciazione filmica e televisiva*, Milano: Bompiani, 1984.

Casetti, Francesco, *Dentro lo sguardo. Il filme e il sou spettatore*, Milano: Bompiani, 1986; *D'un regard l'autre,* trans. Jean Châteauvert and Martine Joly, Lyon: Presses Universitaires de Lyon, 1990. English translation forthcoming from Indiana University Press.

Casetti, Francesco, *Teorie del cinema, 1945-1990*, Milano: Bompiani, 1993.

Chateau, Dominique, *Le cinéma comme langage*, Bruxelles: AISS - Publications de la Sorbonne, 1987.

Chateau, Dominique, and François Jost, *Nouveau cinéma, nouvelle sémiologie: essai d'analyse des films d'Alain Robbe-Grillet*, Paris: U.G.E., 1979.

Chateau, Dominique, André Gardies, François Jost, eds., *Cinémas de la modernité: films, théories*, Paris: Editions Klincksieck, 1981.

Chion, Michel, *La voix au cinéma*, Paris: Cahiers du Cinéma, 1982.

Chion, Michel, *Le son au cinéma*, Paris: Cahiers du Cinéma, 1985.

Chion, Michel, *La toile trouée: la parole au cinéma*, Paris: Cahiers du cinéma, 1988.

Chion, Michel, *L'audio-vision*, Paris: Nathan, 1990. *Audio-Vision*, trans. Claudia Gorbman, New York: Columbia University Press, 1993.

Colin, Michel, *Langue, film, discours. Prolégomènes à une sémiologie générative du film*, Paris: Klincksieck, 1985.

Colin, Michel, *Cinéma, télévision, cognition*, Nancy: Presses Universataires de Nancy, 1992.

Jost, François, *Un monde à notre image: énonciation, cinéma, télévision*, Paris: Klincksieck, 1992.

Metz, Christian, *L'énonciation impersonnelle ou le site du film*, Paris: Editions Méridiens Klincksieck, 1991.

Müller, Jürgen, *Towards a Pragmatics of the Audio-Visual*, 2 vols., Münster: Nodus Publications, 1994.

Odin, Roger, *Cinéma et production de sens*, Paris: Editions Armand Colin, 1990.

Odin, Roger, *Film et fiction effet*, Paris: Editions Armand Colin, forthcoming.

3. Papers

Aumont, Jacques, 'Le point de vue', *Communications*, 38, 1983, pp. 3-29; 'The point of View', *Quarterly Review of Film and Video*, 11, 1989, pp. 1-22.

Bächler, Odile, 'La sémiologie générative au cinéma', *CinémAction*, 47, 1988, pp. 44-51.

Bellour, Raymond, 'Le cinéma et...', *Iris*, 10, 1990, pp. 15-35.

Bensmaïa, Réda, 'Retour du rhétorique, ou le cinéma comme opérateur', *Hors Cadre*, 10, 1992, pp. 239-263.

Bettetini, Gianfranco, and Francesco Casetti, 'Bilan à deux voix', *Hors Cadre*, 10, 1992, pp. 115-124.

Blanco, D., 'Figures discursives de l'énonciation ciné-subjectivité', *Actes Sémiotiques*, documents IX, 90, 1987.

Buckland, Warren, 'Michel Colin and the Psychological Reality of Film Semiology', *Semiotica* (forthcoming).

Burzlaff, Werner, 'Les possibilités phanéroscopiques de l'image cinétique', *Degrés*, 54-55, 1988, pp. f1-f11.

Casetti, Francesco, 'Le texte du film', *Théorie du film*, ed. Jacques Aumont and Jean-Louis Leutrat, Paris: Albatros, 1980, pp. 41-65.

Casetti, Francesco, 'Looking for the Spectator', *Iris*, 2, 1983, pp. 15-29.

Casetti, Francesco, 'Antonioni and Hitchcock: Two Strategies of Narrative Investment', *Sub-Stance*, 51, 1986, pp. 69-86.

Casetti, Francesco, and Roger Odin, 'De la paléo- à la néo-télévision', *Communications*, 51 (1990), pp. 9-26.

Casetti, Francesco, 'Coupures épistémologiques dans la théorie du cinéma après-guerre', *Iris*, 10, 1990, pp. 145-57.

Casetti, Francesco, 'Pragmatique et théorie du cinéma aujourd'hui', *Hors Cadre*, 10, 1992, pp. 99-109.

Chateau, Dominique, 'Propositions pour une théorie du film', *Ça-cinéma*, 1, 1973, pp. 78-95.

Chateau, Dominique, 'Texte et discours dans le film', *Revue d'Esthetique*, 4, 1976, pp. 121-39.

Chateau, Dominique, 'Syntaxe filmique et structure narrative', *Degrés*, 14, 1978, pp. e1-e35.

Chateau, Dominique, 'Le role de l'analyse textuelle dans la théorie', *Théorie du film*, ed. Jacques Aumont and Jean-Louis Leutrat, Paris: Albatros, 1980, pp. 67-71.

Chateau, Dominique, 'Film et réalité: pour rajeunir un vieux problème', *Iris*, 1, 1983, pp. 51-65.

Chateau, Dominique, 'De la théorie à la conaissance', *Hors Cadre*, 1, 1983, pp. 117-29.

Chateau, Dominique, 'Diégèse et énonciation', *Communications*, 38, 1983, pp. 121-54.

Chateau, Dominique, 'La Sémiologie du cinéma: un bilan', *Degrés*, 64, 1990, pp. b-b10.

Chateau, Dominique, 'Le cinéma: un "bon objet"?', *Hors Cadre*, 10, 1992, pp. 125-36.

Châteauvert, Jean, 'Narrer et ne pas narrer', *Poetique*, 93, 1993, pp. 91-111.

Cohen, Alain J.J., 'Le filmique synthétique a priori', *Actes Sémiotiques*, 41, 1987, pp. 52-56.

Colin, Michel, 'Deux ou trois choses que je sais d'elle. (Notes pour une grammaire du texte filmique)', *Kodikas/Code*, 2, 1, 1980, pp. 27-38.

Colin, Michel, 'La dislocation', *Théorie du film*, ed. Jacques Aumont and Jean-Louis Leutrat, Paris: Albatros, 1980, pp. 73-91.

Colin, Michel, 'Etude générative et transformationnelle du champ-contrechamp', *Langues et Littératures*, 1, 1, 1981.

Colin, Michel, 'Syntaxe et sémantique du message filmique', *Iris*, 1, 1, 1983, pp. 83-99.

Colin, Michel, 'Propositions pour une recherche expérimentale en sémiologie du cinéma', *Communications*, 38, 1983, pp. 239-55.

Colin, Michel, 'Coréférence dans *The Adventures of Dollie*', *D.W. Griffith*, ed. Jean Mottet, Paris: L'Harmattan, 1984, pp. 273-82.

Colin, Michel, 'Le statut loqique du film documentaire', *Cinémas et réalités*, ed. J. Lyant and Roger Odin, Saint-Etienne: Cierec, 1984, pp. 253-260.

Colin, Michel, 'Interprétation sémantique et représentations spatiales dans la bande image', *DRLAV. Revue de Linguistique*, 34-35, 1986, pp. 359-376.

Colin, Michel, 'Pour une conception typologique du point de vue', *Actes Sémiotiques*, 41 (1987), pp. 57-64.

Colin, Michel, 'Quelque remarques à propos de la référence dans le documentaire', *APTE. Revue de l'audio-visuel éducatif*, 1987, 2.

Colin, Michel, 'Eléments d'approche cognitive du point de vue au cinéma', *Protée*, 16. 1-2, 1988, pp. 134-38.

Colin, Michel, 'Introduction à une sémiologie générative du film', *Iris*, 9, 1989, pp. 139-57.

Colin, Michel, 'A "Generative Semiology" of Film: to what End?', *Iris*, 9, 1989, pp. 159-69.

Colin, Michel, 'Comprendre l'événement sportif à la télévision. L'exemple de la course cycliste', *Communications*, 51, 1990, pp. 79-110.

Dagrada, Elena, 'Subjectivité et caméra subjective', *Actes Sémiotiques*, 41, 1987, pp. 24-29.

Dayan, Daniel, 'Le spectateur performé', *Hors Cadre*, 2, 1984, pp. 137-49.

Fontanille, Jacques, 'La subjectivité au cinéma', *Actes Sémiotiques*, 41, 1987, pp. 5-23.

Fontanille, Jacques, 'La description du cinéma', *Degrés*, 64, 1990, pp. f-f24.

Gaudreault, André, 'Les aventures d'un concept: la narrativité', *Iris*, 10, 1990, pp. 121-131.

Gorbman, Claudia, 'Chion's *Audio-Vision*', *Wide Angle*, 15, 1, 1993, pp. 66-77.

Jost, François, 'Discours cinematographique, narration: deux façons d'envisager le probleme de l'enonciation', *Théorie du film*, ed. Jacques Aumont and Jean-Louis Leutrat, Paris: Albatros, 1980, pp. 121-31.

Jost, François, 'Vers de nouvelles approches méthodologiques', in *Cinémas de la modernité: films, théories*, ed. Dominique Chateau, André Gardies, and François Jost, Paris: Editions Klincksieck, 1981.

Jost, François, 'Narration(s): en deçà et au-delà', *Communications*, 38, 1983, pp. 192-212.

Jost, François, 'New Tele/visions', *On Film*, 13, 1984, pp. 52-60.

Jost, François, 'La sémiologie du cinéma et ses modèles', *Iris*, 10, 1990, pp. 133-141.

Jost, François, 'Un spectateur en quête d'auteur', *Degrés*, 64, 1990, pp. e-e14.

Kermabon, Jacques, 'Qu'est-ce que la sémio-pragmatique?', *CinémAction*, 47, 1988, pp. 52-55.

Metz, Christian, 'Rapport sur l'etat actuel de la sémiologie du cinéma dans le monde (debut 1974)', *A Semiotic Landscape*, ed. Seymour Chatman, Umberto Eco, and Jean-Marie Klinkenberg, The Hague: Mouton, 1979, pp. 147-157.

Metz, Christian, 'Sémiologie audio-visuelle et linguistique générative', *Essais sémiotiques*, Paris: Editions Klincksieck, 1977, pp. 110-28.

Muscio, Guiliana, and Roberto Zemignan, 'Francesco Casetti and Italian Film Semiotics', *Cinema Journal*, 30, 2, 1991, pp. 23-46.

Odin, Roger, 'Rhétorique du film de famille', *Revue d'Esthéthique*, 1/2, 1979, pp. 340-73.

Odin, Roger, 'L'entree du spectateur dans la fiction', *Théorie du film*, ed. Jacques Aumont and Jean-Louis Leutrat, Paris: Albatros, 1980, pp. 198-213.

Odin, Roger, 'Mise en phase, déphasage et performativé dans *le Tempestaire* de Jean Epstein', *Communications*, 38, 1983, pp. 213-38.

Odin, Roger, 'Film documentaire, lecture documentarisante', *Cinémas et réalités*, ed. J. Lyant and Roger Odin, Saint-Etienne: Cierec, 1984, pp. 263-280.

Odin, Roger, 'Le carré sémiotique du son filmique', *Exigences et perspectives de la sémiotique: recueil d'hommages pour Algirdas Julien Greimas*, ed. Herman Parret and Hans-George Ruprecht, Amsterdam: John Benjamins, 1985, pp. 603-609.

Odin, Roger, 'Du spectateur fictionnalisant au nouveau spectateur: approche sémio-pragmatique', *Iris*, 8, 1988, pp. 121-39.

Odin, Roger, 'L'analyse filmique comme exercise pédagogique', *CinémAction*, 47, 1988, pp. 56-62.

Odin, Roger, 'La sémio-pragmatique sans crise, ni désillusion', *Hors Cadre*, 7, 1989, pp. 77-92.

Odin, Roger, 'Christian Metz et la linguistique', *Iris*, 10, 1990, pp. 81-103.

Odin, Roger, Review of Christian Metz, *L'énonciation impersonnelle ou le site du film*, *Iris*, 14/15, 1992, pp. 201-10.

Odin, Roger, 'L'I.R.C.A.V.: un bilan très subjectif...', *Hors Cadre*, 10, 1992, pp. 89-98.

Ranvaud, Donald, 'Gianfranco Bettetini: the Dual Commitment of an Artist to the New Science', *Framework*, 1, 1977, pp. 8-10.

Ropars-Wuilleumier, Marie-Claire, 'Sémiotique du film ou sémiotique textuelle?', *Exigences et perspectives de la sémiotique: recueil d'hommages pour Algirdas Julien Greimas*, ed. Herman Parret and Hans-George Ruprecht, Amsterdam: John Benjamins, 1985, pp. 639-48.

Ropars-Wuilleumier, Marie-Claire, 'Sujet ou subjectivité? L'intervalle du film', *Actes Sémiotiques*, 41, 1987, pp. 30-39.

Ropars-Wuilleumier, Marie-Claire, 'Ici et ailleurs, ou l'insaissable pragmatique', *Hors Cadre*, 7, 1989, pp. 67-73.

Ropars-Wuilleumier, Marie-Claire, 'Christian Metz et le mirage de l'énonciation', *Iris*, 10, 1990, pp. 105-119.

Simon, Jean-Paul, 'Énonciation et narration', *Communications*, 38, 1983, pp. 155-191.

Sorlin, Pierre, 'A quelle sujet?', *Actes Sémiotiques*, 41, 1987, pp. 40-51.

Vanoye, Francis, 'Nouvelles pistes sémiologiques', *Degrés*, 64, 1990.

Véron, Eliséo, 'Il est là, je le vois, il me parle', *Communications*, 38, 1983, pp. 98-120.

Publication Acknowledgements

Dominique Chateau, 'Vers un modele génératif du discours filmique', published in *Humanisme et Entreprise*, 99, 1976, pp. 1-10. Reprinted by permission of the author.

Michel Colin, 'La Grande Syntagmatique Revisitée', published in *Cinéma, télévision, cognition*, Nancy: Presses Universitaires de Nancy, 1992, pp. 47-84. Reprinted by permission of the publishers.

Michel Colin, 'La Sémiologie du cinéma comme science cognitive', published in *Cinéma, télévision, cognition*, Nancy: Presses Universitaires de Nancy, 1992, pp. 25-45. Reprinted by permission of the publishers.

Francesco Casetti, 'Les yeux dans les yeux', *Communications*, 38, 1983, pp. 78-97. Reprinted by permission of the author.

Christian Metz, 'L'Énonciation impersonnelle, ou le site du film', *Vertigo*, 1, Fall, 1987. This translation first appeared in *New Literary History*, 22, 1991, pp. 747-72. Reprinted here by permission of the editor of *New Literary History*. The translation of technical filmic terms has been slightly modified for terminological consistency.

François Jost, 'Le récit autorisé', Chapter 3 of *Un monde à notre image: énonciation, cinéma, télévision*, Paris: Méridiens Klincksieck, 1992, pp. 49-71. Reprinted by permission of the author.

François Jost, 'The Polyphonic Film and the Spectator' was first presented at the conference 'Subjectivity and Film' at the University of Bergen, Norway, March 20th, 1994. It is based, in part, on Chapter 4 of Jost's *Un monde à notre image: énonciation, cinéma, télévision*, Paris: Méridiens Klincksieck, 1992. Reprinted by permission of the author.

Jan Simons, '"Enunciation": From Code to Interpretation'. Original contribution.

Roger Odin, 'Pour une sémio-pragmatique du cinéma', *Iris*, 1, 1, 1983, pp. 67-81. Reprinted by permission of the author.

Roger Odin, 'A Semio-Pragmatic Approach to the Documentary Film'. This anonymous translation was first published in W. de Greef and W. Hesling (eds.), *Image, Reality, Spectator*, Acco: Leuven/ Amersfoort, 1989, pp. 91-100. Reprinted by permission of the author and the publishers. The translation has been modified by Warren Buckland.

Elena Dagrada, 'The Diegetic Look. Pragmatics of the Point-of-View Shot'. This translation was first published in *Iris*, 7, 1986, pp. 111-24. Reprinted by permission of the author.

Film Culture In Transition: on the series

Film culture in Transition is the name of a new series which addresses the debates around a new and exciting field of study. Never have movies been popular or more ubiquitous, they meet us on television and in the home, at the videotheques, on posters and in advertising. Yet no consensus exists about how the cultural and historical role of the audio-visual media might be understood, and the contest for legitimation among the more established academic disciplines obliges those who teach and research in these fields constantly to question their intellectual foundations and aims.

Film Culture in Transition wants to set new accents, review the state of debates, explore the territory beyond the established topics, but also to consolidate what has been achieved. The focus is on work coming from Europe, continuing the dialogue between the continent's fascination with Hollywood and America's attraction to European aesthetic and critical thought. By trying to shape the debates among different intellectual traditions in Europe itself, the series provide a forum that respects each country's distinctive film and television culture, developed alongside and in competition with Hollywood.

The objective is not a general line, but to provoke reflexion and stimulate research, to give body and substance to the many transitions now centred on the audio-visual media. The elements are in place to make the case for *Film Culture in Transition*.

Thomas Elsaesser
General Editor